DuBay gave us a few more kind words and then turned us over to Sergeant Rider. Staff Sergeant Rider was everything you loved in a Marine. He was big and bad and proud of it. I would later learn he was a sixteen-year veteran of the Corps. He and DuBay were Korean War vets. Rider was tall, about six feet five inches of nasty. But one thing was certain, you knew who was in charge.

"Okay, Marines! I'm here to get some volunteers who want to fight a different war. It's a lonely war. A personal war. I want Marines that can stare a gook down eyeball-to-eyeball. I want you to be able to look 'em in the eye and pull the trigger." Rider spoke my language and kept my attention. . . .

DEAD CENTER

A Marine Sniper's Two-Year
Odyssey in the Vietnam War

Ed Kugler

PRESIDIO
PRESS

BALLANTINE BOOKS • NEW YORK

A Presidio Press Book
Published by The Random House Publishing Group
Copyright © 1999 by Ed Kugler

All rights reserved.

Published in the United States by Presidio Press, an imprint of The Random House Publishing Group, a division of Random House, Inc., New York, and simultaneously in Canada by Random House of Canada Limited, Toronto.

Presidio Press and colophon are trademarks of Random House, Inc.

www.presidiopress.com

Library of Congress Catalog Card Number: 99-90065

ISBN 978-0-8041-1875-0

Manufactured in the United States of America

First Edition: June 1999

For Gloria . . . the Rogues . . . the Corps . . .
and all those who bought the Big One

Map 1. Republic of Vietnam

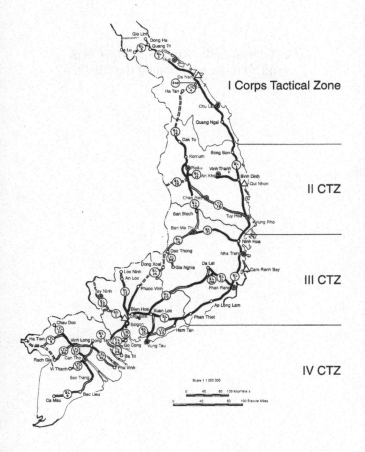

I Corps Tactical Zone

II CTZ

III CTZ

IV CTZ

Gio Linh
Dong Ha
Quang Tri
Ca Lu
Hue
Da Nang
Ha Tan
Chu Lai
Quang Ngai
Dak To
Kontum
Bong Son
Pleiku
Vinh Thanh
An Khe
Binh Dinh
Qui Nhon
Cheo Reo
Ban Blech
Ban Me Thu
Tuy Hoa
Vung Rho
Ninh Hoa
Dao Thong
Nha Trang
Dong Xoai
Gia Nghia
Da Lat
Loc Ninh
An Loc
Phuoc Vinh
Cam Ranh Bay
Tay Ninh
Phan Rang
Bien Hoa
Xuan Loc
Ap Long Lam
Chau Doc
Saigon
Phan Thiet
Ha Tien
Vinh Long
Dong Tam
Go Cong
Ham Tan
Rach Gia
Can Tho
Ba Tri
Vung Tau
Vi Thanh
Phu Vinh
Soc Trang
Ca Mau
Bac Lieu

Scale 1:1,250,000

0   40   80   100 Kilometers
0   40   80   100 Statute Miles

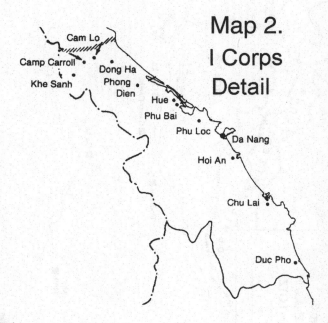

Map 2.
I Corps
Detail

Cam Lo
Camp Carroll
Khe Sanh
Dong Ha
Phong
Dien
Hue
Phu Bai
Phu Loc
Da Nang
Hoi An
Chu Lai
Duc Pho

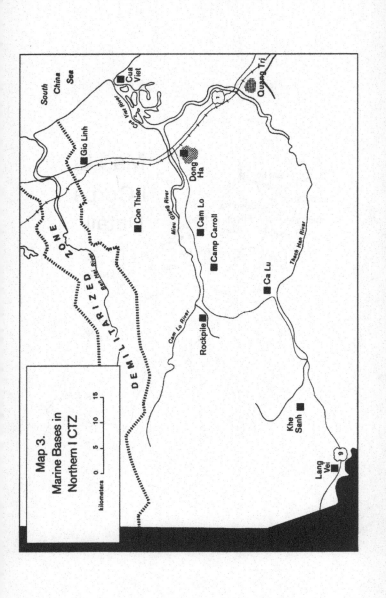

Map 3.
Marine Bases in
Northern I CTZ

kilometers

0   5   10   15

South
China
Sea

Cua
Viet

Gio Linh

Quang Tri

Con Thien

Dong
Ha

D E M I L I T A R I Z E D   Z O N E

Ben Hai River

Mieu Giang River

Cam Lo

Camp Carroll

Cam Lo River

Rockpile

Ca Lu

Thach Han River

Khe
Sanh

Lang
Vei

DEAD
CENTER

Introduction

General Scott suggested that Quitman withdraw and renew the attack with Worth in the morning. Quitman replied that unless he was ordered to do so he would not budge. "The capital is mine," he said to Captain Baker of the Marines. "My brave fellows have conquered it, and by God they shall have it!"

Have it they did. That night, Santa Anna withdrew his beaten army from the city which, in the early morning hours, was surrendered to General Scott. While Scott was still eating his breakfast, Quitman took his 4th Division through the streets to the Grand Plaza, which lay in the shadow of the Aztec Palace. From the windows and roof tops Mexican civilians glumly watched the procession of Americans.

Unkempt, smeared with mud, the soldiers and Marines marched by, led by their disheveled general who had lost a shoe in the mud of the causeway. Before the palace they halted and formed in a ragged line. It was 7 A.M. The commands to present arms rang out over the Plaza as a bullet-shredded American flag

1

was raised above the National Palace where the ancient halls of Montezuma once stood.

The victory—according to tradition—inspired an unknown Marine in Mexico to compose the first stanza of a song. He set it to music of a tune that was popular in those days, taken from an opera called "Genevieve de Brabant" by the German composer, Jacques Offenbach.

From the halls of Montezuma
To the shores of Tripoli
We will fight our country's battles
In the air, on land, and sea
First to fight for right and freedom
And to keep our country free
We are proud to claim the title
Of the United States Marine

Thus the famous marching song was born—The Marine Corps Hymn.

It was cold in Ohio that winter. I sat by the window in Mrs. Lyons's fifth grade classroom at the Gnadenhutten Elementary School. In February, I usually froze by that window, with the ice forming opaque sculptures on the inside of the glass. But I wasn't freezing that day! George P. Hunt had pumped me up with his work, *The Story of the U.S. Marines,* an infamous book at best.

Liking any book surprised me. I hated reading and doing book reports, especially for Mrs. Lyons. I think I hated her more than doing book reports. After all, she was the teacher who had taken my older brother, stood him before the class, and said, "This is an example of how not to be." And I just knew she was out to get me. Especially following the "how not to be" incident, when Mom went over, banged on Mrs. Lyons's front door, and ordered her out of her own house. Mom was screaming "Get out here, and I'll mop the street up with you!" I guess you could say she was real protective of us kids, even brother Butch, who gave her most of her gray hair.

Neither the fact I couldn't stand Mrs. Lyons nor my hatred for reading could stop me from loving that book. My heart raced, chasing away the chill of the windows, as I read of the exploits of the 4th Marines in Mexico. Then I traveled around the world as Mr. Hunt took me on a journey of adventure and excitement with the U.S. Marines. Wow! It was the first book I'd ever loved. And something changed inside me that cold February day.

That's how it started. An innocent kid, in an innocent fifth grade class, reading an obscure book and a dream was born. A dream to be a United States Marine. Somehow, I knew then that I had to be a Marine. I'd show the people of sleepy little Gnadenhutten. I was more than all the fifteen hundred people in town thought I was. Of course, I never expected that less than a decade later I'd be with those same 4th Marines, the ones Mr. Hunt wrote so proudly of in his book. And little did I know I'd fight in a place called Vietnam. And fight not just as a Marine but as a Marine scout-sniper.

This is a book about my two years as a Marine sniper in Vietnam. It's about the wild and crazy odyssey of those two years. It's about how I got there. And it's about "becoming" and "being" a sniper and turning your back on the world. It's about a boy way out in Middle America and his transition from being a small-town kid to a United States Marine. It's a journey inside an eighteen-year-old's mind as he experiences his first combat and the death that comes with it, as a Marine becomes a scout-sniper in a crazy war, as people like me in the death business learn to cope. I did not know how dramatically my decision that cold winter day would impact the rest of my life.

And now that I'm in the rest of my life, I can offer the reader a book that's true. It's raw and straightforward, but the events actually took place. They're often not very nice, but they're real. When they took place is as close as I can get them to the actual time. About as close as a game of hand grenades. Most of the names used are nicknames, the standard military fare, but they're not the actual nicknames. I've changed them to protect the guilty and the innocent. And to respect those who changed their lives and those who didn't. And it's a book about normal people in an abnormal situation, doing shocking things. And it's about what becomes of them when they get together for a war.

And now for a final word on what the book is not. It's not a book about me being a hero or about getting the biggest body count this side of Cambodia. It's not about the glory of war or the disaster of Vietnam. And although you'll read about our time with various Force Recon teams, I was not a member of Marine Force Recon; I did spend a few memorable months supporting them as a sniper. I had to issue that disclaimer since in the past thirty years, I've met enough "former Recon Marines" to populate the entire State of Texas, and that's a bunch.

And lastly, it's not just another Nam book; it's the best damned Nam book you'll ever read!

Prologue

I spent my childhood growing up about as Middle American as it gets. I come from Lock Seventeen, Ohio. I guess it was a bedroom community for Gnadenhutten, where we all went to school. As folklore has it, Lock, as it was affectionately called, got its name being the seventeenth lock on the old Ohio-Erie Canal. I never really knew if that was true. But I did spend a lot of winter days ice-skating on the old canal that came through town. Lock had a whopping seventy-five townspeople. The canal and a railroad ran through the edge of our quaint little farm community. We had a little store, a feed mill, and a beer joint called Poon's.

Poon's was something else. If you could get your head to the bar, you could get served. A couple buddies and I would walk around and collect pop bottles. Then we'd cash them in at Dixon's store for two cents each. Off to Poon's we'd go and buy us a quart of Carling Black Label for a quarter. I had to get drunk . . . that's what Marines did, and I wanted to get started being a Marine right away! So I started early, fourteen years old to be exact. Getting a buzz on Saturday nights walking back from Poon's,

5

sharing slugs on a quart of Carling. Between Poon's and the Saturday night Carlings, I guess I became the one—or maybe there were a couple of us, in our class of thirty-five kids—that you didn't want your daughter to date.

Our family was poor during my early years growing up in Lock, but eventually my dad's trucking venture, the one that kept him away all the time, started to take off. We soon had the only new house on the canal. GoKarts were coming out of California, and we jumped in with both feet. I dropped sports in school and spent my growing-up years on the dirt tracks of northern Ohio racing track rabbits, the Eastern version of GoKarts. We later graduated to karts, and I went big time as my karts were capable of eighty-mile-per-hour speeds.

My senior year came, and thirty-four of the thirty-five kids graduating were wild about their upcoming senior-class trip. New York City! I was never one for crowds or doing what the masses did, so New York wasn't on my agenda. In February that year, 1964, I was off to the re-cruiting station fifteen miles up the road in New Phila-delphia. I'd join the Marines. To put it mildly, my parents weren't keen on the idea. Mom especially. She was a loving, dedicated, but protective and controlling mom. She'd already lost the "be a good kid" battle with my older brother, Butch, who quit school at sixteen, right be-fore they kicked him out. He went off to Pennsylvania to drive a coal truck. He was a big influence on me, and Mom was a little late catching me in time for the crack-down. I always felt sorry for my younger brother, Randy; he bore the brunt of our shenanigans. My sister, Pat, was the oldest of four kids and already on with her life by my graduation. Dad was always gone on business, which he was more dedicated to than to us. He was a product of the depression, and everything was serious to him, especially money. Actually, that's all that ever mattered to him. He was a truck driver who'd done well. He drove trucks, then bought one, then another, and so on, until he had a nice little company going. Those trucks were his babies, not us kids.

Mom worked overtime to make up for Dad's MIA status. I guess since she was an orphan, she was everybody's mom. Her mother died at age thirty-five during the birth of her twelfth child. So Mom and the other eleven ended up in a southern Ohio orphanage. Although she wouldn't talk much about the experience, you could tell things weren't too good at that place. I always figured that explained why Mom about took Mrs. Lyons's head off the day she made an example of Butch. Nobody could screw with her younguns; she was like a momma bear with her cubs.

When it came to the Corps and me, Dad just stood back and let me make the decision. To him, my enlistment meant money he wouldn't have to spend on college. Mom was hopeful I'd flunk the physical and stay home and work in the family business. She always tried to cover for Dad and tell us he was doing it all for us. But five years of Little League baseball and a Dad who couldn't make even one game, left the "he's doing it all for you kids" a bucket that wasn't carrying any water for me. I wanted out of Lock Seventeen and on my own.

Mom's prayers for a flunked physical weren't answered. I was ecstatic coming home from my physical in Cleveland. It was another one of those cold, February nights. I'd used Mom's car to drive the hour to Canton to catch the bus for Cleveland. They put us up in a fleabag hotel downtown. The whole routine was foreign to me. Despite being scared, I was four feet off the ground with excitement at the prospect of where I at least thought I was headed. The United States Marine Corps, and all the glory that went with it, was right around the corner!

The drill they put us through in Cleveland went by pretty fast. As I left, I knew I'd passed, and it felt good. I knew I was leaving home, Lock Seventeen and its seventy-four other inhabitants, behind. The people of Lock had been good to me; all the snobs I disliked were over in Gnaden. But I was seventeen, and I was positive I knew the answers to all of life's important questions. A few years and a few bullets and hand grenades later, I realized I didn't even know which questions to ask, let alone the answers to them.

I'd enlisted under the Marines' Early Entry Program, so my enlistment actually started in February though I wouldn't graduate until May. I had actually made it! I was driving along, higher than I'd ever been on Carling Black Label. I was on top of the world. I rode the hour home with the radio on full blast, listening to the latest musical sensation, the Beatles. They were on every channel, and so was I!

I arrived home, walked in the house, and said, "I'm in!" Mom froze in place. Then she hung her head, as if in defeat, and walked quickly to her room. As usual, Dad wasn't home, but he didn't say anything when he did get there. My aunt and grandma lived with us, and they, too, were disappointed. Mom had three brothers serve in the army during World War II and Korea, so I guess she and the in-laws already had some bad tapes playing about the military.

Time flew by and so did my senior year. May 1964 came and went, and so did I. I attended graduation kicking and screaming all the way. Oh how bad I wanted to blow off that dog and pony show and all the phony people who went with it. "No graduation ceremony for me!" was my battle cry. But Mom had saved her best threats and guilt trips for last; she was determined I wouldn't end up like Brother Butch, so Eddie went to graduation.

Just two weeks later, I was back in Mom's car going on a quiet ride to Cleveland with her and Dad. They took me to Cleveland's Hopkins Airport for my first flight to Charleston, South Carolina, and a bus ride from there to Parris Island. I waved, turned, and walked down the concourse. I was on my way! I was in! Of course, I hadn't the slightest idea what I was really in for, but my fifth-grade dream was about to come true.

The flight wasn't bad, and we arrived in Charleston on time. That's where my plan began to unravel. Right in the middle of the Charleston airport we met a crazy man dressed in a Marine uniform. He was all spit and polish and poster perfect. He was a mean-looking Marine's Marine. He proudly announced, by yelling and screaming at us, that he was there to organize all of us for the bus ride to Parris Island. We were about to become United States Marines! I thought to myself, He doesn't have to act like this to organize me. I'll get in line, just say so! I couldn't figure out what he was so upset about. He continued yelling and screaming, calling us scumbags and maggots. He even said, "You are mere pimples on the face of humanity." I thought he was supposed to be glad to see us. What was the issue? What was going on?

I'd joined the outfit to protect and serve America. I'd heard all the stories about how tough it was, and that if they tell you to jump to the moon, just yell "Yes, sir!" and start leaping. But I thought the Marines would act, well, a little more appreciative than the crazy sergeant. He's telling us how bad we are and what punks we are and . . .

well to shut up and look straight ahead, maggot! Maggot? What the hell is this?

The long ride to Parris Island was made longer by a flat tire on the bus. That gave the madman with a bunch of stripes on his arm more time to humiliate us. And he was good at it. He marched up and down the bus telling us what "pieces of shit" we were and what "scummy civilians" we were. So far, our reception as would-be Marines was just nothing like I thought it was going to be.

Not only had I been trying to drink like a Marine in high school, I had been trying to swear like one. It wasn't a hard skill to learn; I grew up around truck drivers. But that guy gave new meaning to the whole idea of swear words. Could I really be all of those things he was saying? As we rode those last three miles or so over the causeway and onto the island, I reflected on my goal of becoming a Marine. We passed the sentries and the main gate and left civilian life behind. By then, it was nothing more than lights on a distant shore. The bus slithered its way through the humidity of a typical South Carolina summer morning. A morning I'd soon be getting used to. As we pulled up to my new home, I wondered how wise I'd been back in Mrs. Lyons's class that February day, so long ago.

We got off the bus only to have the original "mad man of Charleston" hand us off to a group of very loud, cynical, and nasty drill instructors—DIs. All those men in Marine uniforms, they were like nothing I'd ever had a nightmare about when I was a little kid. They really were mad! Crazy!

In just one day, I found out what a punk I was and how spoiled and coddled I'd been. I discovered I had a long way to go and wasn't sure, just then, if I wanted to make the trip. Where the hell was George P. Hunt when I needed him? What was going on around and to me wasn't how it had sounded in his book, man. I'd even have taken Mrs. Lyons about then.

It took me a while to "get it," to get with the "whole" program. For a couple of days, I was walking around like a guy who'd missed his insulin shot. I was hurtin' for certain. While the big deal took a while for me to figure out, it only took a day for me to get the drift on how the mess hall worked. "Oh, Private Kugler doesn't like our shit on the shingle," the DI bellowed in my ear. He sounded like a wounded moose. "Well, Private Kugler, do you want your mommy to make you scrambled eggs?" I wasn't real quick, but I knew enough either to go hungry or to shut up and eat. I ate.

I struggled, smothered under the twenty-four-hour supervision delivered by the madmen. I really struggled with being told what to do at every turn. I had trouble getting motivated. I suddenly didn't think I wanted to be there. Boy, was I quick! By golly, they couldn't get anything by me. I guess I was a piece of shit after all. I was going downhill fast.

About the three-week point of boot camp, I was sent to sick bay for a dental checkup, but my dental appointment was canceled, so I was back at the barracks before the platoon returned. The quiet was almost more than I could handle. What sheer beauty it was! The DI had been real plain with me about reporting to the PT field when I finished, but I thought I was cute, so I went back and got in my PT gear. I lay down on my rack to relax. I would wait for the platoon to come running down the street, singing, then I was going to hop up and run out and greet them as if I'd just got back. I thought, Now that's a plan!

There were three DIs in charge of our platoon and, unfortunately for me, none of them had been born yesterday.

So here's Kug, stretched out with peace and quiet at my side, when in walks one of the DIs. And what does he find? Private Kugler, lying proudly in his rack, stretched out, hands above his head, relaxed to the max. My butt immediately puckered up and shot straight up into my throat when the soothing silence was shattered by a maniacal scream that straightened my hair. "You scummy, low-life little bastard you. You are a disgrace to my Marine Corps. You thumb-sucking little turd. It's people like you that get Marines killed in combat by disobeying orders just like this one!" Me? Disobeying orders? I was in shock. What was he talking about? What order had I disobeyed? I realized he was about to tell me in terms I'd understand.

I was standing front and center before the captain quicker than a DI can say "scummy civilian." I was sent out of there "mo ricky tick" (military for "right damn now"). I was given the Marine version of a low-level military trial. They called it "Office Hours." Before I knew what hit me, besides my DI, I was out of my platoon and on my way to I knew not where. I had in fact disobeyed an order, an order to go to sick bay and report back "immediately," as in directly afterward. So I was being sent out to the end of the island. They said it was the end of the island, but to me, it was the end of the world. I knew right away that place was a nut ward!

I was in STB, Special Training Branch. And life became a real bitch! It made regular boot camp look like Little League baseball practice. STB was worse than anything I'd ever imagined; I was in Corrective Custody Platoon. It was for people like me that disobeyed orders or just plain couldn't get with the program. STB also housed Fat Man's Platoon, for the overweight, and Motivation Platoon, for the unmotivated souls among us. In CCP, we moved a giant sandpile back and forth, back and forth, every day! Two water buckets, one for each hand! We'd fill them with sand at one end, and then we'd double-time to the other end of the inside of our running track, dump them, and run back. All the while, our DI sat in the middle of the track watching our every move, screaming obscenities as we passed. It was South Carolina in July. At that point in my young life, I didn't know the world got so hot. And the DIs were just whacko. They got off on all that kick-ass stuff. They were building men, but we weren't in the plan because we hadn't got with the program yet.

But one of the madmen tossed me a curve ball that changed my life forever. STB had become more fun than I thought I needed in my life. So one day I decided to go AWOL. I just flat ran away. I hadn't thought it out very well and had no idea where I'd go, except away from STB. I took off when I thought I wouldn't be noticed for a while. It wasn't long before they came looking for me. I hid in some thick brush along the edge of the swamp. Using the recruits to look for me, they made a sweep along the water's edge. I had to lie in the water up to my eyeballs to hide from my fellow recruits. What the hell was I doing? I couldn't believe I'd screwed up so bad.

I evaded everyone and everything for three days. Everything except the scorpions and mosquitos. They were brutal. My life was getting worse, even as I worked my way back along the causeway I'd ridden in on; just over three days from when I'd slipped out, I got caught. The MPs caught me hiding in a car-size bush near the main gate. Of course, it was kind of a relief; I'd spent the last forty-eight hours hiding in that bush. Ouch! They caught me near evening on the third day of my escapade. I'd had no food for three days and drank swamp water when I could. The mosquitos and scorpions got the best of me. I wasn't feeling any too good and was sure I was headed straight for the brig—handcuffs and all.

But the MPs put me in the back of a little pickup truck and drove me back to STB. Then an MP hauled me out of the truck and half dragged me inside, turning me over to the guy I remembered as Sergeant Tarawa, the sergeant in charge of Corrective Custody Platoon. Tarawa wasn't his real name, but he'd always told us stories about Tarawa in World War II. I remembered his bedtime stories, and I remembered that he was crazy as all hell. I knew I was dead meat. He was one tough, mean, and ugly motor scooter. He was going to beat the living shit out of me.

Sergeant Tarawa dragged me in front of the STB crew and humiliated me. Of course, that was standard fare for us screwups. He stood me up and said, "Take a good look; this is what you look like when you try to escape your duty to my Marine Corps." For the first time in my life, I realized I deserved the shit that was happening to me. My public flogging lasted five or ten minutes. After the humiliation, he grabbed hold of my collar and dragged me down the hallway, throwing me into his office like I was a light sack of wheat. I landed on the floor, sitting with my back against the wall and butt on the ground opposite Tarawa. He slammed the door shut!

I thought, I'm on thin ice, and it's about to break. Then came the surprise. Tarawa's voice became soft, almost normal, and the tough old sergeant and serious combat veteran became a human being. It was hard to believe, and I *wanted* to believe it. He was still tough and intense and looked me straight in the eye. Yet something seemed different. I could see he cared. I'd never really felt people cared about me much. That was the first time I "got it." I remember it as if it were yesterday.

"Kid, what the hell is your problem?" he said. And before I could answer, he continued, "Do you know what the hell you just did out there? What have you eaten for the last three days?"

"Nothing, sir," I said. Then he became serious, but caring, almost like a favorite teacher or basketball coach. He said, "Do you know *I* am a Recon Marine, and *I* don't go three days without eating! *I* don't escape and evade like you did!" Then, for the first time, I could see someone who really genuinely cared about me. He cared about his Marine Corps, but he also cared that Ed Kugler became a part of it. He said, "I am going to give you the biggest break of your young life. No court-martial! No brig! You're staying right here with me in STB." Minutes earlier, I would have said I didn't want to do that. But something inside of me changed. I could feel a difference. He went on, "You're going to finish the time you started, plus what you lost hiding out the last three days. Then you *will* graduate boot camp and become a Marine in *my* Marine Corps! Do you understand?"

I said, "Yes, sir!" I got it!

After making me scream the same answer to several more questions, he released me. He went on to tell me I could do anything I wanted to do if I'd just apply myself. And he made it clear that is exactly what he expected me to do: "If I ever see you here again, you'll regret the day you were born." And I never forgot his promise, but I also never forgot those lessons, especially that I could do "anything." The occasion was one of those forks in the road of life, and I knew it would make a difference in mine.

After I left his room, he became the same animal.

Driving, pushing, and demanding that we make the most of ourselves as Marines. While he was the same maniac outside that office, I was a different person on the inside. I saw everything differently for the first time in my life. He had made a difference and, ultimately, had made a Marine out of me. I went back to Platoon 262 and went on to graduate. Despite a couple of wrong turns along the way, I had reached my goal. My parents made the trek down from Lock Seventeen for the big affair. But even on that proud day, things between us just didn't seem to click. It was all bittersweet.

We moved on to infantry training at Camp Geiger in North Carolina. Geiger turned out to be uneventful, and graduation from there brought leave. Then I got a permanent assignment to India Company, 3d Battalion, 6th Marines, "I 3/6." Life as a grunt was fine with me. I was a Marine.

It was the fall of '64, and life in Lejeune with India Company was dull and boring, and uneventful. Talk of Vietnam was the only spice in life. We'd first heard of it back in boot camp as the DIs started telling us to pray for war so we could do what Marines were supposed to do. Life went on, and the war really heated up in early 1965, but we were slated for a Caribbean cruise. We'd make stops in Guantanamo Bay and Vieques Island on our way to jungle training in the heat of Panama. The old salts knew all of them combined ball-busting heat with major boredom.

We took off in April '65 with our first stop in Guantanamo Bay, Cuba, "Gitmo." That's where I found myself on hands and knees, crawling out of my first bar fight. Other than my first fight and being in Cuba, the visit was nothing to write home about. Then we left Gitmo, back on board the USS *Wood County*, bound for Panama, after a brief stop on Vieques Island, every Marine's hell. Vieques was just hot, dry, barren, and full of thigh-burning hills. We eventually reboarded ship for our ultimate destination, Panama.

A day out at sea from Vieques, we got our first mail call, and I got my first surprise: only one letter from home. When I'd left on the cruise, I'd been dating four girls. I first noticed that the return address simply read, in big letters, "US" on the top left corner of the envelope. Naively, I thought that meant it was from the United States. Opening it, I discovered that I'd been "found out." I guess I hadn't been as clever as I'd thought. Dating four girls at the same time from the same general vicinity had apparently caught up with the Kug. The letter turned out to be from all four of them. I guess they no longer all thought they were going with me. They'd each written a separate paragraph, a kiss-off to the "Kug." It was a multiple Dear John. And the US on the envelope meant "us" as in the four of "us."

As fate would have it, we didn't quite make our jungle cruise to Panama; we were diverted for a "police action" in Santo Domingo—the Dominican crisis. We were told there'd been an uprising and a group of rebels had overthrown the government. We'd have to make a landing to save the day! Well, that's what we were there for! All us boots on the ship were pumped up tight with anticipation. We wanted to go in and kick some rebel ass! That is what we were training for, right? The two Korean War vets in our outfit reminded us that we'd just had enough training to get our butts kicked good. "And, no, combat ain't fun like your DI made it sound, either."

We made an unopposed beach landing near Santo Domingo and were met by smiling Dominican soldiers bouncing along the beach as if we had just arrived for a little volleyball. After a brief meeting of the brass, we all climbed on top of amtracs and tanks and, along with our new Dominican friends, rode victoriously into town. The roads were dirt, the air thick with humidity, and the countryside poor.

We arrived at a polo field near the edge of the city. We were told the air wing would make it their chopper pad in the morning. The battalion bigwigs were making their headquarters in a nearby hotel, El Embajador. Our company, India 3/6, would secure the perimeter. It was near midnight by the time we got the order to "dig in." Dig in we did. I awoke the next morning to find that my foxhole was on one of the greens of the hotel golf course. I reasoned that must be why we felt all that "really good" grass everywhere during the night, while we were digging.

We spent a day or two watching the Dominican Air Force, a pair of World War II–era propellor-driven P-51s, dive-bomb the city and the rebel forces inside. What a cakewalk, we thought. Let us at 'em! We're U.S. Marines, don't screw with us. We didn't have to wait long. Our impatience was rewarded by our being selected point company. We'd lead the column as we headed inside the city. We'd come in from the sea side of town, and the 82d Airborne the back side, near the hills. They'd be heli-lifted into place behind the city at dawn.

We lined up on a main street, just outside the polo grounds. We got our marching orders. We locked and loaded and were going in to kick that rebel ass we'd been talking about. There were tanks to accompany us, but someone said they weren't allowed to fire. Tough order to understand, that one: it was war, wasn't it? Something about "rules of engagement," something I didn't understand at all.

Our journey kicked off with Captain Donald standing

tall, high up on a tank and giving the move out signal with a swing of his arm and yelling, "Move out!" Some newsman took a picture of him that would make the papers all over the country. Boy, this must be it, I thought. I was too stupid or too naïve to realize what was about to happen. I just knew that this is what it was all about. That this is what George P. Hunt was writing about.

Our column moved forward, apprehension growing as fast as a field of wild zucchini. I was still thinking, let's kick some ass! We moved forward in two columns, one on each side of the street, with the armor in the middle. We were going down this nice, big street that headed into Santo Domingo. Women and children were sitting on their porches. Men were watering their lawns. There was lots of waving and cheering, and why not—the Marines were there; we'd come to save the day. Yeah, that is what it was all about. I just knew I understood it all—the pride, the commitment, and the history. What a day this'll be, I thought. It's all worth it, I know it is.

Our caravan took a turn and started moving toward Old Santo Domingo. The festive, Fourth of July atmosphere gave way to a sullen, dark, and ugly afternoon. We weren't in the nice part of town anymore, and no one was on the porches or watering lawns or cheering us on. It was okay, not too run down, but something was different. We could hear gunfire up ahead, not far away. We were near a hospital. They said there were snipers up ahead. I thought, Snipers kill people don't they? The cries of "Corpsman!" suddenly sent a wave of fear that filled the hot afternoon air. If the heat wasn't enough, the humidity was terrible, and you needed a knife to cut the tension in the air.

With the cries for corpsmen, and snipers up ahead, we

sprang to action. "Fire teams up!" It was our leader, Corporal Levy; Verdy, a tough kid from North Jersey; Sap, a mountain type from West by God Virginia; and me. The four of us leapfrogged from bush to bush. "Reach the hospital building," Levy yelled. Screams were becoming the music of a long afternoon. At the edge of the building, I tried going around the corner to follow Corporal Levy, my team leader. As I did, shots rang out! My God! They're shooting at me? Verdy made it to Levy; it was time for Sap and me. We had to go! What the hell's this? Scared shitless wouldn't do this deal justice. I could get killed doing this shit. Hunt made it sound so cool. When he talked about it, it wasn't this scary! This is the first damn time, man! Man, this sucks real bad. I try to move ahead by doing the low crawl around the corner of the hospital. Each time I do, a shot rings out, and the bullet strikes right next to my right shoulder, in the dirt! It's almost a simultaneous crack and a thud! This hot afternoon in Santo Domingo is beginning to suck bad. This bastard ain't shooting near me or by me but right damn at me! I slide backward to gain some cover by the edge of the building. I start to reason, which is a dangerous thing when your mind's racing at Indy speeds. But your thoughts hang frozen, like the mosaic of ice I remember on my fifth grade window back in Gnaden. My reasoning quickly says, if he can see me, then I can see his ugly ass! I muster up all the courage I've ever had in my life. I decide to try the low crawl one more time. I start crawling around the hospital corner with Sap nearly up my ass. Verdy and Corporal Levy are already around the corner and somewhere up ahead. Elbows and knees on the ground, wiggling like a snake, I move out and partially around the bush when . . . *wham!* A rifle slug about a foot from my head. Shit on this! I jump and run forward, Sap on my ass, just as Verdy jumps out ahead and nails the sniper in the tree with a burst of M-14 fire. The tree is right in front of us. The sniper was up above, like in the movies. But this sure ain't a movie!

The gunfire stopped, followed by the sound of a dead body falling from a tree. It bounced off limbs and broke branches on its final fall to the earth. It crashed to the ground with a sickening groan. The lifeless body is a heap of motionless flesh and bones, lying in front of us. There's no time for reflection. There's lots of yelling. We're regrouping to head to the bad side of town. The bad side of town? Shit, man, ain't this bad enough? The first person I see killed in my life, and no time to think about it. I guess it's better that way.

Back with my fire team, we advance in formation. We cross a four-lane highway and head out across an open, dirt field. It's maybe a hundred yards across. Looks like it might be a construction site. It has several mounds of dirt lying about like large anthills. We seem to be aimed to cross the field. On the other side were some old wooden buildings. Communications were bad at this point. We didn't know it, but we were headed for the old side of town. And in the old side of town was rebel headquarters.

Our platoon got on line and started doing a textbook sweep across this barren patch of ground. It was hot and dry and really scary out there. We got maybe halfway, a hundred yards or so, when all hell broke loose for sure! A .30-caliber machine gun started raking our assault line. We had a good fifty yards to go before we could get cover in the buildings. We all dived behind the mounds of dirt. Thank God for the anthills! Bunches of Marines, clamoring for cover, returning fire as best we could, not really knowing exactly where it was coming from. It was

pure hell to my right or left. We were pinned! I didn't
want to be there!

The fire coming from the rebel side was withering. I
couldn't figure why our tanks weren't leveling the buildings. I'd later find out the rules of engagement, the ones I
didn't understand, were the problem. The rules said we
couldn't use anything larger than a 7.62mm rifle—our
trusty M-14s. Incredible! Who the hell in their right
minds would do this? That rule would cost more lives on
that afternoon than anyone would ever care to admit.
Welcome to the modern world of warfare, Marine!

The barrage of bullets whizzing by made us want to
burrow our heads down deep in the ground. You wanted
to scream, run—do something. We were trying to shoot
back, but that was tough. Finally, somebody decided to
bring the amtracs out. Those beautiful armored boxcars
rumbled past us then turned around so the opening would
be protected to the back. There was one amtrac for each
squad of Marines. We ran inside dodging lots of hot lead
that whistled overhead and around our feet. The scene
was right out of a damn movie, but we weren't acting. I
was glad to be inside the iron turtle as I heard bullets
ricocheting off its shell. Machine gun rounds were ping-
ing off the sides instead of through my young ass. I was
sure we'd pull back, regroup, and come back for another
shot at the bastards.

But the amtrac made a turn in place and went right for
the buildings! We were shocked. We were charging straight
at the gunfire. We didn't have communications. What the
hell was going on? One of our Korean War vets, a staff
sergeant, looked real bad. He looked out the little windows in the front of the drop door. We were rumbling into
some serious shit. Two of the rows of buildings came together at an angle in front of us, with a street between

them. They were old and eerie-looking. Someone said the machine gun was on the roof.

My heart was in my throat, fighting for space with my butt, which was puckered high and tight. Everyone was hyperventilating, as fear reigned supreme in my amtrac. Without warning, it jerked to a stop. The front landing door dropped, just like in training. But, unlike training, bullets were flying in and ricocheting around from the .30-caliber machine gun perched above us. It was like a shooting gallery for the rebels, as everyone ran outside and into the street. We were assaulting rebels head on! Next damn time, pass the word down, assholes!

I followed Sap, my hillbilly soulmate and M-79 man, straight through a plate glass window. Rifles at port arms, we crashed through, right into a room with a family of four cowering in the corner. We had to get out of the street where there was pure mayhem and certain death. Cries of "Corpsman up!" could be heard from all sides. We'd find out later that we were dropped just one block from rebel headquarters. They were proud of their turf, even if we were United States Marines. The info on the landing was terrible: the "rebels" were part of the Dominican Army that'd gone bad. I'd look back and know leadership was real poor on this Caribbean afternoon. Decisions coming from on high would prove even worse.

Sap and I went out in the street and joined Corporal Levy and Verdy. We moved building to building as a rebel fired at us from a rooftop across the street. I let go with half a magazine from my 14. He flew backward, disappearing from view. Had I killed him? I guess? It didn't feel . . . I didn't feel? Who cares; I hope I killed the bastard for shooting at me! Something died inside me that day. I think it was my feelings. I didn't need feelings

anyway—it was war! We made it past a couple of buildings and turned left toward what turned out to be the
rebel headquarters building. A fire team crossed the
street, with two kids from my old Platoon 262. The street
in front of us was a windowless wall of wood. As the
other fire team advanced along the wall opposite us, the
.30 caliber was back. It tattooed the whole wall with bullets! The bullets were walking down that long, dreary,
windowless wall of wood, on an unnamed street in a sad
town. They stitched holes, chipped wood, and nailed two
kids from Platoon 262. It was amazingly like slow motion
and real ugly to watch. The kid from Jersey took two
slugs in the throat and was lying bleeding, gurgling and
jerking on the pavement in front of us. The kid from up-
state New York, Private Benson, was sitting down against
the wall, dead. His eyes were open, and he had a strange,
almost serene smile on his face. It really wasn't happening was it? A sea-duty corporal with half a fire team
dead was screaming, "Cover me, cover me!" My fire
team leader, Corporal Levy, jumped from our side, into
the middle of the street like John Wayne. He unloaded a
full magazine up toward the .30-caliber killing machine,
positioned on the rooftop above us.

Wow! The kid from Lock Seventeen was now seeing
what it meant to be a United States Marine. It was a real
bitch. Benson was dead, sitting against a wall in the hot
afternoon sun. He still had a smiling face, but a dead one.
Smoked by a rebel with a machine gun. He just sat there
like in the movies. I might die too, I thought and, I remember, I was scared shitless. But the hell with it, let's
get the bastards!

Two guys headed out and dragged the Jersey kid to
safety and a waiting corpsman. I'd later learn he lived
but was sentenced to life with no feeling, paralyzed from

the neck down. A Marine with a life cut short, at least a life as he knew it. Sap and I ran out to get Benson. I couldn't figure it, let's get the machine gun, then the dead guy. But that wasn't the Marine Corps way; you don't leave any dead behind. Period! I'd learn that's a good rule—but I wouldn't learn it that day. As we ran out, each step felt like we were wearing cement shoes. My body seemed heavy, slow, and tired. I remember reaching Benson and turning as we picked him up. I remember he was heavier than any wet bales of hay I ever picked up working at Mr. Leonard's farm up the street in Lock Seventeen. We took off trying to run him to safety. Go! Run before they get you!

I was carrying Benson's right arm in my left. That put me on the machine-gun side of life. Private Benson, who was along for the ride at that point, was in the middle. Sap was on the other side holding Benson's left arm. Just as we took our first step, the grim reaper and his machine gun opened up again. This time, walking deadly hot lead down the center of the street. It was busy chipping up concrete, on its quest to meet us and deliver us to evil before we could carry Benson to cover across the other side. The race might be on, but my life was suddenly in slow motion. Each step seemed like an eternity, each chug of the machine gun got a bullet closer to a burial in Lock Seventeen. Sap and I raced the .30 caliber, as my life flashed before me in living Technicolor. Unbelievable! In a flash, I'm the kid next door at Mrs. Fivecoat's, hiding from mom, racing GoKarts, and skipping school. And I could see and smell the Carling from my drinking days. And the girls, and all the things I shouldn't have done, and even some I should've. And it was live, on stage in the streets of that hot, dirty old city by the sea; it was one bright, frightening Technicolor hurricane that came roaring across the hot, humid afternoon in Old Town Santo Domingo.

Somewhere in the middle of our race for life and before we could cross the narrow street, explosions and machine-gun fire erupted all around us. It seemed like the curtain of our lives was being drawn amid the closing lines of flashes, booms, zings, and all the other sounds of war. Adrenaline was pumping through my veins like a raging river near its crest. In the chaos and struggle that ensued, I was hit with shrapnel from something; hot metal pierced my hands. My right eye started burning, and I couldn't see. Sap screamed, "I'm hit!" as he took two .30-caliber machine-gun slugs in his left arm. The bullets were coming down the street from my side. They'd hit the M-79 rounds I carried for Sap, but the rounds didn't explode! They'd passed by me and hit Sap. He dropped Benson, who by then had been hit twice more by the machine gunner. The guy in the sky with the machine gun was, so far, winning the afternoon.

We'd gotten Benson halfway or more, when we were taken out of the game. Marines everywhere jumped out to cover us. Two more Marines ran out to get Benson's body as I followed Sap around the corner of the building to help with his arm. There was no corpsman to yell for; it was standing room only, waiting for medical help. I sat down next to Sap, who was leaning against a wall. I grabbed his badly mangled left arm and laid it across my lap. He leaned his head over on my shoulder. His head was back, and he was looking at the sky. He was staring into space as a low moan seeped from his lips.

People were being dragged by us, as the casualties mounted. I needed to take care of Sap and fast, real fast, but I hadn't seen anything like his wounds before. One look, and I knew he was in deep trouble. Blood was pumping everywhere, covering me, Sap, and the concrete around us. I was having trouble seeing. My eye was bad, and it was burning. I could see with just one eye. I quickly took out the compress from the medical kit on the back of my belt. I knew enough to try a pressure bandage, but his wound was enormous. Opposite his elbow, the two bullets had torn all the meat and muscle from the inside of his arm. As I pushed the bandage in to apply pressure, my whole hand went inside the wound and into his arm. I wanted to vomit right there, but there wasn't time.

My hands were burning from the shrapnel, but I couldn't see any cuts because of all Sap's blood. Or was it mine? There wasn't time to find out with my best friend in my lap and dying fast. I could sense Sap getting weaker as he was telling me it felt like a bee sting. I kept telling him not to look. I kept telling him he'd be okay, even though I didn't see how he would. I had to stop the bleeding or he'd die in my arms. He was looking gray and pale, and still the blood rushed from his body like water from a fire hydrant, filling the street beneath us. I took my K-bar and what was left of the bandolier that held the M-79 grenades I'd carried for Sap. I hastily fashioned a tourniquet, placed it around his arm, and was soon able to control the bleeding by twisting it tight, just above the elbow. It meant risking his entire arm, but I had to do it for Sap.

All things considered, as the amtrac rolled up the street to pick up the wounded and dead, he was doing okay. We were covered in blood by the time I got him to his feet to get into the iron box. Just then, he looked down and saw the extent of the damage to his arm and became hysterical. We were both evacuated to the polo grounds and then onto the USS *Wasp* offshore. A night on the *Wasp*,

and we were on to Puerto Rico and eventually Womack
Army Hospital in Fort Bragg, North Carolina.

I remember lying in my rack at Womack thinking,
Man, have I made a serious career mistake. People can
get killed doing this shit. Maybe I was slow or something,
but war was tough. Sap would recover but would never
regain total use of his arm. He'd later thank me for saving it and him. Me? I was grateful for his thanks. Corpsmen, back at the polo grounds, had been critical of my
using a tourniquet; I'd seen it as the only way.

Well, my wounds were minor, some shrapnel to the
hands and the powder in my eye, presumably from the
M-79 round that was hit by the bullet. It would screw my
eyes up for a short while, but in the end, it was one of
many cheap Purple Hearts rendered amid the confusion
of our first combat. My poor Mom, who didn't want me
doing this stuff anyway, had a bad time when she heard
what happened. The government somehow mixed up the
telegram of the kid from Jersey, paralyzed from the neck
down, with my telegram. My injuries were to the eye and
hand and no big deal. In Nam, I got worse and didn't
even get evacuated. But as I called home the second day
I was in Carolina, she was crying, as I told her all was well.

She said, "Ed, I have prepared myself, so just tell me
straight." "Mom, look I'm fine. I walked out here and
called you." "Knock it off," she said. "I know you can't
walk, and I am prepared for it." It took some doing to
undo what the government had inadvertently done and
to convince her there must be a mistake. It's really not
good to mess up the sending home of notices of wounds,
dismemberment, and death.

I recovered and rejoined the 6th Marines, but I was assigned to Mike Company instead of India, which had already staffed up by the time I got back. It was back to

being a grunt again. The highlight was a NATO cruise to Norway, Denmark, Sweden, and Germany, with a stop in Dublin, Ireland, along the way. I'd made it through Dublin to the mountain training in Norway when I received word of my oldest brother's death while driving a truck in Indiana. I had to depart the ship and fly home, although I got there too late for the funeral. While home on emergency leave, my hard drinking caught up with me. Drunk, I was in a bad car accident, and suffered a concussion and several stitches here and there on my head. Back at Lejeune, I was placed on medical waivers in late '65, a time when the first Marines started rotating back from Nam. Hearing the war stories of Chu Lai and Da Nang from those early birds of the war, the spark started burning inside me again. Sergeant Tarawa back in STB was still strong in my mind as I went home that Christmas. It was then I decided that I needed to go to Vietnam, wherever the hell that was. I just needed to be there. My parents never understood and wouldn't talk about it at all.

Back from holiday leave, I went in to volunteer to go to the Nam. I remember the lieutenant asking me if I was sure I wanted to do that. And I said, "Yes!" Since I'd used up all my leave between the holidays and my brother's death last fall, I had no leave left. My CO agreed to let me have a seventy-two-hour pass on each of the four weekends remaining before going to California to report for jungle training at Camp Pendleton. My dad agreed to let me use his former business partner's car to drive back and forth on weekends.

It was a 1965 Buick Wildcat with a 455 engine and a four-barrel carb. It would pass anything but a gas station. It's a good thing I left when I did; I figured I was going to Nam, what could they do to me? I lived hard and drove fast. In those four weekends, I managed to get speeding tickets in Ohio, North Carolina, Virginia, and Pennsylvania. When it was all said and done, I was ready for Nam, whatever and wherever it was. Time does heal your wounds, or at least buries the memories until they come forth another day. Which indeed they would.

When I was done at Lejeune, I had five days to get from there to Camp Pendleton. I drove the Wildcat home to drop it off, figuring I'd better do that while I still had a license. Then, a little partying, and I had another long ride with Mom and Dad. We went back up to Cleveland's Hopkins Airport. California, here I come! Vietnam, hell, you can't be far away.

PART ONE

Becoming a Marine Sniper

CHAPTER ONE

Snipers Up . . . Hell Yes!

It might be January, but it's hotter than hell. The sun's streaming through the trees, creating shadows that streak across the sergeant's face. He's working himself into a thick lather as he describes what Nam's like. It's for the education of trainees like me in the audience. "At night, it's blacker than the inside of an ape's ass at midnight!" he bellows. He's dark with a Nam tan; his looks betray his irrational nature. He works to impress the fifty or so of us, the fresh meat, seated on makeshift wooden benches. It's jungle training, it's Camp Pendleton, and it's weird.

My mind drifts away from his antics to my arrival in California just two days earlier. I'm back sitting in a little park just outside the bus station in Oceanside. I'm fresh in from the frigid January winds of Cleveland. And I love the warm, short-sleeve weather of Southern California. I sit, listening to someone's radio playing "Monday Monday." Me, the Mamas and the Papas, and all this wonderful weather, how can it be? I'm sitting in Oceanside, waiting for my bus to Pendleton, and I think, Man, this'll be a good place to come when all the Marine and Nam stuff is over. This is nice, it's damned nice!

Well that was a couple days ago, and this is now. I'm listening to a sergeant rant and rave about our fate, how half of us are coming home flat-ass on a stretcher or dead, dumb, and cold in a body bag. He's screaming at anyone who falls asleep. He blasts one Marine with, "You asshole, you're gonna get people killed." I don't know if it was the heat, the Mamas and the Papas, or "California Dreamin'," but none of what he was saying registered with me. I just wanted to get through the shit and get it on. We were in "jungle training," California style. I guess it was all the Corps had on short notice; the Nam buildup caught everyone off guard. We were in jungle training, but there wasn't a jungle within a thousand miles of Camp Pendleton.

Our training would last four weeks. Then, we'd each be individual replacements for Marine units already calling Vietnam home. For the grunt trainee, peacetime life in the Corps sucked. It was major boring. And jungle training for Nam was no exception. We'd split our days getting Nam ready, physically and mentally. Then we'd learn the skills necessary to stay alive and kill gooks when we got there.

Getting in shape was a major ball buster. We'd be out back of the camp some damn place, humping the barren hills in full battle gear all day long. Between the heat of the California sun and the weight we were humping, our thighs were always burning. The climb up those bastardly hills was a major ass kicker. "You assholes get in shape," the sergeant would scream, "or you'll get your ass left behind in Nam!"

The very thought of being left behind in Nam kept most of us going. Who the hell wanted to be left behind in

Nam or anywhere for that matter? What the hell is Nam anyway? I didn't know, but hell, I wanted to go anyway. I wanted to serve my country. That's what the Corps was all about. That's why I joined. We all felt that way.

Training with all the guys I didn't know was boot camp all over. It didn't have the restrictions, but it was a foreign affair for me. I only knew a couple of the guys out of the hundreds going through training. I was never one to just join in with groups I didn't know; I usually had only one or two close friends at a time. Jungle school was no exception. I occasionally saw a couple of guys who were in Santo Domingo with me, but it was rare. It was all like starting over. I felt the Corps could do better with units that were formed and trained intact. But it wasn't to be.

Before long I struck up with a kid just out of boot camp. He was from Houston. I knew him only as Thompson, his last name and the universal military tag.

Thompson was a really nice kid. Like me, he'd joined the Corps at seventeen, but he went to boot camp in San Diego, then got his orders for Nam. He wasn't as excited about the prospect as I was. He was seventeen years old, and I was eighteen, and I had Santo Domingo under my belt, and that made me an old salt to him. Thompson even looked young. Too damn young to be married! I couldn't believe that when he told me. Told me he married a Mexican girl he went with in high school. Did it as soon as he found out he was going to Nam. What the hell was he thinking?

I didn't need to agree with him to like him; we hit it off from day one and stayed together all through training, beside each other every step of the way. Up and down, up and down as we humped endlessly through the hills around Pendleton. Marching every morning to get in shape. Each afternoon, we tried to keep each other awake in the face of our instructors' endless droning. We'd get their drift early on, but that didn't stop them; they made the "gooks," as they called them, out to be purely invincible. They told us story after story about how the Viet Cong could sneak up to a sentry in the middle of the night, slit his throat, then be gone before his buddies even knew he was dead.

Even with all of us knee-deep in boredom, some stories began a wave of emotion that would wash over the half-attentive audience, drawing responses from the disbelief of "Give me a fucking break," to the fear of "Oh my God, how will I survive?" Thompson worried a lot. He just wanted to go to Nam, do his duty, and get back in one piece. He talked endlessly of the life he wanted to build with his little lady. He didn't want some gook sneaking up and ending his dreams. I had no dreams like his but I still didn't believe some little bastard could sneak up and slit my throat without my knowing about it either. They were human weren't they?

I'd have to wait 'til Nam to know for sure. Training continued to be a drag, but the mock-up of the booby-trapped village got my attention. It was the next to last stop in training at jungle school, and the instructors were enthusiastic Nam vets. After my first walk, I was paranoid for sure. And if I was paranoid, then Thompson was a basket case. He hadn't looked forward to Vietnam before, and after all the stories of gore from the booby traps, he was down for the count.

They said the booby-trap village was a replica of what we'd find in Vietnam. It had grass huts and trails and everything else needed to simulate what we would run into as Nam grunts. I wanted to go to Nam, but I didn't want that cannon fodder bullshit that I'd seen in Santo Domingo. Grunts are beautiful, but they're usually the first dead. The booby traps focused my attention better than all the lectures we'd endured. I could look at a punji pit with its razor-sharp stakes and see firsthand what a bummer that'd be. The idea of the stakes alone was bad enough without having to worry about some gook rubbing his shit on them to infect my wounds.

We'd been training hard and we needed a break; we'd had daily early morning runs, hikes that lasted all day, and hour after hour of afternoon lectures. By the time we had finished the hands-on booby-trap training, two weeks had passed, during which we'd spend lots of evenings in the pool, taking swimming tests, so we were ready for a break. Lighten up, guys, we'll be ready for Nam . . . a break, okay, just a break?

Finally word came that the next weekend was ours: a seventy-two-hour pass! I'd run into an old buddy from Dom Rep and the 6th Marines. He suggested we go to Tijuana, Mexico. The old salts called it TJ. All I knew was that it was south of California somewhere. Thompson didn't want to make the trip, but I convinced him to come along and have some fun. "What could it hurt?" I said. My Dom Rep friend, Hanscomb, brought along a buddy of his, and the four of us were off to TJ.

First thing Saturday morning, we boarded a bus from the base to Oceanside. There, we changed buses for the two-hour ride south to Tijuana. It was a gorgeous day. The more I saw of California, the more I loved what I saw. The ride was great, the time raced by, and we soon passed through San Diego and on to the border. We got off the bus on the U.S. side, right at the border.

Hanscomb said he knew the way; he'd been there on his last tour at Pendleton. He was elated, said he couldn't wait to see our faces when we saw Tijuana. His buddy played along with him; either he'd been there before or didn't want to let us first timers know that he hadn't.

A few steps inside Mexico, and life began to change. Wow! People are real poor; they beg and live in the dirt. It looked a lot like parts of Santo Domingo. Thompson wasn't happy at all, told me that we shouldn't have come. I was looking forward to getting drunk; it'd been a long time. We walked a mile or so before reaching downtown Tijuana. The language didn't seem to be a real barrier, the people made you feel welcome, and the bars seemed like bars in any other sleazy town I'd been in. I said, "Hanscomb, what's the big deal here? Looks like lots of places I've been, just poorer." Hanscomb just smiled. Vendors were everywhere; the place had a carnival-like atmosphere. Then I noticed a big difference: it wasn't everywhere that little boys came up to sell you their sisters. Now that was different!

We hit the first bar, sat down, and ordered some beer. As we were being served, several Spanish girls came over to get us to buy them drinks. Hanscomb, the old salt, immediately explained the game. They'd order an expensive mixed drink, it's really Kool-Aid, we'd pay, and they would split the profits with the bar. We declined. Undeterred by our rebuff, one of the girls, at about thirty the oldest of the bunch, picked out Thompson as the baby of our group. She waddled over and sat right on his lap. I was laughing along with the other two, but poor Thompson wasn't having any fun.

Before you could spell w-h-o-r-e, Thompson was out of there. He mustered the strength to push her off his lap and run for the door. Hanscomb and pal were in hysterics. I chased outside after him. Thompson was angry and embarrassed, and I was feeling about snake high for making him come along. He just wanted to catch the bus back up to Pendleton. He couldn't stand to be in the midst of life that low. He told me to stay with my friends and that he'd be okay, then he headed back north, and I headed back inside. I was a Marine; I could take it. I drank the rest of the day away and most of the night. I experienced some things that stayed with me through the drunk of the night.

Late Saturday night, I caught a bus back north to Pendleton. I slept all the way, arriving early Sunday morning. Back at Oceanside, I decided to catch a taxi back to base rather than wait for the bus; I was beat from being up all night. Of course, when I arrived, Thompson was happy and fresh; he had just talked to his wife and felt good about coming home. Screw it all, I thought, I don't want a wife, and I survived . . . I think?

Monday of week three came, and our training continued. More hills to climb, more runs to make, more boring lectures to attend, and more booby traps to figure out. Days on end of listening to our instructors, who were all trying to give us a message. Some telling us to go and kick some ass, others telling us "good luck," and a few letting us know "this ain't what you think it is." Hanscomb and I made one more weekend to Tijuana, just for the hell of it. Time moved on, and so would we, very soon. Then, as with all the new meat, we were divided into companies to board ship for the journey to Vietnam. The last thing I remember about jungle school was a sign with an arrow pointing west that read, VIETNAM 10,000 MILES.

We packed up and headed off in buses, bound for the ships in San Diego. My last thought of San Diego was passing through it on my way to Tijuana. I really hadn't seen enough to know what the real city was like. We arrived at the naval base and laid eyes on our big ship for the first time, a merchant marine ship, not regular navy. I didn't know what that meant, or even if that mattered. A ship was a ship from a Marine's-eye view. They told us the trip would take thirty days. Since it was late February, that meant we'd arrive in late March 1966. After a couple of days of loading our seemingly overloaded vessel, we were off for Vietnam.

Life on board ship was about as boring as boring can be. It made the lectures at Pendleton look exciting. Thompson was close by, but Hanscomb I rarely saw. There were nine hundred Marines on board this ship, and it felt like nine thousand. There was a line for everything. You got in line for breakfast, and by the time you got through it, you had to get in the line forming for lunch, and then repeat that for dinner. A line for haircuts, to take a shower, to buy a comb, or take a shit. I'll bet you'd have to get in line to die on this big mother.

I tried to pass the time by reading and playing chess. I read a couple of psychology books, the most interesting by Maxwell Maltz, called *Psychocybernetics*, which I enjoyed and which gave me some insight into myself. I thought I was getting pretty good at chess until a kid from Georgia came down to my area and beat me with what he called fool's mate. It was humbling and embarrassing. I was back in a flash to *Psychocybernetics*, while trying to figure out how I got my clock cleaned so badly. I never did figure it out, but I also never opened my mouth again about how good a chess player I was.

Life aboard ship was like the other two times I'd been on board. Hurry up and wait! Only this time it was a long wait. Thirty days at sea crossing the Pacific was a bit much. Three times longer than crossing the Atlantic when we'd gone on the NATO cruise to Norway the previous fall. The worst part was the unending boredom of guard duty.

In the compartments down below, life was a bit close for me. There were eight to ten Marines in one row of bunks that ran vertically, from top to bottom. The bunks were about a shoulder-width apart. So you can imagine how cozy it was when all nine of us were in the bunks at the same time. I was six foot three and weighed in at 190 pounds. If I was on my back and wanted to turn on my stomach, my shoulders hit the guy above me on the way around. It was not for the claustrophobic. It was all an adjustment in living and a time to develop your patience. Guys coming and going at all hours and having to climb up or down to get to their racks. You'd have to slide in and out horizontally to make it all work. The aroma of quarters so close could be pretty bad. But we all survived.

As we grew closer to Nam, we started having meetings to tell us what to expect. By then, we were so bored that the meetings were a welcome break. You could only watch so many clouds and whitecaps out across the ocean. We learned we'd all be replacements for guys coming home. Guys who would be coming home, we realized, one way or the other. Some came home on the passenger jets as they rotated back to the World. Still others raced home on hospital planes, lying on gurneys while hooked up to plasma. They came home to loved ones waiting, terrified, of they knew not what. And still others made the trip home in coffins.

As we came ashore at Da Nang, it struck me that the place could just have easily been Santo Domingo. It had pure white beaches and looked green and lush. It was hot and very humid. I didn't know if we'd need our K-bar knives for fighting, but they'd come in damn handy to cut through the humidity. It was just incredible, as if a wall of warm jelly hung in the air.

The only good thing I could see about landing was getting our feet back on solid ground. And then there was knowing that, if you were lucky, you'd never have to sleep that close to another man again in your whole life. The fresh air was a treat, and we enjoyed the breeze blowing near the coastline.

There must be something about landing on a beach these days that draws "friendlies" to the welcoming party. We were met by a few Marines already ashore, as well as a small contingent of little, queer-looking people in military uniforms. We'd soon learn they were the ARVNs, troops from the Army of the Republic of Vietnam. They were the home team, and we were there to help. They sure looked like they needed some help. They didn't look very fearsome to me, a tick or two up the scale from the Dominican Army maybe.

Exiting our floating home, we were just a big mob. Nine hundred kids, from all over the country, arriving to fight a war most of us knew nothing about, in a country whose location most of us couldn't have found on a globe. It took several hours to get us organized and moved inland to what was becoming the Da Nang Air Base. Once there, we were told we'd spend the night. In the A.M. we'd be divvied up and sent to our new units. We were all set up in squads and platoons and given wood hootches with metal roofs. Word had it these were built by the Seabees (U.S. Navy construction units) and they'd be "as good as it'd get." But those old wooden cots were a welcome sight after thirty days on board ship.

I was trying to settle in for a last night of security when Thompson came by to say good-bye in case he missed me in the morning. That was nice in a place where nice was usually absent. He was a good kid who didn't want any part of Marine life as I knew it; he didn't want to drink, run around, or go for the glory of it all. Yet, we'd somehow got along and become friends in the process. I often found myself wishing I were more like him. But I was still chasing the Marines I'd learned about in the fifth grade. As I did, there was shooting starting up, off in the hills somewhere. I sat up and walked outside. In the distance, tracers pierced the night sky and grenades boomed. Then the sounds of Marine artillery going off nearby brought me face to face with the reality of war. Nothing like a huge explosion or two to wipe the smile off your ugly face. It was then that I really felt ten thousand miles from home.

Inside, I lay back in my old wooden rack. My mind raced, filling with anticipation. What was it like out there? What was all the shooting? Was it always like that, every night? The screened sides of our hootch let in a slight breeze, and that was the only comfort we could get from the stifling heat that had swallowed us whole. Most of the land around the hootches had been cleared, leaving fields of bare earth as our resting place. I could only lie there trying to imagine the world I would enter in the morning. Sleep wouldn't come easy that night, but it was nice being in semifresh air and out from under eight other Marines.

I lay back, thinking only of getting my tour of duty done. I just wanted to race and chase women. But, for reasons I didn't understand, I needed to finish doing the Marine thing. But long term, my life would be racing and working my way up to the Indy cars. My dreams were interrupted by the sound effects echoing from somewhere off in the night. Then I was transported by my overworked imagination back to the hot and heavy streets of old Santo Domingo. There I was, with Sap, Verdy, and

Corporal Levy. And all I could think was that I'd volunteered for the same bullshit again.

It was a long night. With each sound of war that pierced the night, I'd relive Santo Domingo and Sap, Benson, and the quadriplegic from Jersey. It was a night of action for me, old action experienced a second time. Action that weighed me down most of the night.

Reveille came at 0600. I got up like the other 899, not knowing just where I'd be the next day. We gathered our seabags and fell out in company formation. Placing our seabags next to us to mark our spots, off we went to the chow hall for breakfast. As I walked along, I thought that it would probably be the last breakfast for a few of us; I didn't feel a lot like eating.

The talk was all about where we were headed. The fact was, with nine hundred of us, we were heading off in all directions. The hotshots, the guys who thought they were in the know, were always speculating on the downside: big battle looming up north; the hot stuff is down in Chu Lai. I didn't spend a lot of time on that kind of speculation; the Corps didn't care about where an individual went, nor should it. But I did know that I didn't want to be cannon fodder again; I really wanted some control over my young ass. I didn't want some sea-duty corporal without a clue telling me to charge another fucking machine gun. I knew that if I was going to die, I didn't want it to be for nothing. So I tried to steer clear of the breakfast banter at the Da Nang induction area.

Chow behind us, we fell out to bake in the morning sun. It was the first time I was really able to look around to the horizon in daylight. There were hills in the distance; helicopters were as common as butterflies, and F-4 Phantoms were coming and going like United at Cleveland on Thanksgiving. The air was electric with activity as I stood in the melting sun awaiting news of my fate with a few hundred others. I saw Americans were everywhere. Where the hell were those ARVN characters?

I was snatched from my daydreaming when we were called to attention, which, in the sweltering heat, was cruel and unusual punishment. Then the lieutenant in charge of our destinies turned to address us. Two Marines were standing next to him. "At ease, men. I want you all to know we have your assignments, we have the outfits you'll be going to as replacements. We'll tell you where to fall out and report for your lift out to your outfit. Some of you will be going out this morning, some this afternoon, and the remainder sometime tomorrow. Before I read off the list, I have these two gentlemen here from 4th Marines headquarters who need to talk to you about an opportunity they have available. I give you Gunnery Sergeant DuBay and Staff Sergeant Rider." With that, he turned the time over to the two tanned and grizzled Marines. I didn't know what was up, but I assure you I was all ears. I still hadn't ponied up to the idea of being a replacement.

Gunny DuBay was a small, grandfatherly man. But he had the Marine Corps–issue deep voice required of all gunnys. He started by saying, "Marines, I'm Gunnery Sergeant DuBay and this is Sergeant Rider. We've been given the assignment of creating a new outfit for the 4th Marines. We have been tasked with starting what will be the 4th Marine scout-snipers. This will be a unit of some thirty Marines just like many of you. We are taking volunteers. We have a few on board in Phu Bai already. I'll tell you, this work is not for everyone. We know that, and we want you to know that. We only want people that want to do this work!"

He still had my attention. I had no idea what a scout-sniper was, but I sure as hell wanted to know more. Snipers? All I knew was from the movies, where some Nip would climb a tree to shoot at John Wayne, or pop up from a spider hole. But it sounded better than charging machine guns in broad daylight. I stood up straight to hear better; there was chatter all around me as most folks had already heard enough. One of the first things you learned in the Corps was *never* to volunteer, but I'd already broken that commandment a couple of times. One guy mumbled, wanting to know, "How anyone could be so stupid as to volunteer to be a sniper and go out and fight the war one-on-one."

Something about being called a replacement bothered me. I mean, if I was replacing him, what the hell happened to him? Obviously, lots of us out there melting away in the morning sun were replacing folks who'd bought the proverbial farm. I was all for fighting the little bastards and kicking their asses, but I wanted to be smart about it; I'd learned that from my first afternoon in the sun dodging rebel bullets in Dom Rep. What I remembered most about the assault on rebel headquarters was how damned dumb lining up and charging a machine gun in broad daylight was. Macho, maybe, but none too bright. I left there with a *big* learning: that there's gotta be a better way to fight a war.

DuBay gave us a few more kind words and then turned us over to Sergeant Rider. Staff Sergeant Rider was everything you loved in a Marine. He was big and bad and proud of it. I would later learn he was a sixteen-year veteran of the Corps. He and DuBay were Korean War vets. Rider was tall, about six feet five inches of nasty, coated, full-length, in bullshit. But one thing was certain, you knew who was in charge.

"Okay, Marines! I'm here to get some volunteers who want to fight a different war. It's a lonely war. A personal war. I want Marines that can stare a gook down eyeball-to-eyeball. I want you to be able to look 'em in the eye and pull the trigger." Rider spoke my language and kept my attention. He continued, "First off, you must already be qualified as an expert on the rifle range. No expert, no volunteer, *no* exceptions!" he bellowed like a DI having a real bad day.

I'd scored a 223 in qualification, just by the 220 cutoff for expert rifleman. Not bad for a kid who'd never fired more than his Daisy BB gun before. In basic training, when it came time for the rifle range, I was all ears, standing front and center. I wanted to know how to do it right. My dad was a big time deer and moose hunter, but since we were never close, he never taught me, and I never asked. When the Parris Island instructor got hold of me, he got hold of a cherry: "Great! You don't have any bad habits for me to break." I guess I didn't. I was never prouder than when I made it—an expert rifleman in the U.S. Marine Corps! Hot damn!

Rider was in command and on a roll. He was laying out the details of what he wanted and when he wanted it. It all boiled down to his need to know "right now." If we volunteered and signed up, we'd go with him and the gunny first thing in the morning. We'd go to Phu Bai and attend the first sniper school for the 4th Marines, the second for Nam. The first, he said, was in Chu Lai under Captain Russell. He told us the Marines only had snipers during wartime, and we'd be among the first organized since the end of World War II. Now that was reason enough for me, but he continued the sell job: "You young men have a chance to make an impact and be part of history. You can come with us and be part of the best. And as the gunny said, it's not for everyone. It's a lonely job; you'll work in two-man teams, alone. The risks are high. You'll be trained in land-mine warfare and in demolitions. You'll be trained to call in air strikes and artillery. You'll learn to be self-sufficient and survive in the bush. You'll fight a personal, one-on-one war. *You* have to decide if you think you can handle it."

Man, this was the chance to do something few have done. Hell, *no one's* done it since World War II. How many people have *ever* done something like this? It was my chance to do something special and maybe even make a difference. It was a chance to be somebody. And it seemed to offer more control over my life than being just a grunt.

Then my flashbacks jumped out of the shadows again. It was Santo Domingo, and Private Benson was taking a direct hit in the chest right before my eyes. Sap's blood was splattered all over me.

My flashbacks were chased away when Rider yelled over the voices. The debate raging in my mind stopped. I was scared, but I was holding my hand up.

Rider noticed me first and motioned me forward to stand with them. Of the hundred or so standing with me through the recruiting pitch, I was the only one who volunteered. As I reached the front and stood with Rider, I noticed a couple of other Marine replacements standing off to one side. Like me, they were waiting for the sales pitch to finish. They were volunteers from a previous pitch. By the time Rider and DuBay were done pitching the nine hundred replacements from our ship, they'd found only five, five volunteers to be scout-snipers. I walked over and joined the others. One was a kid from Baltimore with a boxer's nose and a bad attitude. He'd joined, as he put it, "to kill some gooks." The other was a kid from Texas. He seemed like a nice guy. He was big into hunting and thought his dad would be proud.

We joined Rider and DuBay as they walked from platoon to platoon. Rider did most of the recruiting. DuBay was just in charge. My mind started to wander all over again. I wanted to kick ass. I really wanted to excel. I wanted to do something special. And I really didn't want to be a number charging up some nameless, godforsaken hill.

The day wore long, hot, and tired before Rider and DuBay got their recruits. Done selling the replacements, they took their catch to a nearby tent. It was obvious by then that unless we really fucked up, we were theirs! Inside, they each sat down at a little makeshift table made of ammo boxes. Nearby was another guy who didn't look like a Marine. He looked a little more intellectual, more educated. He was a navy psychiatrist. I asked Rider, who said the psychiatrist was there to "observe."

The process was pretty simple. One by one we sat down. First in front of DuBay, and then in front of Rider. Both fired questions at us, as the intelligent dude sat at a table watching the goings-on. I was third to go on the firing line. DuBay was first. He turned out to be a fatherly type, especially for a gunny. In the brief time we had, I actually got to like him. He was quiet, almost kind. He asked me to talk about my family, my upbringing, and my experiences. What stood out in childhood? "Why the Marines?" he said. He asked a lot to find out about my personality. But all in all, it was an easy interview. He wanted to know us and who we were since he'd have to train us, I guess. The interview was a surprise to me; I'd expected to be harassed and challenged. I liked the gunny, but he wasn't what I expected. As I moved from him to Rider, I wasn't disappointed anymore; Rider scared the shit out of me.

Rider looked at me and said, "What makes you think you can cut being a sniper in *my* platoon, Kugler?" Now that was a helluva good question. Could I, the kid from Lock Seventeen, really shoot some dink between the eyes? Before I could answer, he says in his patented, smart-ass tone, "Why the hell do you want to be in here anyway?" He grilled me for close to an hour, but I took it the whole way; I was a Marine, and I was used to shit, lots of it. Before it was over, I loved the guy, even if he wasn't too sure about me. I was still scared of him, but I loved him.

I learned early that the truth, however painful, is always the only way to go. In one exchange, I said, "Sergeant Rider, I was in Santo Domingo and got wounded there. I got on line with my platoon and charged a machine gun. We got pinned down in the middle of a field. It was sucking some serious wind doin' that shit. I'm not sure what you have going, but it's gotta be better than the shit I've been through down there." He laughed at my honesty, then challenged me on whether or not I could shoot somebody straight up, straight on, right between the eyes. I sat for a moment, looked him in the eyes, and said, "I don't know, but I sure believe I can. As near as I could tell, last time around, death doesn't bother me much."

We went on talking for longer than DuBay liked. He came by twice to try and move us along. I told him how I felt about the chance to do what so few people in all of history will ever have the chance to do. "How cool has that gotta be, Sarge?" I asked honestly. On that note, the expression that hung on his face betrayed his words; he clearly thought I was a nutcase. But he decided I was okay in his book. I left him to go sit and await my fate with the other volunteers. We'd all gotten off the ship the morning before, and we were now baking in the afternoon sun like a few thousand other American kids in Vietnam.

It was a couple of hours before they finished with the five of us. They then had to confer with the navy dude, who'd been sitting around like a cigar-store Indian all afternoon. He just sat and watched the goings-on, apparently as bored as we were. In the distance we could see the last remnants of our nine hundred or so replacements. They were breaking up, to travel to their new homes on day two of 395 days in Vietnam.

Eventually, Rider walked back in with DuBay right on his ass. It looked like Rider ran the place, not DuBay. You couldn't help but like DuBay, though. I'd never had a grandpa; mine died in a railroad accident long before I arrived on the scene. But if I could have picked one, DuBay would've been a good choice; he was a genuinely nice fellow. Rider on the other hand was the kind of guy you wouldn't let near your family. Unless, of course, the shit was about to hit the fan, then you'd want him living right next door. He was the kind of Marine I'd read about back in Mrs. Lyons's class a lifetime ago: a badass, kick-ass Marine.

Rider and DuBay started out by giving us the usual Marine Corps shit about not being sure if we could hack it and not being sure whether we'd make it all the way through training before they announced, "You're all in. For now!" I was elated! I wasn't sure why, but I damned sure was.

Rider took off to check out our transportation. DuBay explained we'd be flying to Phu Bai in choppers. Phu Bai, a couple hours north of Da Nang, was where the 4th Marines was headquartered. Rider would take us up, where we'd join some in-country Marines from the grunts who'd already volunteered. DuBay, being a decent human being and all, welcomed us to his outfit. He told us he was proud of us for stepping up and being willing to be part of something, he believed, could make a difference in the war. I couldn't help but think that the two men were as different as ice and water. Oh they were technically the same, both being Marines and all, but that's where the similarities ended.

DuBay would stay behind and continue recruiting other in-country Marines to fill out his platoon. I got the distinct impression that there weren't a lot of volunteers to be had. Rider returned with a 6 × 6 truck (pronounced "six-by-six" or, more simply, "six-by") he'd commandeered from Motor T. Five of us, all newly appointed snipers, piled in the back of the truck. Rider and the driver were up front. The six-by roared off in a cloud of dust. We were on our way to the airstrip to catch our chopper for Phu Bai.

I stared around me, taking in all the newness along with a mouthful of dust. I couldn't help but wonder how long it'd be before I'd be out shooting people that looked just like the ones walking along the road. Could I do it? What if I couldn't? Hell, why was I worrying? I didn't have any trouble shooting at people in Santo Domingo. When your ass was on the line, it wasn't hard to pull the trigger. Then I thought, what if your ass *isn't* on the line? What if you're just hiding someplace and have to shoot a person? Wouldn't it just be like now, riding along looking at people who look strange to you and *bam!* You shoot their ass out of this life and into the next! I'd shot the rifleman on the rooftop in Dom Rep, but he was shooting at me.

We rode along for forty-five minutes, and my mind wan-

dered the whole time. We traveled through some part of
Da Nang and eventually into the bigger part of the Marine base. Despite the occasional sounds of war off in the
distance, we could've been visiting any tropical island
with a U.S. base on site. It was heavy military all the way,
and there was an air of activity and excitement all
around. It had the feel of adventure but without the omi-
nous threat I'd imagined during my flashbacks the night
before.

At the chopper pad there were green helicopters by
the dozen, in all shapes and sizes and in all states of repair. There you could easily distinguish the old salts from
the rest of the Marines working on and around them.
The salts wore an attitude of "fuck it" so obvious you
could spot it from a passing six-by. I wondered how long
it would take me to get in the "groove" of the war. I
wondered deep down inside if Rider was right when he
asked if I could do the job. But I caught myself. Shit! I
can do it, dammit! I remembered Parris Island and STB.
I learned from Sergeant Tarawa, and I remembered the
break he gave me. I also remembered that he taught me I
could do anything.

After a few miscues, we arrived at the part of the air
wing Rider was looking for. I got the feeling that Rider
had been a supply officer in a previous life; he seemed to
know everyone and everything and how to get it. We'd
soon learn that he did know everyone and how lucky we
were to be with him. Especially when we needed something, anything. The six-by finally came to a stop for
good. We jumped off, dragging our seabags as we went.
Rider hurriedly directed us to the chopper for the lift
north to our new home.

The chopper was a UH-34. One of the old gas jobs

where the pilots are way up high and the troops underneath. Every time I got in one, it reminded me of a mosquito puffed up, full of blood, out of shape, and looking like it can't get off the ground. And the one Rider got for us was no cherry either. It was green all over and looked worse for the wear it'd experienced during its time in Vietnam.

We got inside, and I got the first of many surprises about life inside a combat zone. The inside of the chopper was bare: no seat belts, no seats, no nothing. It was the five of us, Rider, and the door gunner with his M-60 and his bad-ass attitude. Oh yeah, there was the floor, where we all sat down and held on to whatever we could find, which was not much. We sat back for a little wait while they warmed up the engine. It wasn't long before we got the thumbs-up.

With a deafening roar, the UH-34 took us airborne for the first time in Nam. The roar of the motor reminded me of the medevac out of Santo Domingo. That one had carried us offshore to the USS *Wasp* less than a year ago. The chopper shook so violently on takeoff that I was sure every bolt holding it together would either break or vibrate loose. Suddenly the tail was up, the nose was down, and we were a few feet off the ground and moving forward. The flight smoothed out as we picked up speed. Damned if the thing didn't fly!

I can't say the noise ever got any better, but the vibration seemed to subside with altitude and airspeed. As we raced through the early evening sky, our door gunner was vigilant. I got the feeling he wouldn't require a lot of reason to blow the shit out of somebody. Flying along, I looked out over the countryside and scanned the horizon. It was a gorgeous day, too damned humid, but at least here we had some wind coming in through the open chopper door, and that helped a lot with cooling. Peering out the window, I was struck by the beauty of the South China Sea and Vietnam's magnificent white coastline. The ground was either brown or a lush tropical green. In between was a patchwork of water-filled squares that had to be rice paddies. I'd never seen rice paddies before. We whisked along north to Phu Bai. As we did, I reflected on the beauty below and what a contrast a war must be in a place like this. My mind drifted back to Oceanside and "the World," as they called it in Vietnam. I knew I had work to do. But then it was home to the States. Back to my dream of racing cars and bikes. My daydreams were fueled by the peace of the moment. The sound of the engine on our UH-34 became my mantra. I drifted deeper and deeper into my world to come. Hell, I got just 394 days left in Nam. Maybe I'll just stay in California when the war is over and party for a little while.

Reality returned as I gazed out the chopper's window. We were cutting through the air on our way to Phu Bai. We were going to be in sniper school with Sergeant Rider. There he was, slouched down across from me, hat over his face, sleeping, not a care in the world as we whirled northward, flying into we knew not what. Somewhere down below a war was going on. That day it was not for us. But the war down there was waiting. The skies were a brilliant blue, just beginning to darken as we flew. Puffy white clouds dotted the evening sky as we whirled our way toward our new home.

CHAPTER TWO

Phu Bai, Sniper School, and Well . . . This Ain't Your Father's Oldsmobile!

I might've dozed off like Rider, but reality zoomed back when I nearly fell over on him. The chopper was in a steep bank as we descended into Phu Bai; they wanted to drop right in over the airstrip without risking a long descent, which was a magnet for bad guys. The door gunner yells, "Snipers, you know!" pointing to the ground around the airstrip. I think, hell no, I don't know, I just got here, asshole. The irony hits me that we have a chopper load of snipers and would-be snipers and he's yelling his guts out worrying about snipers. Rider must've read my mind when he screamed, "You ain't snipers yet!" He had a way of keeping us honest.

As we swirled through the steep bank, I could see some clues of what life would be like down below at that place called Phu Bai. As the turn continued, out my window I saw the last glimpse of the South China Sea a few miles off. Then I saw the mountains, big mountains, a few klicks west. Even from the chopper, they looked mean and ugly. Phu Bai was a lot farther from civilization than Da Nang had been. It was a step deeper into the mud and muck of war. And I didn't know the half of it.

As we revved for final descent, the roar of the motors was deafening. Out of the corner of my eye, I saw the outline of an old building. Then we came down out of the sky with a smash and hit the ground hard, creating a huge dust billow all around us. The dust came down on us like it was raining sand, but felt good to be on the ground again. We gathered our wits and our things and, one by one, piled off the helicopter. We were home.

Rider was off first, leading the way toward an old French hangar. It was tall and open and had a little office in one corner. Around the office stood an equal number of U.S. Marines and those ARVN characters. The area was busy, alive with people going everywhere, but it was a lot different than Da Nang. Da Nang was big and getting bigger. It was official. This was unofficial. What struck me the most was those folks had things to do. No makework there. Military formality as I had known it hadn't gotten on the chopper with us. Even Rider was more relaxed than I'd seen him. He was laughing, talking, and running around. But right then he was about to leave us all behind. His six-foot-five-inch frame and long legs were making some serious time. It wasn't long, and five new snipers were sucking wind. We walked along behind Rider, pushing ourselves to keep up, which was quite a chore.

As I struggled along behind, seabag on my shoulder, my only thought was how damned hot it still was and how filthy and dirty everything was. Dust and dirt were in abundance. Helicopters were everywhere, just not as many as at Da Nang. Vehicles of all kinds, shapes, and sizes were everywhere. Some just roaming around, others sitting about. So why the hell were we racing along on foot?

It was flat around Phu Bai. There was lots of dirt divided by lush green tree lines and hedgerows. I could see
that much. A few Vietnamese were around as well. The
Vietnamese were a strange looking people, small, unkempt, and dirty looking. They wore silklike, baggy outfits, and some had what looked like rags wrapped around
their heads. I walked along wondering why so many Vietnamese were on the base. Aren't we fighting them over
this oven of a country they call home? God it was hot! It
was so hot that caring about anything else was a chore.

Eventually Rider's forced march ended when we all
arrived at a row of well-framed, perfectly squared tents.
As I walked inside, I could see the secret. Somebody had
built a tent frame out of two-by-fours and laid the damn
tent over it. They had wooden floors and screened sides
so you could roll up the tent sides and get air. Not bad!
Lots better than that fucking ship we were in. But air? If
there was any air to get, I'd be gettin' it. Sweat was rolling
off me, and my clothes were soaked a couple of times
through.

We were glad to reach the tent identified by Rider as
our hootch. We walked in behind him. Wooden cots lined
most of one side and all of the other, ten or eleven cots in
all. Personal items were lying all over the place. But
there wasn't a swinging dick to be seen anywhere. Where
the hell was everyone? It was about 1630 hours, and the
five of us were looking for the bunkmates Rider'd been
talking about. Maybe they're at chow. Then Rider bellowed, "Okay, assholes, drop your gear and follow me;
we're going to a meeting."

We tossed our gear on the floor, then raced out to
catch Rider, who'd stepped from our hootch and taken off
like a streak. He had five sweating, confused, and hungry
soon-to-be snipers trailing behind. We walked down a dirt

area between rows of hootches, including some with shiny metal roofs. They were like little houses with screened sides. As we walked, a noise grew louder with each step. The more we walked, the louder it got. Finally we turned a corner on Rider's heels and ran smack into a group of Marines. They were everywhere. Laughing, talking, Budweisers in hand; they were in character, as Marines with beer will be. We were elated—it was the club, not another meeting! Rider waded right into the middle of the group, and bodies parted like the Red Sea at the sight of Moses. Rider was obviously a big deal there. He knew everyone and their dog, too. I thought, Hell, I hit the big one on this deal. Rider's team was the right choice all right. He dived nearly headfirst into a cooler filled to the brim with ice and beer. He got us each a cold Bud. It was cold and it tasted good. Rider said, "Drink up, fellas, and get as drunk as you want. But we still start tomorrow at 0600." Now he was my kind of guy.

The cold, cold beer was a serious treat. It hit the spot dead on. It also made being new in town a whole lot easier. Da Nang was long ago. We'd missed lunch, and I was near dehydration from the sun, which felt like it was an inch or two from my head. All those things combined to insure we got a buzz on pretty quick. Rider told us to drink up while the supply lasted. They'd overlook the usual two-beer ration. I just knew Rider had something to do with that one; I could tell rules weren't his strong suit.

We noticed a big commotion in the far corner of the club tent, with lots of yelling and screaming going down, and I imagined crawling my way out of another bar fight like the one back in Gitmo. I mustered some gumption and walked closer to check it out, a couple of the new snipers trailing behind me. The uproar was a chugalug contest, and it was already down to the last two guys; both were zonked out of their minds. They were shirtless, heads back, foaming at the mouth, guzzling away, their Buds straight in the air. Beer was gurgling out of their mouths and running down their bare chests. People were yelling and screaming; I thought I was back in Tijuana for a minute. Then it was over in a few seconds. A guy with a barrel chest and a pair of wild eyes was declared the winner.

We weren't surprised when Rider walked out and put an arm around each of them. He was proud as a new parent and why not? They were both snipers from our outfit. We found out it was Rider's thing: we needed to win *all* of the chugalug contests. Period. He didn't want excuses, just victory. He'd declared it! The two contestants needed help getting around, and Rider gave it to them. He was heading our way. The winner with the barrel chest was a lance corporal they called Zulu. The loser was his boot-camp buddy from eastern Maine. He was a wild one, too. He wasn't as big as Zulu in body, but made it up in spirit. Rider came over and said, "Fellas I want you to meet Zulu and Wiener. They're our chugalug champions. One of 'em wins every night. You'll be expected to carry the tradition on." With that, we all met up with each other for the first time.

Zulu was actually personable, even when dead drunk. Wiener could care less. He just said his hi's and byes and headed off with an "I'll catch you all later." Zulu was ever the perfect host. He shook our hands and made the rounds to find out where everyone was from. He even asked, "Do you have an old lady back home?" He was a bit weird, but I liked him. He talked with a real intensity. With him, you got more than his undivided attention; you got Zulu, straight up. You could tell he was a bright dude. But boy, he was really different. Eventually, to my surprise, Zulu came strutting up to the end of our circle, looked all of us over, then stared at me. "Kugler, huh? Well, you're now Kug. Come with me; we need to get to know each other. See you fellas around." Arm around my shoulder, Zulu takes me off to have a beer. Turns out, he's in search of a partner.

He walks me over to a bunker where we take up residence by standing alongside and holding it up. Zulu leads us through the usual bit of where you from, how long you been here, and what's Nam about. I learn Zulu is from a small town in New Mexico. He was a high school wrestler, football player, and cockhound. He thought it'd be cool to join the Marines and kick some ass. He was intrigued by my small-town roots and really got off on my shit in Santo Domingo.

We drank the twilight of an early evening into the total darkness of a Nam night. There wasn't any action in the neighborhood, but Zulu said it was coming soon. He'd been in country about six months as a grunt. He'd volunteered to join Rider and be a sniper. He loved Rider. As a grunt, he'd been with Kilo 3/4 and faced down a human-wave assault by the NVA. There was definitely something weird about the guy. He told me how eerie combat was, how it freaked lots of guys out. He explained the thousand-yard stare and described where it comes from. As he told me, he almost watered at the mouth with excitement. He actually had a twinkle in his eye . . . but I liked him. The lectures of Professor Zulu ended about midnight, and we weaved our way back to the sniper area. I couldn't remember which hootch I'd put my gear in. I followed Zulu into his area. He was more than a little under the weather when he said, "Fuck it! Take this rack next to me, we'll worry about the details tomorrow." Then, without a word, he just lay flat out on his back, sound asleep. I was left to do the same. I wasn't sure where the hell I was. I'd soon learn that doing whatever he wanted, to whomever he wanted, whenever he wanted, was Zulu's trademark.

Sleep was an elusive target that night. In my semiconscious state, I could hear explosions in the distance, and I wondered if someone out there had just bought the farm. Zulu's stories of the bush were fresh and alive and raced through my mind. He talked in such graphic detail, I felt like I was there. He talked about girls back home. I wondered what they were doing about then. That kind of life was far away and seemed so long ago. That part of my past was a life very different from Zulu's. Now the days were filled and overflowing with new and strange goings-on. The days . . . what day was it anyway? Wednesday, I think. I didn't know. It wouldn't be long until days and weeks and months would mean nothing. Right now, I needed to get through my first night in Phu Bai.

It could've been a bull moose in heat, but it was Sergeant Rider invading our dreams. It was 0530, and man, morning came early around there. He came screaming in our hootch with his personalized good morning. We'd learn that greetings from Rider were always special. This one was a surprise. It was just last night he told us we wouldn't get started 'til we filled out the platoon. But it was still the Corps so we were up.

We were up and at 'em everyday at 0530 just as Rider had promised. It made no difference that we didn't have anything to do all day. But that was the Marine Corps way. So our first few days, every day, were filled with early reveille and late taps. As Rider and DuBay assembled the troops, the rest of us drank the night away in wait. When I wasn't drunk, I wrote a few letters home. I needed to pass on my new address so the folks back home could catch up with me. By the time I left the States, the girlfriends were falling like flies. When I left for the Corps, my high-school flame had gotten married, and another member of my Caribbean foursome had since joined the married ranks. Letters home were to Mom, Dad and, now and then, my younger brother. My older sister was already pretty distant, so we didn't have much in common. Aunt Florence and Grandma lived with us, and they were faithful supporters, always interested in what I was doing. But the girls ... well, Zulu had a more active pool of followers than I did. And I didn't need the hassle just then. The days were slow and hot. I couldn't get over the heat. The old salts kept telling us we'd get used to it, but that didn't seem possible to me in the beginning.

The platoon was growing, but not fast enough for me; I wanted to get on with life and get to training. We had a pug-nose Polish kid from Baltimore, a tall Texan we called Trip, and another Polack from Chicago we called Corporal Ski. Then came Royal, a nice, cultured kid from Virginia. Then there were Wiener and Zulu, who'd been friends since San Diego boot camp. But they didn't like each other enough to bunk or be on a team together. They also disliked most of the new guys coming into the group. They really hated the big, whiny kid from Kansas City. I didn't like him much either. His world revolved around him. He might as well have walked around with a mirror hanging in front of his face. All he could talk about was "his" parachuting and "his" tough life back home and "his" shooting. The nicknames were just the standard military fare. I guess it was a way of not getting close enough to care. The guy next to you might not be standing tomorrow.

It was at Phu Bai that Zulu introduced me to Nero

Wolfe, the consummate detective. Of course, I hadn't heard of him. Zulu was just amazed. "Where the fuck have you been, man?" he yelled. "What an asshole. You don't know Nero Wolfe!" He went to his footlocker and produced several books featuring his hero. He waved one around and headed my way. "Kug, you asshole, if we're gonna be partners, then you gotta know about my man Nero." Shiiit! I gotta read this shit . . . but what about this being your partner? Zulu had decided I was the guy. He and I had about as much in common as a cheap whore and the Pope, but . . . Zulu had spoken.

We lost about a week while the platoon waited for troops. Rider and DuBay were looking for a whole platoon of men for the 4th Marine scout-snipers. But, come Monday morning, Day One of sniper school, they had eighteen volunteers, twelve shy of the thirty they were after. The recruiting would continue forever. But the group was real interesting: we had people from all walks of life, all areas of the country, and every reason for being here you could imagine. The one thing we had in common was that we had nothing in common. Lots of unique people together to kick ass and kill gooks: some couldn't wait to kill, others didn't know if they could, but all were ready to try.

By Monday morning, I was ready. Sitting around, telling endless stories, reading Nero Wolfe, and getting drunk were all wearing old. I was ready.

Sniper school, Day One, was not my idea of fun. Interesting, yes, fun, no. It was hot, humid, and tiring. We sat in a tent trying to learn about our new weapons. Hell, we couldn't even keep them dry, sweating the way we were. It was frustrating as hell: we had to know about our weapons, but wanted to go out and *do it*. We bitched to

Rider. He said tomorrow was it, and we'd wish we were back in the tent. The saving grace was Rider himself. His one-liners and tall tales made life interesting. DuBay was the weapons man and confined most of his talk to that area. Rider was the operations guy. He knew the field, and he loved our weapons. The problem was they both wanted us to love them, too. And the one thing that'd get Grandpa DuBay's dander up was to not care for a weapon. He'd go from nice to nasty in about three seconds from a standing start if he saw a dirty rifle. Those lifers were all the same. I expected us to break out in that Parris Island favorite "this is my rifle, this is my gun, this is for fighting, this is for fun!" any minute. Complete with grabbing our dicks just like Parris Island.

The day wore on like a bad boot while we talked about the history of Marine snipers. They were successful on the islands in the big one, World War II. We talked about the philosophy of snipers in Vietnam and how that related to the island warfare of World War II. Rider told us the purpose of our platoon was to put snipers out in the bush so they could harass the gooks the same way the gooks were doing to us. To do that, you had to have the head for being a sniper first. Rider could teach us to shoot, but mentally, we either had what it took to be a sniper or we didn't. Period.

They gave us an article from the *Sea Tiger* about Captain Russell, who'd started Marine snipers in Nam. The article read, "The ability to go long periods without food and water, to control emotions and to kill 'calmly and deliberately' without remorse are the main qualifications of a good sniper." It went on to say, "A good sniper is born . . . not made." It said that snipers should undergo psychiatric examination, and I guess we had. At least, the navy psychiatrist had been listening. The article said we had to have "certain essential skills," that we had to be intelligent enough to learn a wide variety of skills such as ballistics, radio, calling in artillery fire, map reading, and the collection and reporting of intelligence information. Since sniper teams operate alone and go for long periods of time without contact, they have to be self-reliant. Captain Russell is quoted as saying, "Sniping is a very personal war. A sniper . . . must kill calmly and deliberately, shooting carefully selected targets and must not be susceptible to emotions or anxiety. They will see the look on faces of the people that they kill."

DuBay had been on the Marine rifle team, and we'd soon discover he knew his weapons. When the platoon got going, he'd act as the armorer. He offered us a choice of weapons. A Winchester Model 70, 30-06 was the basic weapon of choice. It was a match rifle put together specifically for our work, and it was a beauty. It had an extended barrel, lengthened an extra four inches to give us more accuracy. It had a floating barrel with an oversize and very heavy stock to give us more stability. It looked a little like my dad's deer rifle, so it sounded fine to me. Zulu and I decided right away to be Winchester men.

The other rifle option was a resurrected version of the old M-1, an age-old favorite of gun lovers everywhere. But not this kid. It looked old, and was even older than it looked. It was reliable and proven. It was an excellent weapon. It just didn't light my fire. Zulu and I looked it over but decided to stay with Winchester. Hell, at that point in my experience, looks alone did it. Model 70 just looked like it'd shoot a helluva lot farther than the old-fashioned looking M-1.

For the Winchester, we'd choose between two scope

options. The recommended was a long, skinny, odd-looking thing with a weirder name. The eight-power ($8\times$) Unertal. Or we could get a basic three-by-nine variable (i.e., the 3×9). The M-1 guys, and there were a few, got only one choice, a little toy of a thing, just a two-scope that mounted on the side of the rifle. It was great for ruining your eye if you didn't hang on to it. That little mother would get you when you fired off a round and the rifle recoiled.

Now that we could see and touch our weapons, our excitement started to grow. We had something besides each other to be pissed at. We had a reason to focus and something in common besides "back home." We each chose a rifle setup that we'd start off with. Of course, as we learned more, we could change. And we began to see that we had a lot to learn. And I was glad to be learning alongside Zulu. I was getting pumped.

Zulu was different, but I knew from Dom Rep that when the proverbial shit hits the fan, it's good to have a whacko by your side. You didn't want a bookworm that knew how it "should be"! They didn't have an ounce of common sense and would be of little use when lead was flying. There were lots of those around, but not many had held up a hand for our outfit. Thank God for small favors.

We finished Day One looking, feeling, touching, and nearly tasting the weapons at our disposal. Zulu and I had already decided we were Winchester men, so that was a done deal. We picked the rifles we wanted and signed them out, attesting and avowing with our blood, sweat, and tears, to allow our balls to be cut out person-ally by Rider if we ever lost the things, in combat or not. "Die with the bastard," he said, "but don't you ever let it fall in the wrong hands." Rider ended by telling us we'd be on trucks at 0630 and on the range by 0700. We were to take two canteens of water in case "the mule" didn't show up as promised. With that advice, we were free to keep our record going at the club and win another chugalug contest.

The nights at school went as usual for Nam. Darker than dark, like sleeping in a sauna, and the only saving grace was it was drunk out again, so sleep was possible. The drinking fit me at the time. I'd always needed my booze. I started back at Poon's, what seemed like a lifetime ago. Somehow, the booze seemed to make it all go easier. Problem was, I was never sure what "it all" was. I could only lie there wondering what tomorrow and the training range would bring, and stare out through the side screens of the hootch and up at the star-filled night sky of Phu Bai. I lay there for a while, floating in a Budweiser-fueled dream, wondering what my old girls were doing. Would they bother to write, or were the bridges too badly burned? I loved looking out at the night sky and imagining it was a giant mirror, reflecting our image to someone on the other side of the world who was peering up at the same stars. Then the screaming of Rider interrupted my mental odyssey. It was morning. Oh man!

Five-thirty is too damned early to do anything except be zonked out, especially for a bunch of eighteen- and nineteen-year-olds with hangovers. I was hurtin' for certain. I needed sleep, but sleep didn't need me. Sergeant Rider did, though! He got us up, cleaned up, and ready for our six-bys in record time. It was a record for me and Zulu, anyway.

At 0630, after a horrible breakfast at the mess tent, we grabbed our gear, our weapons, and our asses and piled into two six-bys. It was already steaming. Rider was in charge, sitting in the cab front of one truck, with DuBay in the cab of the other. We peons were left to sit, stand, or lie all over the back.

The dirt road ahead wound lazily across scrubby, rolling hills leading west of the airstrip. Along lots of it, Marines were digging hastily fortified positions, lots of foxholes and a growing number of sandbags. The area was protected by concertina wire laid in rows at the front of the Marine perimeter. That made us realize we were in a real war. As we bounced along, I was thinking that *The Story of the U.S. Marines* had become real life for the kid from Lock Seventeen.

The two dirty, dusty trucks and their cargo, a light platoon of would-be snipers, passed through the main gate of the Phu Bai base camp. The five or six of us who had just arrived in country a week or so earlier sat up to take notice. We were leaving what felt like our only security. Looking around, I could see for a long way across barren rolling hills. I wondered about the enemy's snipers. Weren't they a threat? Zulu laughed when I asked that, put his hat back over his face, and lay back down. I wondered how on earth he could rest. We were outside the base weren't we? Didn't he care? Clearly, he didn't. Only us new guys in country cared, and we were left to wonder and worry in silence.

We soon pulled up on top of a small hill that had a couple of strange-looking cement monuments surrounded by what looked like grave markers. The hills formed a little bowl with the marker to one side behind us. Our trucks chugged to a stop, brakes squealing, leaving us sitting in a thick cloud of dust. It was 0700 when eighteen coughing, choking, and filthy Marines piled off. We looked around but saw only dirt and rolling hills.

Rider jumped out and quickly took charge. He told us

no grab-ass, just get over here and sit down. We all sat down with Zulu. Rider said, pointing to his rear, "You see that bowl behind me? It's formed by those two hills, there and there." I looked but saw nothing more than dirty hills adorned with a few scrubby bushes. To the rear and behind them were mountains, green as a golf course, but they looked like major ball busters to me. I could see them. But a *bowl* in front of me? What is he talking about?

We all must have looked like a blank screen. Frustrated, Rider started waving his arms and shouting, "It's right there!" But it wasn't quick enough for Rider. He said, "Look, assholes, it's right there!" I think we started getting a clue, I know I did. And pointing once again to the "bowl" it started to make sense. We were still too slow for Rider. He says, "Fuck it, follow me." He tells the two Motor-T drivers to watch out for snipers. The rest of us were to follow him. We go chasing this guy who could chew up the ground like a damn Rototiller. Man, could he walk. And man, were we trying to keep up.

It took us a lot of sweat and a little time to get to the bowl he was talking about, the sides of two hills that came together to form a U facing "our" hill. Rider had had the engineers come out to map out our range. They'd driven tall metal fence stakes in the ground at various distances. The stakes were the kind you might use for a snow fence back home. I looked back at the Motor-T guys. It was a helluva ways back to the trucks. It was going to be one long shot from back there. Rider was explaining as he took us on a tour. The first set of stakes was set at four hundred meters. There were two or three stakes at each distance, placed ten or so yards apart. That distance was doable; we did five hundred meters in boot camp with open sights.

Rider had us carrying 105mm artillery casings. He took one of them and placed it, open end first, down over the top of a metal stake. Then he covered the other two at four hundred meters. The way they'd been driven into the ground, they stuck up four and a half or five feet in the air. Rider said, "You see, guys, this canister represents the killing zone of your target. It's about chest high. When you learn to hit this, you'll hit them."

He called Rooster over, the Baltimore kid with the pug nose, short little bastard, about five and a half feet high. Rider had him stand beside the "target." The canister hanging over the top of the fence post. Well I'll be dogged. It's chest high on Rooster. Hell, that makes it gut high on me; I'm six foot three. Rider explains that most gooks are about Rooster's height. He tells us the canister is about eighteen inches long and six inches across. He says that's roughly the center of mass of a man's chest. That's where we were to learn to aim. "That's our dead center," Rider says. "If you can hit this canister, you can nail a gook right where it counts," and he pointed to his own heart. The excitement was building in us as fast as the heat from the morning sun.

We followed Rider in a walk around the bowl, identifying each and every stake the engineers had set for us at one-hundred-meter intervals. At each one, Rider placed a canister over it. We set targets at four hundred, then set five hundred, six hundred, seven hundred, eight hundred, nine hundred, and one at a thousand meters! A kilometer! I turned around and looked back at the trucks. I got excited just thinking about mastering that distance. It was a challenge, but I knew I could do it. I was really psyched! Zulu just smiled. The walk back went a lot easier because it was fueled by our anticipation. Rider made the dirt hills of his firing range come to life with the possibilities.

We joined DuBay back on our little rise, where he'd been setting things up. He was more cautious than Rider, so he wanted constant security. We'd take turns, two of us at a time, going off to watch out for enemy snipers in what turned out to be a Buddhist graveyard. Zulu and I got first duty because he sucked up to Rider, saying he'd handle it to start off. DuBay had the others filling sandbags with dirt to use for rifle support. They were needed to sight our rifles. The sandbag affair would take an hour or so, time Zulu and I spent "guarding" their efforts.

I wasn't the brightest bulb in our lamp, but I could see real fast that Zulu knew his way around. To his mind, guarding beat filling sandbags in the hot sun. From the Buddhist cemetery we could see down and around the area surrounding our range. We had our sniper rifles and our 7×50 binoculars. The binoculars were the important thing. With them, we could scan the horizon for bad guys. I was pumped. "This is cool shit, man," I said, turning around to Zulu. And there was my crack partner, lying down inside this cement ring, hat over his face trying to get some Zs. I was astonished! I said, "Zulu! What the fuck are you doing, man? We're supposed to be standing guard out here!"

With the half-evil, half–Eddie Haskell smile that I learned to love to hate, he said "Kug, relax, man. There are no bad guys out here. Rider is just covering his ass with DuBay. Just look busy but relax. Let me get some Zs, and then I'll sit up and look busy while you get some." He smiled, picked up his hat, and started to lie down.

"How the hell do you know there aren't any bad guys out here?"

"Look around, Kug. There ain't shit out here. It's all

dirt for hundreds of yards. The little bastards can't shoot that straight and that far. Trust me, man. I won't steer you wrong. I like you. Now do what the fuck you want, I'm getting some Zs!" I sat on the edge of what turned out to be a pagoda, scared as hell, scanning the horizon and protecting my platoon. And I was also wondering what the hell I got myself into.

It was about 1030 hours before Rider and DuBay were satisfied that we were ready. DuBay was a safety freak. He was nice about it, but real serious. Rider was a safety freak but not so serious nor so nice about it. There was to be no grab-assing or screwing around of any kind.

We paired up in teams of two. As partners, Zulu and I were "heaven sent," according to him. After my recent pagoda experience, I thought he was a madman, yet I wanted him next to me in the wilds. I could tell by the look in his eyes he'd be there for me. He must have felt the same way about me or why the hell would he have chosen me?

The game was, we'd all pair up and start shooting. All the while, DuBay would work his way around and zero in each of our rifles himself. Rider would coach and generally keep us straight. Zulu and I paired up for our first shots. I told him to go first. One man would spot and call the adjustment and the fire for the other. I'd start by using the 7×50s and spot hits for Zulu. Then he'd do mine. Rider and DuBay each had 20× ship's telescopes mounted on tripods. They moved up and down the line, watching each of the teams and providing their own brand of feedback.

From there on in, our days were all the same: shoot from 0700 until about 1500, usually eight full hours. We'd rotate and take a break here and there and eat some C rations, but generally, it was shoot, shoot, and more shoot, eight teams of two shooting at a time with one team in the pagoda. DuBay coached four, and Rider four. They'd switch off so they both worked with all of us.

When 1500 rolled around, the Motor-T guys would be back, and we'd bounce our way back to Phu Bai, eating dust and dirt all the way home. Once back, we'd have an hour to check our mail, clean our weapons, and kick back. At 1600 we'd all head for the club. We'd be sure to get at least two beers, lots more if any of us could work a deal. The club visit would end about 1730 with the daily chugalug contest. Then came the dreaded trip to the mess hall to endure whatever slop they'd dreamed up that day. Chow done, we'd be expected front and center with either Rider or DuBay around 1900 hours. We'd spend a couple of hours debriefing the day and learning about the tactics and strategy of being a sniper. At around 2100 hours, it was free time, knowing we had to be up at 0530 to start all over again. Our recreational choices were a bit limited.

I began to lose track of the days since they were all the same. I decided I'd keep track on a calendar, the popular way to count down the days until you returned to the World. The United States was a faraway dream and my mind was consumed with becoming a Marine sniper. Yeah, I wanted to go home and race and all, but just then, I was becoming a sniper. In the annals of time, how many people had walked our earth as a sniper?

Our first day ran into our first week. Some days I'd come back from the range and wonder if I'd ever hear again. We fired round after round of hand-loaded match ammo. Expensive shit for sure. One-hundred-eighty-three-grain bullets. Boom. Eight hours of nothing but firing or spotting for your partner. It was hours of booms to either side of the head. Headaches were common, but the 1600 club calls usually took care of that, at least until morning. Then we had headaches the size of Kansas. The end of Week One brought us a day off. By then, a day without the range was hard to imagine. It must've been a Sunday, and we got to sleep in 'til 0800. Then we worked on our weapons and talked tactics. I could tell that we were getting closer, developing a common perspective on what it meant to be a sniper. We needed more than the drinking to bring us together, it just took us up a step. The shooting brought us closer, closer as a team, and closer to the reality of the war. We weren't just training anymore; this was it. And, in all probability, some of us weren't going home to live the hopes and dreams we shared when we came. Some of us were going to die.

The end of the week also brought our first mail call. Zulu, Wiener, and the guys who'd been in country for a while had lots of mail. The rest of us had just a little. Me? I had a letter from Mom and one from Dad. It was nice in one way and sad in the other. It was just like being there. I hated how it made me feel. Mom passed on the gossip from her circles. Dad talked of his business as if I were still sitting there pretending to listen. They both expressed horror that I'd volunteered to come to Vietnam. They said they didn't understand why. Mom mentioned that if I needed "help" I should "get it." At least she was more direct, Dad avoided mentioning Vietnam directly. He just said that he wished I hadn't made "that choice." I wished I could be there to see their faces when they opened my letter to learn I'd again volunteered—to be a scout-sniper. What the hell did they think the Marine Corps was supposed to do? Why the hell couldn't they ever just be fucking happy for me?

Week Two was much like Week One. We'd start each

morning by going out to the range. We'd do a walk-around to insure the gooks hadn't booby-trapped our work area. With the area secure, we'd be on our bellies, in the heat, firing round after round into the hillside. Zulu and I were nearly always together. We'd begun to build a real bond. So he was royally pissed when Rider announced we'd be switching off partners. Zulu complained, but it was part of the plan. He complied, but let it be known it was for training only. When we went to the bush, it was he and I. The switch turned out to be a good thing. It was another step in getting closer, becoming better, and getting ready.

We'd started shooting at the four-hundred- and five-hundred-meter targets the previous week. By week's end, we were trying our hand all the way out. We were okay out to about seven hundred meters, but beyond that was an art form we hadn't yet mastered. By then, we were firing so much lead into the canisters we had to replace them every day. Rider let us loose to work our way to a thousand meters during Week Two. It would be our first serious work at that distance. It was a real challenge, to shoot at something you could barely see.

After Week One, we had to lock in our choice of equipment. I chose to keep my Winchester Model 70, 30-06, and I also stayed with the 3×9 variable Marine scope. Zulu matched my choice of weapons. He'd played around with the M-1, but after a day or so he decided against it. The M-1 was a good and reliable weapon. It was also very accurate. But we weren't able to get the distance out of it that we could with the Winchester. We Winchester men had serious sniper weapons. We could hit the thousand-meter canister with a degree of consistency by midweek. At that point, I wouldn't have wanted to be standing out there when we were firing.

Among us the debate raged between the Unertal 8× scope for the Winchester and the 3×9 variable. Zulu argued for and got the Unertal. I stayed with the 3×9. DuBay stood his ground, arguing that there was no right choice, only the one that worked for the shooter; it was a very personal thing. Zulu and I made up our minds about the choice of equipment early; most of the others fretted, debated, and argued the fine points of their choices. In the end, the Unertal was the most popular scope, the Winchester was the rifle of choice, and the M-1 was the chosen winner of only a couple.

The hot and muggy days on the range wore on us as bad as we wore on each other. The heat was having an impact. I left the States with 195 pounds on my six-foot-three frame, but already I could feel I was getting skinny, and I really hadn't done shit yet. But day after long hot day, baking in the sun, drinking piss-warm water from a mule or canteen, didn't exactly serve to fatten us up. The days were just hard work as we lay in the hot sun, firing endlessly at imaginary bad guys. The hard part wasn't the physical work but the physical conditions. Our bodies had to make major adjustments to survive life in the Nam. And it didn't get any better anytime soon.

The heat was worse when we were on the ground shooting. Work on the firing line required focus. Lying out there in the prone position, rifle resting on the sandbags, rifle butt pulled tight into your shoulder, and then repeating that a few hundred times a day. All the while baking like a Japanese lobster stuck on a hot grill. The work required extreme concentration. It required control of our breathing. It required us to empty everything out of our minds. For a few precious seconds, we had to zero in on the target's dead center. I knew I had to be in control to win. And I had to win to stay alive. I knew that DuBay and Rider were right when they said being a sniper was as much mental as it was physical. I had to win the mental game. To do so, I'd have to change.

We worked day after day, and nearly everything we did was repetition. Prone position, rifle at the ready, rifle butt tight to shoulder, stock of the rifle just kissing your cheek at that sweet spot, and everyone had a sweet spot. Clear your eyes, focus, gently place the crosshairs on the target . . . there . . . just right. Now breathe in a nice, slow, deep breath. Then let it out, not all the way, just halfway and now . . . hold, hold it gently . . . now, the grip on your trigger needs to be gentle, "Like you'd squeeze your girlfriend's tit," Rider used to say. Now that brought it all home. Then he'd add, "Let the barrel float ever so slightly in a small circle around the kill zone. When the crosshairs touch the kill zone where you want it, you squeeze off the trigger as soft and gentle as when you'd touch your girl's nipple." Boom! The round rockets off, hitting the target dead center.

It was almost a natural high. It's nearly poetic, an art form. It wasn't long before we consistently put nine out of ten rounds in the canister at four hundred meters. Then five hundred, six hundred, and seven hundred meters. The zero on our rifles was set at six hundred meters. For shorter targets we'd hold down, below our dead center. For longer range shots, we learned to hold up. I learned real fast that the sniping business was really as much art as it was science. The weapons were certainly top-notch and had superb support equipment. Learning to use the weapon properly, with artistry *and* skill, was the key to being an expert sniper. We didn't walk around and impress people with being a sniper. We wanted to go out and deliver the mail via long distance. We learned to work with the weather. The wind was the toughest variable to overcome, but the heat was a factor, too. We had to work in all wind conditions. Rider retaught us the flag system used in boot camp. If the flag is straight out, it's twenty miles per hour plus. Each click of the flag down from the horizontal is less wind velocity. We wouldn't have flags in the bush, but we'd have grass and treetops to use. Again, we're dealing with art. You just had to learn to feel it. There wasn't a tree or tall bush for miles, so Rider placed homemade pennants in the distance to teach us how to judge the speed of the wind. They were an inexact tool but better than nothing. They taught us to use a lot of common things to get the job done. We had to judge distance. We learned to visualize football fields in our mind. We'd flip 'em over, end-for-end, to judge how far a target was from us. It was really important to get the distance close, right on, if we could. We had to know whether to aim up, down, or dead center. We had to judge windage close for the right and left. We needed distance information for the up, down, or dead center. We had to develop serious judgment skills. The necessary skills reminded me of what it took to be a shooter in basketball. Pure shooters had to have touch, and touch came from the head and the heart, deep inside. Pure shooters in Nam were no different. They had to have it, too. And I did!

Toward the end of Week Two, Friday or Saturday, perhaps, we stayed in for Land-Mine Warfare and Demolitions School. DuBay told us we needed it for our own protection. Rider added that it was part of the "scout" part of scout-sniper. Despite the course title, the training was actually a makeshift affair set up by 3d Engineers for folks like us in Nam.

We spent four or five hours with the demo guys learning to identify common booby traps found in I Corps. Most were more particular to Quang Tri Province. We worked in teams, and Zulu and I were together, identifying and learning how each worked. We spent a lot of time learning how they were made. And then we graduated to the double booby trap, where the booby trap was booby-trapped. We learned about the signs used by the enemy to mark the presence of booby traps. The enemy didn't want to blow up their own kind. It was fascinating business. I loved every minute of it. It was intense and serious, and amazingly, not one of us was fucking off. Going in, Zulu had told me to learn as much as I could from it. I did, and demo school was over too soon. They told us we'd be back late next week for more. We needed to know how to set some standard explosives. The demo folks wanted us to know how to recognize the ground weapons used against us and then know how to take care of them, how to disarm or blow them up. I couldn't wait for more, and most of us felt the same way.

With demo school done, and Week Two on the range, we welcomed sleep 'til 0800. But we awoke to the usual weapons work, map and compass work, and more sniper tactics and strategy. Our second mail call came to Sniper Platoon. No letters from the honeys yet, but there was another from Mom. It was bittersweet and much as I'd expected. She was behind me, she said, but she didn't understand me. Why did I get myself involved in something like being a sniper? Dad wrote a short note, never mentioning my choice. He just told me of his battles with the Teamsters Union. Home seemed a very distant place already. I needed to be "here" and not worry about "there."

The other good thing about being at Phu Bai was being clean: It was good to have a day without getting so damned grungy. I had a shower under the fifty-five-gallon water drum that served to wet us down. It was the navy shower—shower on, get all wet, shower off, soap up, shower on and rinse. There was never enough water to keep it running like back home. Still, it felt great. The water was piss warm, but it was at least wet. After the shower, all clean, I went in and lay back for another night of stargazing. Our day off, we didn't do the drinking we did on other days.

I was feeling good, but apprehensive about where I was. I was learning to knock it dead on the range. I was consistent at all the target ranges. I was enjoying learning the strategy of sniping. I loved the mental part of becoming a sniper. But what would things really be like when I got out there? Could I look another person in the eye and pull the trigger? I had on Santo Domingo, hadn't I? Of course, there they were shooting at me.

Another 0530 morning brought the beginning of Week Three, our last. Along with it came the realization that I had to change. I woke up knowing that I wasn't where I needed to be. To do the job right, I would have to eliminate all emotions from my life. I couldn't afford feelings. I'd start immediately by working on my weaknesses. Week Three was crunch time for all of us, but riding to the range I felt good. I knew what I had to do for sniping to work. And I knew I could do it.

We'd all gotten closer over the past two weeks, including DuBay and Rider. DuBay was always worried about us. He didn't want any of us getting hurt. You could feel that he cared more than most. He preached about camouflage techniques, about being careful, and about being prudent when they cut us loose. Rider's counsel was more about kicking ass and doing what had to be done. Those two were a lot like Heckle and Jeckle. They also complemented each other, and we learned to like and respect them both.

Our third week was in mid-April. The old-timers were saying that the hot season was coming. What the hell had we been living if not the fucking hot season? On the other hand, with just over three weeks in country, I felt I might have begun to adjust to the heat.

Week Three was devoted to honing our skills. We got serious shooting for accuracy at long range. We had to do all the range markers that week. *We* judged the range then we zeroed in and made the hit. The targets were different, and we quickly learned that Rider had been out moving targets on our day off. He knew the distance of each, but we didn't. So we rolled those football fields, flipped them end for end. We used the method and learned it well. And it worked. It took us to the next level on our journey to becoming Marine scout-snipers. We were almost home.

To pass on with the big guy's blessing, we were expected to hit each canister on four of five shots. We had to zero in at each yard marker. It worked real well. It wasn't fancy, it was tacky actually, but it was damned effective. A couple of guys struggled early in the week, but Rider brought them around by week's end. The incessant *boom, boom, boom* of us firing our 30-06s, and an occasional M-1 shot, had paid off. All eighteen of us could ding a canister at a thousand meters on four of five shots.

Our final round of shooting took two days. On Day Three, we went to the engineer battalion for the afternoon to finish our work in demolitions. I thought about the quick tour of demo school and all I didn't know. I remembered hand-to-hand training back in boot camp. The instructor told us we'd learn just enough hand-to-hand to go out into the world and get our smart asses kicked. I laughed at the thought of learning just enough to get our smart asses blown into tiny little pieces then be shipped home in a cigar box. What the hell, you had to have a sense of humor to survive.

Demo school started with a review of the previous week's flyby. Then we worked on disarming some of the more basic booby traps. The bulk of the time we spent learning to work with C4 (malleable "plastic" explosive), det cord, and blasting caps. We needed to know how to fashion light explosives. The engineers wanted us to be able to blow the booby traps we found so others wouldn't get killed. Some guys really got off working with explosives. I mean, their eyes lit up, and they got all happy. It did weird things to people. It was interesting as hell to me, but I knew how dangerous that shit was. I was intrigued but not off my nut about the prospect of blowing things up, especially if the "things" had a good chance of including my young ass. I was just nineteen and had hopes of making twenty or so. So I listened up real good.

It was a long afternoon with the engineers. When we finished, we went back to the platoon area and got good and drunk. Our group was much tighter by then. One benefit was having more people look out for you when you couldn't find your way home. And that night was one of those nights. Zulu and I planned on working together, starting the next week. Calls for sniper support were coming in. I'd also gotten close with another kid we called Pearl. He was young and baby faced, but physically and mentally tough. He was from a very small town on the shores of Lake Superior. He was an avid hunter, loved the outdoors, and just wanted to be a game warden when he went home. He'd joined snipers to make his dad proud. They'd hunted together since he was young. He said he knew his dad would want him to do it. Pearl was a nice guy. I liked him a lot. He didn't drink much and had no desire to whore around. Pearl was my second choice for a partner. He helped me home from the club and into my rack, near him.

Our last day, we spent at the artillery battalion on Phu Bai, where we had a crash course in being a forward observer. We worked all day learning how to call in artillery and air strikes. And that was a real power trip. Man, the power you felt laying out your map, getting on the hook with the bad guy's address, and laying heavy metal out there, lighting up the countryside. Does it get any better than that? It was downright intoxicating. I loved it, but calling in arty required serious map skills. Lots of folks struggled. I learned the average Joe doesn't always get it when it comes to map reading. The skills don't come naturally, and if you couldn't read a map, you were not going to excel at calling in arty and air. A day wasn't a lot of damn time to learn that skill. It's a real art, but there was a war heating up, so we had to do the best we could. I left there knowing just enough to get going. I'd pick up the rest as I went.

Our artillery live-fire training was out back of Phu Bai, over toward the mountains I'd seen from our range. We set in on a little hill overlooking a valley. The FO instructor walked us through the basics one more time, then he called in some live hits of his own to show us how it's done. Zulu, Pearl, and I thought it all looked easy enough so we knew we could do it ourselves. All of us could shoot the eyes out of a pig at six hundred meters, but I was not sure about raining bombs and arty all over the valley. Having artillery falling every place we wanted was a real rip, but some of our guys had a tough time with calling it. I was one of a few who picked it up right away, and I was real proud that I got very close after a couple of tries. Then they told me that, "Close only counts in horseshoes and hand grenades." I must say, though, that it *may* count with the 155s. What a hole *they* blow! I passed off on a good note.

The arty day turned out to be another *long* day. A long day killing cubic yards of dirt and centuries of trees in a nameless valley. Arty over, we returned with one more day of work left. Then we'd be officially deemed ready. Our last day was spent going over our weapons one more time. DuBay watched over our shoulders to see how we were maintaining them. He was really concerned about what would happen to them in the monsoon season. He kept telling us that it will rain for days on end, and we'll have floods. It was hard to relate to that when we were standing ball-high in dust and it was so fucking hot we could light a candle just by looking at it hard.

Finally, after three long, hot, and dry weeks, we were at the end of training. We were snipers! Marine scout-snipers! DuBay chaired a formal meeting and pronounced each of us ready, trained, and real live, bonafide snipers. And damned if we didn't think we were. Gunny then sat down for a fireside chat. He gave us a grim outline of the action ahead. We'd been hearing that a buildup at the DMZ was coming soon. The DMZ ran along the North Vietnamese border, fifty miles or so north of us on

Highway 1. The gunny wished us well and expressed his concern for our safety.

Then Rider stepped up and congratulated us. It was short and sweet. He said, "Follow me!" With all his snipers trailing behind, he charged off across the base at Phu Bai. We didn't know where the hell he was taking us. It wasn't to our club; that was in the other direction. We walked across an open area of a couple hundred yards. On the other side, we came into some more hootches, all nicer than ours. It turned out he was taking us to the Seabee area. He had cut a deal for us to party in their club. The deal included unlimited beer, so party we did!

That night the Seabees' club got real, real, drunk, real fast, and real early. The Seabees were great guys who worked hard and played hard, and they welcomed us with open arms. They were fascinated by what we did. Well, to that point we hadn't *done* shit, but I guess they were fascinated by what we were going to do. The night soon became a blur of stories and tall tales and more stories, all washed down with gallons of beer. I don't know how long it all went on or who stayed on, other than just a few. What I do know is that when I tried to wake up the next morning, I knew something bad had happened to me. Something real bad had happened.

I couldn't tell which way was up or what time it was. I just knew the hot sun was beating down on me forcefully. I was in a Budweiser-induced stupor that my consciousness was desperately trying to overcome, but my body was refusing to cooperate. I wasn't just missing a beat, I wasn't hitting on *any* cylinder. None! I couldn't move. Each time I tried, pain shot throughout my body. It was so intense, I was afraid of what it might do to me. Something was very wrong. I could feel the warmth of the sun rolling from head to toe, so I realized I was lying someplace. It felt like the ground. I could only think, open your eyes, asshole, and find out. Seemed reasonable, so I tried. I could get only one eye open, my left. I could only see dirt; it seemed to be all around me, an inch or less away. I closed my eye and lay there trying to figure out what was wrong. Where the hell was I? Dirt, sun . . . I must be outside someplace? I built up the courage to look again. This time, I managed to raise my head a little. That enabled me to open my other eye. With both eyes now processing, I looked to my left because that's the direction my head happened to be pointing, so it worked out. I started processing data again. I could see I was in a sandy field, I could just make out hootches off in the distance. Then I heard a *whomp, whomp, whomp* noise. It was a chopper! I was in bad shape, real bad shape. I turned my head around and found someone lying next to me. I'm in the dirt, it's morning, and someone's lying next to me? Then it all started to come back.

The party! It's the party . . . yeah, the party, the one with the Seabees. But what am I doing in this field? I got it! I must not have made it back to my hootch last night. Good thinking, Kug, but who the hell is that body next to mine? Zulu, it's gotta be Zulu. I'm starting to come to. I call out his name and as I do, I feel much pain in my throat. It's drier than the damn dust bowl I live in. Nothing, not a single sound came from the body in the dirt next to mine. I call out again, "Hey, Zulu."

There was slight movement as his head turned my way. His eyes were shut; a groan came out of his mouth. "Fuck you, let me sleep."

Then I got the big picture. I was facedown in the dirt, hands at my sides, hurting like I'd just been run over by a freight train. I raised myself to one elbow in disgust. Eventually I worked at it and got myself up to a sitting position. To my surprise, behind me and to the right lay Wiener. There we were, a trio of snipers dead to the world in the dirt. The three of us apparently had made it that far on our way back across the field. I tried waking Zulu and Wiener but nothing worked, that is, until I saw Rider striding toward us from the sniper area. By the time he reached us, he was laughing his ass off. I endured his shit for a few minutes as he congratulated us on our drinking skills. Eventually we got it together enough to get Rider's blessing. Then the four of us walked across the great divide to our hootch.

Along the way, Rider informed us that requests had come in for sniper support. The teams would be dividing up and heading out in a day or two. Zulu reminded him that it was he and I. Rider concurred, so I knew he liked us. He said, "I came out here because I wanted to tell you two something personally. The major from Force Recon came by and wants two snipers to go out on their recon patrols. It's crazy shit they do, but they're really good. I wanted to see if the two of you were interested before I offer it to the whole platoon. So, what do you think?"

As we walked, it became clear that it wasn't a good day for thinking and a worse day for making decisions. I'd been conscious all of maybe ten minutes, Zulu five, and Wiener even less. Wiener whined because he couldn't have first chance. I wanted to talk with Zulu and think about it. I thought the assignment would be cool but didn't know enough about Force Recon. Zulu hadn't said two words since coming to life, but suddenly the crazy SOB says, "Sure we'll fucking do it. When do we leave?"

"Hey, asshole, don't I have anything in this?" I said.

And then here we go on a, "Kug, trust me; I know what the fuck I'm doing. These guys are pros. It's much better than fucking around with the grunts all day. Now trust me, we'll do it."

By the time we reached Rider's tent, I gave in. Why not go learn with the best? Force Recon here we come. Rider told us to go down for an interview that afternoon. I was excited all right, but I was scared as hell.

PART TWO

Becoming a Nam Marine

Becoming a
New Marine

CHAPTER THREE

Force Recon Comes Calling

Zulu and I passed on the club, hit the showers, and got wet under our fifty-five-gallon drum. We dried off, then headed over to 3d Force Recon. We reported in to the lieutenant in charge, a big dude, dark, I think Italian. He offered us a soda and said to sit down. I noticed his tent was a lot nicer than mine was. Hell, he had soda on site. In fact, the whole neighborhood was a click or two better than ours, and ours was a step up from life as a grunt.

The lieutenant was a very serious man; he was concerned about being in charge of life and death. He was sure about himself but not too sure about us. He quizzed us on our background, time in the Corps, and combat experience. He wanted to look inside us. Zulu gave him a taste of "up time" with 3/4, the human waves, and all the bullshit life brought as a grunt. I gave him a flyby of Santo Domingo. He seemed satisfied with both of us. Those bastards were serious about their work, but at the time, I knew little about Force Recon other than that they ran their asses off. Every time I'd ever seen them they were running and singing, "Recon, recon . . . have

you heard . . . we're gonna jump from the big-ass birds."
They were skinheads, always working out and running.

The lieutenant said he'd give us a try but they'd have
their eyes on us. He got up and welcomed us to the team.
He said he'd get Sergeant Lich. He walked out, and I
looked at Zulu. He was just smiling like a damn lunatic. I
said, "What the hell is so funny?"

He smiled. "Kug, this is the best. Stick with me, man."

The lieutenant returned after a short time. Following
behind him was a Marine's Marine, probably late twenties, skinhead, tall, and tanned. One serious looking dude
is all I could think. The whole outfit had that "serious as
shit" air about it. I didn't *know* why, but it was pretty
damned easy to guess the reason. And I could see they
were about to tell us.

Sergeant Lich took the two of us out and down recon
row to his hootch. Inside sat some more serious dudes.
They'd just received word of their next mission; we'd be
going along because they wanted to see if snipers could
be effective with recon teams. Lich took us over to his
rack, and we sat down. He introduced us to a couple of
other recon Marines who'd be going on the ride with us.

I was high with an adrenaline rush. My heart was
racing. I was ripe with anticipation and covered in fear.
Fear of the unknown. Fear of the known. This was a
damned war. A real war. It wasn't like the four-day shoot-
out in the streets of Santo Domingo the previous year.
We were going out hunting for bad guys. All around me
in the hootch lay commo gear and weapons of all kinds.
Maps everywhere and men in varying stages of acceptance of the situation we all found ourselves in.

Sergeant Lich told us he was a lifer in the Corps, but we
could see that; hell, the whole outfit's professionalism was
obvious. Lich's professionalism outshone them all. He

was serious as a heart attack about what he did. He let us know we'd better be serious too. I was impressed with his patience and his caring; there wasn't a lot of that to be found. He was from Houston, Texas. He was single and just had a mom and dad back home. He let us know he'd return to them again. That was a guy I could believe in.

I sat listening to his directions. While I did, I found I could only think of Mom and Dad. I wondered what they thought about me and what I was doing. I wondered what it would be like to feel the way Sergeant Lich felt about his parents. He'd told them he was stationed in Okinawa; he didn't want them to worry. I couldn't relate, but I didn't really know why. If my letters were any indication, my parents would find all this interesting, but at best a minor irritant.

Lich outlined that we'd need to be over at recon at 1000 hours the next morning. The mission would last seven days. We'd be inserted into a valley to the west, near Laos. He said it was near A Shau, whatever the hell A Shau was. He told us to get some rest and come fresh in the morning. "You'll need to be here to go over the operation. You'll each be paired with one of our men as a split team." Prime time was getting closer by the minute. He said, "We do that in case we're hit and have to split up. We'll split in teams of two and make our break. We'll regroup later. It's all planned ahead of time."

Zulu and I took off back to our hootch. He was psyched to the max. Me? I was overflowing with a mixture of emotions. On the one hand, I was bursting with pride and anticipation, and outright stone cold fear on the other. Just being with Force Recon was something special to me. It was a long way from STB. Hell, I was fired up! Knowing I was about to take a chopper thirty miles into nowhere and be dropped off for seven days made me want to puke my guts inside out. It was the terror of what I knew and what I didn't. Hell, I was going out there with one guy I met just a month ago and six I just saw for the first time an hour earlier. I wondered what the hell I was doing.

True to tradition, Zulu was off to the club. It was near 1800 hours by then. He'd have to hurry. For the first time since I arrived in country, I passed on the booze. I wanted to get ready for the mission. I wanted to make sure my weapon was as ready as I was. I cleaned it and went over it very carefully. I laid out my gear for the morning. I studied the maps they gave us. I was psyched! Zulu came back and had a good laugh at me preparing for my first patrol. He had that special knack of making you feel like shit. Then he could laugh and bring you back in. He looked at me with a sly grin and said, "Kugler, Kugler—it's just a war. Throw your shit together in the A.M. We'll go get 'em. It'll be fun. You'll see." I didn't know what to make of him.

Rider had just started his nightly card game, so Zulu was off to win some of the big guy's money. Cards weren't my thing, so the big nightly game was nothing more than a spectator sport for me. But whether you knew cards or not, you knew they were Rider's thing. You knew you wouldn't win unless he wanted you to. That fact quickly became apparent to most of the snipers, but a few macho types continued to believe and profess that they would beat him. None ever came close. Zulu quickly became his recruiter, bringing others from outside our group to the game. Rider wanted to expand his winnings without bleeding his own troops. That sort of thing was frowned on by the Corps, but we'd all go and buy him money orders so he could send home his sizable winnings without attracting too much attention to himself. He took care of us, so we took care of him. It all worked out in the end.

Morning came, and Zulu and I realized we had a problem. We were about to go out with eight guys to the badlands and we were carrying nothing but our sniper rifles. The 06 was a wonderful weapon for the war of distance. But we questioned what we'd do in a small group. What would happen if the day went to shit? Shouldn't we carry .45s or something? At least a pistol would give us some personal protection and a little more firepower. It was a question no one had thought about, and no one was prepared to answer just yet.

DuBay was against our going with recon. He felt it was too dangerous. He and Rider, who had set up the deal, debated. I heard Rider telling him, "These guys *want* to do it. They'll be okay. Third Force is a good outfit, and they stay out of the shit and do their job." We really *did* want to do it. For me it was an ego thing. I wanted, maybe needed, to prove to myself that I could do the recon thing. I remembered old Sergeant Tarawa at Parris Island. When I was single-handedly fucking up my life, he believed in me. He told me I could do anything. I'd hid out for three days. Didn't eat a thing. It was then that he took a chance on me. He told me I could do anything if I just put my mind to it and *did* it. And by God, I did, and I would again there in Vietnam! DuBay reluctantly agreed that we could go but said he couldn't get us approval for side arms but that he'd work on it for us if we kept doing things with recon. Whoopie.

At 1000 hours, we were back, front and center, with Sergeant Lich. We met the rest of the team, a professional and bad-looking group. They welcomed us and told us where we'd fit in. Zulu would pair in the middle of the group with a really strange looking corporal who looked like he'd been on one too many missions. Sergeant Lich was the tail-end Charlie, and I'd pair with him. That was fine with me; I trusted him already.

We all went inside the tent that served as recon headquarters. There was an official briefing area with a wall map mounted on a board leaning against one wall of the tent. There were some chairs strung all about. We formed a circle around the lieutenant, who was to be our patrol leader, and sat down around him to learn what was about to happen.

The briefing lasted most of the day. By the time we went over equipment, maps, escape routes, codes, artillery preplots, and aerial photos, it was a full day. It was all new to me, but I was impressed. I was scared as hell, but I was also drunk with anticipation. I wanted to get out there and knock some little bastard dead on his ass! I wanted to be damned good at the sniping business. And I was fascinated with the details of what was happening. Being fascinated put me in the minority. Most just wanted to go do what they were told and get back in one piece.

The aerial photographs were excellent. It was hard to imagine some plane somewhere could take shots like this and we could have them fresh today. We had a series of eight or ten black-and-white photos of the LZ where we'd be inserted. The lieutenant said, "The chopper will come in and set down facing this direction." He pointed to a spot on a picture. "When you exit the door, you'll see this tree and hedgerow." He again pointed to the photograph. Then he detailed who would come off the bird first, second, third, and right down to Sergeant Lich, the last. The detail of the plans and the team's attitude toward the work was a real confidence builder. Those men knew their shit. I was glad I became a sniper. I was glad I was paired with Zulu in sniper school, and damned glad I was starting out with Force Recon, where I could learn how to fight the war and survive. At least that's what I was counting on as we ended the day. It was the day before liftoff and the day before my first actual patrol in Nam. I was ready. I didn't know for what or who, but I was ready for something. In fact, if it hadn't been for the weight of all that stone-cold fright I was carrying around, I'd have been on cloud nine. I'd have to learn how to balance fear and ecstasy at the same time.

By the time recon was done with us, we could recite details of their plan in one of our drunken stupors. We'd lift off at 1800 hours from Phu Bai carrying sixty to seventy pounds of gear. We had enough grenades and ammunition to survive a night alone; sometimes that was recon's luck of the draw. Grunt companies were on standby to come in and kick ass if we got waxed, but rallying one could take up to an hour or more. The Sparrow Hawks, as they were called, were lifesavers when they could get in. But that wasn't a sure thing. If you got hit during the night, they couldn't get in till morning. We'd have to fend for ourselves. We all had maps and knew how to use them; we had a partner and planned rally points for every day. If we were hit real hard, we'd split up into teams of two, withdraw, and regroup at a rally point later. Patrols like that aren't for the faint at heart. We'd be out for seven days. Our food had to last that long plus a day or two as extra insurance. Weather, heavy contact elsewhere, or any of a large number of unknowns could keep us out longer. It looked to me like Force Recon thought of everything; we'd soon find out.

Zulu and I walked back home to snipers. It was club time, so we went straight over for our usual watering down. By then, there were only a few snipers left, the grunts were calling, and it looked like we'd all been put to work. Zulu got drunk. I had a couple, then went back to the hootch. I just wanted to get a buzz on, go write a few letters, and contemplate the mission. I was really getting into that sniper stuff. I worked hard on burying my emotions. I needed to chase out any feelings I had about life and death in favor of indifference. To do that work, I needed control. The next eighteen hours would be a trial of my ability to overcome my own fear, a trial of patience, as we waited for a lift into somewhere near Laos.

I was experiencing a strange mixture of fear, excitement, and boredom. The combination generated feelings I had trouble understanding. I went outside and lay down, my body stretched across the top of a bunker. There were only four or five of us inside the hootch, but I wanted to be alone to think about my life. It was after midnight, and it was still hot and sticky, almost unbearable. But as I lay there on my back staring up into the starry sky, I found comfort in the expanse of space. I could always count on my mirrored galaxy to come to the rescue, especially that time of year.

My mind wandered to my racing days. It was May and a new season was starting in the Midwest. I loved racing around at eighty miles per hour an inch or two above the ground. Now that's a rush! C-Open-class karts just flew on the ground. But hell, that's nothin' compared to the rush I knew I'd get the next day flying into an LZ thirty miles from nowhere. My mind was popping. I must have dozed off. When I woke up, I was actually a little chilly, and a surprise breeze was blowing lightly across my bunker. I rolled off the bunker and went back in the hootch. It was nearly 0300 hours.

I went inside and crashed. It was near 0930 when I regained consciousness. I blinked and realized someone had turned on the damned oven again. I was sweating furiously and hadn't lifted a finger. I looked over; Zulu's rack was empty.

I got up and scrounged around for some C-rat, ham and eggs from a B1 unit, our breakfast of choice. I needed a B2 to rip off some cheese. I liked to cook them together for a C-rat omelet. Hell, whatever we did was better than the mess hall. They could fuck up a wet dream on a rainy night. I finally got my Cs and set out to cook them and eat my breakfast. I wondered what the hell I'd be eating the next morning.

It was about 1000 hours when I finished. I was ready to get off some letters before I left for the bush. I was scared as hell and proud at the same time; I was here doing what I'd set out to do in the fifth grade. I started to write, but the paper kept getting wet from the sweat dripping off my arm.

I sat, sweating, for a couple of hours, all the while writing home. On the one hand, I wanted to let it all go. I wanted to be this emotionless machine doing what I was trained to do. On the other, I couldn't help but think of the folks back home. I wrote Mom and Dad and told them where I was going. I tried to explain how it felt and why I wanted to go. I wanted them to understand and accept what I wanted to do. But even as I wrote, I knew it would fall on deaf ears. They cared about me, just not about what I was doing. I guess I was looking for support or reassurance that what I was doing was the right thing, that I'd be okay. I'm not sure. I also wrote a few letters to girls I once knew; I just wanted to see what was up.

Zulu came walking in a little after noon. He had a grin plastered all over his face. He was as happy as if he was headed off to Disneyland. I said, "What the hell did you get into?"

"Kug, my man, I've just been off visiting some of my

old buds from the grunts. Catching up on old times ya know."

"So why the hell are you so happy about that?" I asked, half irritated. How could he be so lighthearted on such a serious day? He let out a loud belly laugh that had an evil tone attached to it. His laugh trailed off through the afternoon's searing heat, and then he walked over and put his arm around me. I pushed him away with, "Come on, asshole, I'm hot enough already."

"Kug, let me teach you a thing or two about going to the bush. Hell, you don't know if any of us'll make it back. Right?" I stared at him thinking what a complete piece of shit he was for saying that. Before I can answer, he says, "Come on, am I right?"

I agreed, technically the asshole was right, I guess.

"I mean, Kug, it's all a big game, and we're just bit players. Let's have fun and make the most of it. I just went over and told a few old cronies of mine good-bye. Hell, I don't know if I'll be back from the recon deal, and neither do you. So fuck it! Deal with it and have fun—for tomorrow we may die!"

With that the world's number one Nero Wolfe fan waltzed off to visit one more old buddy and bid him farewell. I was left dripping with sweat and about to piss my pants from the fear he left behind. I was alone, sitting on my rack, and I wasn't in the mood to write anymore. I was left to sit, sweat, and ponder the wisdom passed on from one weird dude, Zulu, my partner.

I got up and went outside. I wanted to walk and clear my head. But as I was leaving, I bumped into Zulu, strutting along, beaming like a kid coming down for Christmas morning. I told him we had to be serious; he just smiled and suggested we take a walk over to recon to check in. I thought that was a good idea; if I got involved in the work of getting ready, I'd forget about the stuff racing around in my head.

At recon, we reconnected with the guys on our team. We were ready, but I wanted one final check; I was as nervous as I'd ever been. Zulu headed down to the chow hall for what he called his Last Supper. He was a regular fucking comedian who cut no slack for the new guy. I couldn't imagine what he'd be like in the bush. The more I got to know him, the less I could imagine him in the Marines.

Zulu came back from the mess hall full, fit, and ready to go. We were packed, ready, and checked out for the big show. Gunny DuBay came in to wish us well. He gave us some last-minute pointers about staying alive, then checked our weapons inside and out. Man, he liked those Winchesters. Rider stopped by to give us his own brand of encouragement. Then we were ready, and off we went to the airstrip. The choppers were waiting, and we met recon there. Each man carrying sixty pounds or so of gear, weapons, C rats, and grenades, we all looked like pack mules. We were dressed for the kill: our faces painted shades of green and black; we could tell by the stares of passersby that we looked the part. We could also tell they didn't want to come along. Hell, I understood how they felt. I was scared shitless or I'd have filled my pants by then.

We boarded the choppers right after the recon lieutenant and the pilots did a check of the plans. The UH-34 felt old and rickety as it roared, shook, and rumbled us into the early evening sky. Every face on board wore the intensity that masked the fear boiling deep inside. All eyes were bright and wired. Those who could were staring down, searching the ground, already several hundred feet below. I was frightened as all hell.

The ride to the insertion point was about thirty minutes. As a deceptive move to confuse the bad guys, the chopper would dip into three different LZs; we'd get out at stop number two. The ideas was if gooks in the area saw the chopper coming in, they wouldn't know which LZ they dropped us in. Sounded good to me, but it was a bummer for the pilots who had to go in and out; approaches and takeoffs were the most dangerous part of their mission.

The two Huey gunships on station with us provided escort enroute and cover when we flew in. Above the Hueys flew two F-4 Phantoms. They'd stay up, away, and on station for a few minutes after insertion. Their job was to come in and blow the bejesus out of anyone giving us shit. The whole show was directed by a Bird Dog, a small Cessna or Piper, that slowly circled the LZ. They'd stay on station and direct the fire if we needed support. This gig was professional from the git-go. I felt good about the superb planning, great support, and excellent coordination. It was a pleasure in a land of displeasure. But all that was about to end.

The fleeting security I felt from all this support was yanked from me as the chopper banked hard to the left. We were going in! It was just stop number one, and already my ass was puckered tight. We were all wearing soft-cover bush hats, which meant we couldn't take our hard hats off and sit on them the way we were taught Stateside.

The 34 dropped into the LZ. The engines were revving out the roof. We came in with the nose high, tail leaning down, and then we were in with a thud! We were shadowed by tall green trees and all but swallowed in giant yellowish grass. That's all I could see. I didn't hear any shooting. Then we were revving up again, shaking violently as we climbed up and out. Airborne again, we circled our way up and along the treetops. We lunged forward, speeding along the dark green, foreboding hillside. The mood in the plane had begun serious and suddenly switched to dead serious. "Lock and load," the lieutenant yelled. Sergeant Lich hit me on the arm and gave me the thumbs-up. We were going in! This was our bus stop and we were ready for the real thing.

I leaned over and looked out as we banked another hard left. Everything I could see was green. We were coming in along a steep hillside. Hell, it could've been the hills around the racetrack back in Ohio. Thicker, maybe greener—uh oh—here we are! Grass all over! We came in hard and fast, smashing to the ground. No time to bounce around; we're outta here!

I jumped—and slammed to the ground right on my face. I didn't know the grass was five feet high. With the weight of the world clinging to my back, I struggled up and ran to the tree I was assigned. Sergeant Lich beat me there. I was still fighting to regain my breath. It had been a rude awakening to have all my gear smash my face in the dirt. And the Winchester had smacked hard on the ground. So much for the scope's being sighted in. But fuck it! Recon's on the ground and Kug's with them!

With the roar of the chopper, I experienced the first big breeze I'd had in a month. The blade wash on their liftoff nearly blew us over. At least it was a short relief from the stifling heat. The humidity in the grass was crazy. With the chopper airborne, the grass jumped back to normal height, and we disappeared. It was tough as hell to see. Heads of recon Marines popped up all around. The place actually looked a lot like the aerial photos, but it was scary. It was a lot different from looking at a map and thinking how cool an op is going to be!

Recon's point man gave us the hand signal to move out. We were supposed to beat feet for an hour to put distance between us and the LZ in case the gooks descended on the place. That had been explained by Lich before the mission, but I didn't know we'd be in a fucking race. The point disappeared in the tall grass as the rest of us followed at a trot. Sergeant Lich was tail-end Charlie, and I was his cover. That put me next to last, a lonely place to be.

We were on a forced march. As we made our way from the LZ, I heard the choppers circling overhead. I heard the jets up there, too. We were marching hard through tall elephant grass. We'd stop just for a second, listen, look, then be off again. We soon reached the river we were looking for. We took a sharp left along the riverbed. It was scary as hell out there, but so far, so good. We only had an hour or two of daylight left, and it was getting creepy all around, like a bad monster movie.

My first outing in the Nam was turning out to be a major ass kicker. My lungs were burning; my legs and thighs were on fire; I was pushing myself to keep up. I was already sucking some serious wind, and we were barely past the green flag! My mind raced between the unending possibilities of what might lie ahead in the mass of green life surrounding us and the necessity of keeping my eyes glued and ears locked on the jungle ahead.

The patrol slowed down, and I could barely make out the sound of someone talking. What the hell was going on? We were told time and again *never* to talk out here. Then I could hear . . . it was the lieutenant on the radio. Something was happening? What was it? I was wired to the max! Are gooks up ahead? All of a sudden—chaos came raining down like cold raindrops in a sudden storm. *Vrooooom! Bang, brrrp, brrrp! Whooosh!* A horrendous series of loud, terrifying sounds roared up the river to our right. I was face down in muck, and I realized that the trees were raining shells. They were dropping like heavy leaves all around us. A fucking F-4 had flown nearly right up our ass, roaring up the murky river while unloading 20mm cannon on an enemy still unseen by us. I was sure that I was dead meat! Fear hung in the air all around us.

Shells were still trickling through the trees when we got up to check out the area. They passed word back; the spotter had seen enemy troops up ahead. They were along the river a hundred yards up. Hell, that's where we were headed! Did the fly guys get them? Do we check? No time to find out; we were off to the races again, charging ahead, right up the river. With our plans already compromised, I wondered if we'd go ahead. I secretly hoped they'd come and get us out; the bad guys knew we were in the neighborhood; how could we do reconnaissance? I fought hard to hold my fear in check.

My hopes of early extraction were dashed as the patrol took a sharp left. We headed straight up a mountain. I mean it could've been the side of a skyscraper in Cleveland. By that time, I was running on pure adrenaline. My thighs were past the burning stage and were toying with giving out. I'd already sweated so much, I didn't know how any liquid could be left in me. Sergeant Lich moved up toward the front of the pack, and a young, tough-looking black guy switched with Lich and moved back. He and I were tail end. Lich was like a cat that knew the neighborhood, so they needed him up front. The jungle was tough but loosened up after forty-five minutes on the run. It was a little more open on the ground, but the canopy above covered us like a blanket. We hit a trail near the top. It felt like we were on top of a point. I needed a break in the worst way. I thought about nightfall, which had to be close. We'd have to break then . . . wouldn't we? I was wiped out, and we'd just started. I'd already gone farther than I'd ever dreamed I could. Patrolling was going to take some getting used to. But the more time passed, the more I was starting to feel better about my safety.

The mountain leveled off, and we'd walked a little farther down a trail when the column stopped. None too soon for me. The thick canopy continued, but I could still only see twenty feet back from the trail. They passed the word back with hand motions—two hands held as if breaking something—that we'd break. It worked. We were trained not to talk. My new tail-end Charlie motioned me to sit. He wanted me to watch one side of the trail. I sat down and lay back on my pack. That gave me minor relief from my aching shoulders. I could lay back for relief, but I'd never take off my pack unless told to do so. I looked over in surprise. Our new tail-end Charlie was leaning back, lighting up a cigarette. Sergeant Lich would never have done that—*what* the hell could that guy have been thinking?

I scanned my part of the jungle world . . . nothing. I glanced at my watch. We'd been in just over an hour. I was dead on my ass, staring into deep, green space. My breath came hard. I was spooked by the silence, and just then the world to my right exploded. *Brrrp-brrrp-brrrp!* The blast from a submachine gun erupted from the right rear. I spun with my Winchester and started firing. *Bang-bang-bang!* My fucking single-shot, bolt-action, long-range rifle was hurtin' for certain. Sergeant Lich was already at the side of tail-end Charlie, who was lying on the ground, moaning. Bullets were flying all around me. *Thud!* My backpack took a hit, and the impact jerked me to one side. I went *bang-bang*, emptying the last of my five shots. I saw the silhouette of a figure scurrying down and out of sight. Silence seemed the victor for now. It was again quiet except for the sounds of the struggle for life. I'm a damned sniper and there I sat with a damned peashooter. I was trying to fight in thick jungle, and all I had was a single-shot rifle. Fuck!

Sergeant Lich was holding tail-end Charlie, who was looking pretty bad. It looked like he took two hits in the arm and shoulder. Another recon guy across and behind me took one in the leg. He was moving around, and it looked like it might have been a graze. So we were already down two. The lieutenant regrouped the team. Zulu grabbed an M-14 from the badly wounded tail-end Charlie. That left me the lone gunman with a single-shot, bolt-action rifle. Furious about being undergunned, I reloaded my rifle with five more rounds.

We had to move out of there. We got up, started moving, and *brrrrp*—all over again! We were down on our faces, and Zulu yelled for me. I look up as an M-14 came flying through the air. The recon guy slightly wounded had taken another hit. By then he was real fucked up. I grabbed the 14 and returned fire, along with Zulu. Lich was moving his wounded guy down the trail as Zulu and I covered the team that was now moving out. We were shooting up the jungle, and firing the 14 made me feel like I was on the first team again. I got some confidence back. Maybe it was false confidence, but it felt good.

Silence returned as Zulu and I took off to follow the recon team down the trail. We alternated covering each other until we reached the team. Lich was half dragging, half carrying the wounded guy. He had an arm around his neck. The guy was hardly moving his legs. The lieutenant was on the horn calling for a medevac. We were still in thick canopy as nightfall began to swallow us whole. I knew there wouldn't be a medevac before dawn.

Our patrol crept along, turtlelike, through the early night. Zulu and I covered our tracks at the rear. The little bastards who fucked us up were probably off somewhere kicking up their heels by then. They'd get us when we were weak. Now that's a lesson to learn. I looked around. I was in deep, dark Vietnam. Who would live out there? There just couldn't be anything for miles. Just the assholes who ambushed us. We moved along, and as twilight gave way to total darkness, we reached a low point in the trail. The lieutenant decided his guys couldn't go any farther and we'd spend the night right there.

We'd hide up in a thick area off the trail where we couldn't be found. The black guy was losing blood, and his condition didn't look promising. I didn't know if he'd make it. I thought about what Zulu had said. He was right again; you really didn't know if you'd come back from any mission. We crawled into a mess of undergrowth and it was like crawling through a bag of pretzels. It was thick, twisted, and clung to you like it was alive. It was a killer on the wounded. I was thankful it wasn't me. I was still in one piece, and that was good.

The lieutenant finally got his call back. No choppers were comin' out that night. It'd require a basket drop to penetrate the canopy. That wasn't happening at night. It started raining and just poured bucketfuls of water from the sky, which was welcome while it lasted, all of about five or six minutes. Then it was like being in a greenhouse during growing season. The humidity was stifling. I didn't know how the wounded were coping. I couldn't imagine it. They'd been filled with morphine and just contributed to the silence of the night.

We prepared for the night by putting the wounded in the center of our small circle. Sergeant Lich was there to watch over them. The rest of us lay prone, weapons facing out, and our feet to the center. There were just four of us to guard the perimeter. Our wounded and their caretaker were in the middle. We'd gotten ourselves in there so we could be safe from bad guys trying to sneak up on us. The theory was we'd have to hear them coming. With so few of us left to fight, we'd all stay up on guard. It made sense, but oh what a bitch. I was already burned out.

The deep, dark night brought with it the sounds of the jungle. They were unnerving, covering the spectrum of frightening possibilities. I lay prone, rifle in my shoulder, aiming at unknown targets in the night. It was dark as a night with no stars, and we couldn't make out shapes or silhouettes. When I looked straight up to the sky, I could only faintly make it out. Lying there in the black of night, I was left to pretend I was okay. But I wasn't okay. I wasn't anything but scared. I was fucking frightened well out of my wits. There was the constant drip of rain from leaf to leaf, all across the jungle floor. My energized imagination fueled itself with visions of people walking nearby. Were they walking? Were they real? Were they taking steps in the night? Were they getting closer to the crazies from America, the crazies who came to fight here in no-man's-land? Soon I was fighting for mental control of myself. I knew the game was mental, but I hung on the edge of mental anarchy. My mind would suddenly race off into the night. Gooks would come running into our tight little circle. They'd do a rain dance on our heads until our last breath of life was completely stomped out of us. Then they'd run out, leaving our lifeless carcasses to ruin the day of our loved ones a world away. I fought to bring reason back to the party. But what if the gooks could sneak up and cut your throat and not be heard? What if all the bullshit they fed us in jungle school was true? What then? Control was all I needed. Then I'd survive.

It was a wicked, black, and horrible night. My fears danced on my head while the ghosts of the night seemed to attack again and again. I was wired and needed support to calm my growing concerns with the jungle noises out front. I was completely beat. I had to have some sleep. I was dragging ass slower than an old alligator. I quietly crawled over to Zulu. He was sound asleep the way I was going to be, sleeping like a baby in the crib. How the hell could he sleep so soundly out there in gook heaven? I reached down and shook him awake. "Zulu, it's your turn," I whispered. He mumbled that he'd take care of it. I was glad they'd switched us to a 50 percent watch. I go to move and notice he doesn't move an inch. What the hell is this? I'm dead. My eyelids weigh ten pounds. He'll get up, I think. I slide back over to my position. I decide to try and get some Zs. I lay facedown with my rifle tight in my shoulder, trying to doze off, when I realized Zulu hadn't moved an inch! I can't see him, but I can tell he's asleep. I pull my aching ass up and slowly slide back over. The bastard was sound asleep.

I grabbed his shoulder. "Zulu! You're supposed to be on watch, get up!" I couldn't see him very well, but a hand grabbed my head and pulled it down to his. "I am."

"You *am* my ass," I said, a little too loud. We're trying to whisper to each other, but it's tough.

Finally, Zulu said, "Kug, relax. No one's coming through this shit. Go to sleep. I'm responsible, okay? Now let me the fuck alone." His hand pushed my head up and away.

He then lay back to enjoy some more Zs. What an asshole! We were in the middle of nowhere, with gooks all around, and he was asleep.

I knew the bastard was going to stay asleep, so I decided to stay up all night. I lay down and slipped the 14 back in my shoulder. I'd stay up forever if I had to, I thought. Fear and doubt again fueled my imagination. I imagined hundreds, if not thousands of little slant-eyed bastards surrounding us. They'd come in, but I'd be awake, dammit! He could sleep, but I wouldn't. My nerves were rattling like a bad muffler. They stretched out well ahead of the tips of my fingers. They felt like radar in the night. I'll feel the little mothers out there in front of me. I'll stay up and stay awake. I'll do it!

I did stay up all night. It was terrible. It rained again, but the weather seemed to be clearing up. The night was still real dark, and I still couldn't see anything of our surroundings. In Nam, time doesn't move, only events, and they just happen. I lay looking around and everything was quiet. I was all ears. The wounded behind me in the center had either died or were sleeping real sound. Maybe they were high from the morphine. Who knew?

Morning light also brought some relaxation. It appeared we'd successfully ditched the bad boys who screwed up our well-planned patrol. The lieutenant said we could try and eat something as long as it was odorless. Hell, the only odor in my pack was from a bullet hole right through the heart of a can of meatballs. I quickly took it out of my pack and buried it. I ate a can of peaches and called it breakfast. I was off to a roaring start with my life in the Nam. I was also flat burned out, and it'd only been a day.

The jungle floor came to full life with the brightening of the morning sun. I was dead on my feet but still alive to go at it another day. Zulu and the rest of the recon team came to life, but one of the wounded didn't. The night had been too long and hard for him. That'd sure do it, I thought. The other guy was faring okay, all things considered. I divorced myself from the dead guy. I decided that life in Nam was just that way. Whatever emotions I had, needed a cement vault to hide in. And they would hide, even if I had to push them in and shut the door. Sometimes you win and sometimes you lose. Winners got up in the morning; losers didn't.

We packed up and went on our way. Sergeant Lich led us in search of an LZ. We were in tough country. Finding a spot with no trees was no small task, even for those guys. We used up most of the morning locating a suitable extraction point. Finally, we called for a chopper with a winch. It arrived a short time later, and the wire-support basket circled overhead. I could barely see it up where it was waving in the breeze. I wished I could ride up in the basket. As I stood there, I actually harbored illusions that they'd take us all out. I mean hell, we were surely compromised now.

We got the dead and the wounded up and on board for the ride home. It looked like a tough ride up and out of the canopy. But soon they were gone, and we were alone again. There were six of us left, but no one knew how many of *them* were left. I knew more than six. It was now four recon, two snipers, and an unknown number of bad guys. Zulu and I both had M-14s. The problem was, we had to carry them and our sniper rifles. It was tough trying to walk through a jungle with a big barrel sticking up to catch onto everything. On the other hand, it was also pretty fruitless to carry a weapon that could shoot for over a thousand yards in a jungle where I couldn't see twenty feet. I hadn't seen anything farther away than twenty feet since the chopper had dropped us off. And the distance wasn't the only problem; the five-shot, bang-bang machine was a serious fucking health hazard.

The rising chopper was our last glimpse of freedom for a while. We'd lost a lot of time. We regrouped and cautiously set off again toward our original objectives. We were saddled up for the long haul. Off we went to observe the activity in a small village a couple of grid squares to the west. We snaked and sneaked our way, slicing through the beautiful silence of the jungle floor. It was hot, thick, and steamy with an occasional shower along the way. The jungle canopy choked out the light, keeping everything below in daytime twilight. The constant humidity made the march feel like taking a hike in a sauna.

We got to take our long-distance look at the village. We sat there swimming in the heat for three days straight. We stayed hidden at the jungle's edge, high above the village. People came and went. Some had weapons, and some didn't. I didn't know where the hell we were, but it was way the hell out in bad-guy land. At least we got some rest. I started to recover and feel better. That was a scary thought. The heat prevented me from eating much. Patience became a severe necessity. Zulu and I took turns on the binoculars. We'd watch people down below, living their lives, oblivious to the dangerous eyes watching them from above.

Zulu and I asked permission to take one of them out down below. But that came back a loud "negatory." The lieutenant said he didn't want to compromise our observation post. Made sense to me, but why the hell did you bring snipers then? I didn't know. I didn't know a lot about Vietnam, yet I found myself glad to be with recon. I was glad I had survived the little action we'd had. After three days, we moved out to set up and observe another area, and the Phantoms came streaking in with napalm and daisy cutters. It was a helluva sight. As we moved on, I thought for a moment of how the lives of the people I'd been scoping out were either snuffed out or dramatically fucked up forever. I realized mine was changed as well. I decided not to worry about it and put more cement on the vault of my emotions.

Our next site was about as exciting as watching me build stick huts. The choppers came after us a day late. We were out for eight days instead of seven. By that time, the mission was just a minor frustration. Those old UH-34s were a beautiful sight coming in, flashing those blades in the early morning sun. We'd spent the night before curled up in a thicket alongside the clearing where the chopper was to pick us up.

After first light, we saddled up and waited in the tree line next to the clearing. Finally, the sweet noise of rescue hung in the air. We popped yellow smoke, and it was prime time. We raced out from hiding to meet the chopper, piled in, and were airborne immediately. We ascended into the beauty of the morning sky, visions of home and cold beer and soft covered wooden racks filled our heads. Then sniper fire filled the air around the chopper, and the door gunner opened up, blasting the countryside as we flew away to freedom. Our first patrol with recon was nearly over. We'd survived to fight another day!

Arriving back at sniper headquarters, we were greeted like we'd done something big. Gunny DuBay had heard about the firefight when it first happened. I could tell from his face that he'd been worried sick since hearing the news. His line of work had to be a ball buster if he cared. Then, with a few of our guys who were just back from the grunts, we went to the club to compare war stories and see who got the first kill. No cigar and no kills for the 4th Marine scout-snipers yet. Zulu and I did the usual and drank ourselves silly; we had to celebrate the fact that we'd made it back from our first recon mission.

First thing next morning, DuBay came by to talk with us about our recon assignment. He really questioned whether we could be effective as snipers for them. We didn't tell him how we felt about our rifles up there; he'd pull the plug. Zulu and I wanted to stay with recon, so we had to talk our shit. As we talked with DuBay, recon called to make it official. They wanted the two of us permanently assigned to them until further notice. We said, "Hell, yes," but DuBay said he'd think it over. We went to Rider and put the arm on him. He was a good guy. He demanded a lot, but he was there for us. He said he'd handle it for us, but he didn't want us doing anything stupid and getting ourselves killed. "DuBay will have my ass," were his parting words.

Rider worked fast. We got our way. We were out with recon in just three days. That would become our routine: seven, sometimes up to ten, days out and three days back. Ten out, three back, and we had a deal. The problem we wanted fixed right away was the lack of side arms. According to our boys, Rider and DuBay, we couldn't have a pistol or anything. They weren't authorized for snipers. Of course, the M-79 grenadier carried a .45 for protection. Why shouldn't we? After all, the grenadier traveled with an army of grunts; we were nearly alone. No matter, the argument was in vain. And if Rider couldn't get them, they couldn't be got!

So we turned to our new friends in recon. They seemed to be able to get anything they wanted. When we prepared for our next patrol, they offered us whatever we needed. I think they liked our willingness to do whatever needed to be done. They'd seen us in action; they'd asked for us permanently. We went over to their armory with Sergeant Lich. Zulu and I were like two kids in a candy store. Right before our eyes was an array of weapons like I'd never seen before. One of them was a Thompson .45-caliber submachine gun. Now that was right out of the movies. If I'd had that dude out in the bush last week, I could've cut some brush and kicked some ass. "Give me one a' those!" I said. And Zulu agreed. We checked out Thompsons, eight magazines, and the magazine pouches to carry them. We knew we were bad. Back at snipers, we were the envy of our platoon.

We got word that our next patrol would be in and out in seven days and somewhere near Laos again. It was unforgettable. Zulu and I jumped out of the chopper, sniper rifles rigged to our backs and Thompsons in our hands. We had three hundred rounds of .45 ammunition on our belts. I hit the ground and nearly broke my knees. The weight of the Thompson and everything else was astonishing. Between the Thompson, the ammo, and the chow, it was like carrying a damn washing machine on your back. Carrying that momma'd make a man out of me fast. The mission was a learning experience, but uneventful. We snooped and pooped over near Laos, but nothing was happening. We came home to some more changes in the game plan.

Recon got word of some big stuff coming down to the north. Our next gig was to be up north toward the DMZ. They'd be up there for a couple weeks or more. They wanted us to go. It might be a temporary transfer; they weren't sure. Who the hell cared; we'd go. We set off to let Rider know the score. He'd deal with DuBay. We gladly turned in our Thompsons in favor of something lighter, some automatic M-14s. At least we could carry those without getting a hernia. The Thompson was good for the ego but the 14 was good for the soul. The gunny reluctantly agreed to our excursion to the north, and we were off.

I'd begun to lose track of time. I didn't know what day it was, and I didn't care. I knew it was near the first of June. I slipped a few letters home between recon trips and updated the folks. The letters on the rebound weren't very supportive. It was clear they didn't want to hear much about the Nam. It was also easy to see that just as my life was progressing, so were the lives of everyone back home. The World seemed farther away each day.

Zulu and I joined up with our recon team and moved to a small northern outpost called Dong Ha. It had a short, steel-matted airstrip and some dilapidated French buildings that sat across from a fortified U.S. Air Force radar station. There we were, sweating our asses off, and those flyboys were living like fuckin' kings. The place was fortified with concrete bunkers and had a machine-gun emplacement every thirty feet. They had mines and concertina wire all around. They lived in air-conditioned billets that looked like house trailers. They might as well have been in L.A.!

We flew into Dong Ha for one night. The choppers were to pick us up in the morning for the insertion. We came in late and spent the night sleeping outside the flyboy compound. Recon was staging out of the old, deserted French buildings. Zulu and I slept on the cement floor with the rats. There weren't enough of them to fuck with recon Marines. We could hear 'em running around, but they didn't bother us. The flyboys next door were gracious hosts and had us in for an unbelievable steak dinner. I didn't know people lived like that anymore.

We had a short night. We were inserted around 0700 hours. We were going into the mountains west of Cam Lo, above Highway 9, the road leading between Dong Ha and Khe Sanh. Intelligence believed there was a major buildup of NVA troops coming across the DMZ. Our mission was to go in, observe the area, report on activity, and if given the opportunity, capture enemy documents. I could tell by the stress levels obvious in the recon leaders that the mission would be a big one. One of their teams had already got shot up and lost a couple of guys. Now there was us, and we were in the fray with them.

We spent three uneventful days up on the mountain. It was another ass kicker. We didn't see jack shit or any of his companions. It was hot, humid, and boring as all hell. Word came down for us to get in position and assault a small hilltop outpost where the flyboys had seen some activity and thought there was a chance there might be some information to be had. It took us a whole day to get in position. We couldn't be seen, heard, or smelled. We crawled straight up a waterfall for more than four hours. The noise of the falling water covered our noise and our trail. We reached the top and holed up for the night. At dawn, the F-4s came to strafe the area and cover us for the assault. We stayed way back and let the 20mm cannons do their work. It was a beautiful sight. Debris flying everywhere made us glad we were on the home team. We quickly crawled the last fifty yards to the edge of the hillside. Splitting into two teams of four each, we were ready to rock 'n' roll. I was scared shitless with anticipation. Crawling, we got within twenty feet of the target. It looked like rice cooking. Smoke was rising in the glare of the early morning sun. Hell, it could've been a Boy Scout camp. We spread out across the ground on our side of the hill. We got on line, and we ran quickly from hootch to hootch. There were three bodies, all dead. Rice was cooking and ready for the dead. We looked around quickly, but nothing of note. We'd assaulted a dead outpost. A deeper search, and we uncovered some maps and documents. As quickly and silently as we came, we went. We needed to be out of there fast; we never knew how many brothers the dead guys had around the corner.

The day of our extraction, we were on a hill high above the Cam Lo River, waiting on the chopper, when I saw sampans moving along the river. They looked really suspicious, and they had to be bad guys way out there. They were maybe seven hundred yards away when I requested permission from the lieutenant to take out the two sampan drivers. It was time; Zulu and I needed to knock one of these little bastards off. The lieutenant took the 7×50s to see for himself, then turned and told us that was a "negatory." No fucking way, not again. What bullshit! Disappointed, we caught our chopper back.

Back at Phu Bai, recon got word they were moving temporarily to Dong Ha. The 3d Marine Division was preparing for some big shit in June and needed on-site recon support. Zulu and I were granted permission to move with them. Despite our restrictions on shootin' gooks, the patrolling skills we were learning with recon made the experience worthwhile. We didn't own much, but we packed what we had and flew off to a new home in Dong Ha. It was in the north of I Corps. We flew up from Phu Bai in a C-130 transport. By the end of the first week in June, we were in our new digs at the Dong Ha airstrip. The flight up was fine, but we learned it was a white knuckler landing on the short steel-matted runway of Dong Ha. It added a little more excitement to our lives. The planes came in and nearly screeched to a stop.

Zulu and I went back to our old digs in the French

compound. The officers got the best of the worst, the recon guys took next dibs, and Zulu and I brought up the rear of a bad dog. We made our home in the bombed-out end of the building. Our room had no roof and two walls. The other two were crumbling, only half-standing. Well, it was the dry season. At least I could look up at night, see the starlit sky, and do my mirror routine. I made my bed on what was left of the hearth of an old fireplace. Zulu, on the other hand, pushed the debris back and slept in the corner on the floor amid what looked like ancient ruins.

The French compound wasn't bad if you weren't there much, and we weren't there much. We were running our patrols, the seven to ten days out, three days off. The three days back we cherished. Many of the teams were getting hit hard on insertion, but we'd been lucky so far; we'd get in before we got shit. Activity in the area was picking up, and it was becoming more like a freeway out there. Large units were being spotted all over the area. We'd run patrols around Cam Lo and Con Thien and would always report back large sitings of NVA. The pucker factor was getting real tight. We'd sometimes go after the NVA with artillery, but the answer was still negative when we requested to fire our sniper rifles. Still no fucking kills for the good guys.

In June, 3d Mar Div brought on the grunts. A large part of the 4th Marines was moved to the DMZ. Everything was in place for some big action. All our recon work had led to the launching of Operation Hastings, a battle between the NVA's 324 B Division and our 4th Marines. The 3d Battalion of the 4th Marines led the spearhead into the middle of the 324 B Division. The bulk of the fighting took place between Con Thien and Cam Lo. I'd been in there lots of times with recon. It was tough country with high and low rolling hills and lots of dense underbrush and serious vegetation, and it was scary as all hell. The heat was stifling and the casualties high. Kilo Company 3/4, Zulu's old unit, was point company in the battle, and they'd already seen some serious shit.

It wasn't long before the casualties were mounting. We got word that they'd been overrun, but fought back valiantly. The battalion held, and the 324 B was chased back across the DMZ. We'd won the first set-piece battle with the bad guys from up north. At least they went back for a time. But the casualties were high on both sides. When it was all over, 3/4 came back to Dong Ha for a rest. Since Zulu and I were between recon runs, we went by to check it out. His old platoon had lost eighteen men. Their staff sergeant was a Sergeant McGinty. Wow! Before my antics in boot camp, he had been my DI back at Parris Island. I saw him walking out of the headquarters tent. He didn't know me, but then, he didn't really know anyone. He looked bad, real bad. He was thin, gaunt looking, like a sick old man. His face was a pasty gray. He was maybe thirty or so. They said he was a hero and that he had rallied the troops against human-wave assaults. I learned later that he was meritoriously promoted from staff sergeant to lieutenant. And then one day, I heard he was put in for the Medal of Honor. Everyone said he deserved it. I hope he did. They also said he was never the same again.

Hell, was anything worth all that? I don't know if it is or isn't. Looking into the faces of the Marine survivors was painful enough for me. I sat next to a good friend of Zulu's. He just sat and stared out in space, talking with us the whole time. He rambled on, emotionless, about his fear when the bugles blew. He became distant as he told us of the screams and curses of the NVA as they ran through the Marine lines. That guy survived, but survival hadn't been good to him. McGinty had looked bad; this guy looked worse.

Zulu and I walked back to our French home. We were shook up but in awe of what we saw. Even Zulu was moved by what the battle had done to his friends. The usual grin didn't grace his face this time. We walked past the makeshift med station between the airstrip and the French compound, where for a few days we'd been helping move the casualties and the bodies of the fallen Marines from Hastings. They'd all arrived in a hurry and lay in disarray. We'd come back with recon with our work all done before the shit hit the fan for the grunt masses, so we helped out wherever we could. It was the least we could do, a small price to pay to remain the sanest ones in a crazy place.

Between the mangled bodies of kids like me and the stories and looks in the eyes of the men of 3/4, something inside me died. My faint capacity to give a shit went somewhere far, far away. I hadn't fired my dead center shot just yet, but I knew when I did, I'd have to be cold and hard. To deal in death, I just might have to be dead inside myself.

Hastings lasted the better part of two weeks. It had been the biggest operation yet. The war was young, and Hastings was history. It was late June, and we had about five weeks on the job, and we'd yet to fire a shot as snipers. We'd fired some as recon Marines but the sniper deal hadn't happened yet. We loved recon, but our work with them was restricting and kept us from doing what we were trained to do. Zulu and I talked about packing it in, going back to our unit, and taking our chances. Recon didn't want us to leave, and we didn't want to. They felt like things'd change and we'd be used more. We just wanted to shoot the shit out of somebody.

Zulu and I were on a three-day break. We hadn't been back down to Phu Bai for quite a while. Rider had sent word that we shouldn't get too distant from the outfit, and Gunny DuBay's tour was about up, and he wanted to see us. We went to the airstrip at Dong Ha and hitch-hiked a ride to Phu Bai with some air force C-130 jocks. I wondered if it was like this in the Wild West. Hell, we'd go down, hang around the airstrip, and just bum a ride to Phu Bai. The Marine pilots all stuck to the "rank" thing. They'd rarely talk to us. But the air force guys were regular folks. They'd take us down with no scheduled trip of their own and drop us off. We'd set a time for us to be there in the morning, and they'd come by and give us a ride back north. At Phu Bai, we'd get drunk, get our mail, see the gunny and Rider, and be on our way the next day. We set up a routine, and it kept Rider quiet. It was wild and crazy, and we were free. That was living, if you were in Nam.

DuBay had a serious fatherly chat with us. He was sure recon was bad work for snipers. But we were just as sure we had to keep it up. I knew the lessons were too valuable to miss. Lich and the whole team were a model of professionalism. They taught us the art of camouflage and the best way to hide out in the bush. They taught us how to apply all the classroom lessons, like calling in choppers, air strikes, and artillery. The discipline of holding your finger on the lid of the C rat so the slight click from your P-38 couldn't be heard as you opened it. Lich was like a cat playing in the tall grass, as he taught lessons in stealth. It would have taken years to learn with the grunts.

After a long chat we convinced him recon was the right thing to do. I'd learned so much from them; I didn't want to give it up. It pissed me off that I was behind in the kills department but, hell, you can't have everything. I was good, and I knew I'd catch up. The letters-from-home department was a bummer. They were starting to talk about how I'd changed and was not like I used to be, and all that nonsense. I really needed preaching when I was out there in the bad land. The gulf between the World and me seemed to be widening with each passing letter, but I didn't have time to care. I had work to do.

The big break for us came the last week of June. We were on patrol with recon just north of Highway 9 and a few klicks west of Cam Lo. I think the mountain was called Dong Hoi. It was supposed to be the headquarters of an NVA division. We didn't find much of the division, but we did find a strange mountain peak to our west. It sat in the middle of a valley and jutted straight up with cliffs on all sides. The tree line stopped about halfway up, and it was gray, rough-looking rock from there skyward. It was in the middle of valleys and mountains in every direction. It'd be great as an observation post. We all agreed that this peak showed promise.

Back at Dong Ha, the recon leaders proposed setting up an observation post on top of the peak we'd seen. The big dogs bought the idea, and we were about to be launched. Our recon team would be placed on the peak that became known as the Rockpile, and our drop on the Rockpile coincided with the kickoff of Operation Prairie, a big grunt operation in the mountains south of the DMZ. It would be in and around the Rockpile. It was the perfect place from which to direct air and artillery strikes on the valleys below. We worked hard on the plans and set them in place in record time, then saddled up for what we were told would be a seven- to ten-day stay. There'd be six Recon Marines and two snipers, eight of us in all. I couldn't wait. That was hot shit.

We were picked up on the morning of July 4 in two

Chinook CH-46 helicopters. We had lots of gear to get up on top of the Rockpile: cans of water, cases of C rats, heavy radio equipment, and all our personal gear. Zulu and I were taking one of our ship's telescopes; with a fixed base to work from, it could be valuable. We were weighed down with our heavy ammo. We wanted to be ready.

When we got there, a strong wind was whipping across the top of the seven-hundred-foot mountain peak, and the pilots were having a hard time getting the chopper properly lined up and holding it in place. The first couple of passes, we were literally blown away and over the mountain's edge. That's when they decided we'd have to jump down; they just couldn't get the chopper to sit there. The ship came around and over the top of the peak. It was just a small flat spot, maybe fifteen feet long and five or six feet wide, right on top. The tops of the rocks were all jagged and sharp. Someone said it looked like granite. I don't know what the hell it was, but it was sure as hell evil looking. The pilot came up and held the chopper in the air, hovering six or eight feet above the little clearing. The chopper was swaying in the breeze just over the top of the seven-hundred-foot peak as we climbed out the side door of the Chinook. The door dropped out of the side of the chopper and hung by two cables. I held the cables as I edged down the steps to the bottom. At the bottom, I held the cables and leaned out, ready to drop, the third man out behind two recon guys. I leaned, jumped, and landed real hard, sending pain rippling up my legs and back. But fuck it, I was there. A couple more guys had jumped off when I looked up to see that Zulu was next. He was leaning out, hanging onto the cables just as I had. He was ready to jump, a leg hanging out, when a gust of wind pushed the chopper off the

top. It fell fast, making a sweeping motion out and
around the valley, as it descended several hundred feet
above the valley floor. Zulu was hanging on for his life.
The crew chief right behind him was reaching out, holding his pack. I'll bet that wiped the shit-eating grin off
Zulu's face. He hung out there while the chopper gained
control and climbed back up in a big circle. Zulu was sitting in the doorway for round two. There was just him
and a couple of recon left. The 46 came up and held fast.
Zulu bailed out, followed by the rest of the team.

Life up on top was never easy. Getting supplies up on
the Rockpile was very hard. The winds made it treach-
erous for the pilots every time. The next day, they came
with UH-34s, the old reliables. The pilots learned they
could lower the front two wheels onto the rocks, with the
tail flapping in the breeze. As they sat there, the crew
would toss supplies out, fast. That technique worked
most of the time, and we never lost any choppers doing
it, but more than one pilot probably had to clean out his
flight suit after a resupply.

Life up on the Rockpile was unique. We ordered up
sleeping bags so we could sleep at night on the rocks.
We'd curl up in a rock and blow some Zs. The rocks were
so jagged, it was next to impossible to sit or lie. The
sleeping bags cushioned the blow, and we'd use them to
make little beds; no one had space enough to lie down.
But we could get some sleep up there. We'd leave one or
two men awake at night, but the cliffs on all sides were so
steep, we knew no one was coming up. Near the end of
our first week of life up in the air, one of the guys woke us
all up, screaming! It was the middle of the night and dark
as a coffin. We couldn't just run to his aid, unless we
wanted to chance a fall of about seven hundred feet.
When we finally reached the guy, he was hysterical. And

so were we when we realized what had happened. A rock ape had climbed up in the black of night and just slapped the shit out of him! He was sleeping and *wham!* it just started beating him on his legs and feet. The little rock apes didn't know what to make of us invading their home. We'd seen them before on a neighboring peak, but never dreamed they'd come over and attack us. On the other hand, it was a welcome relief to our boring existence high in the sky.

The boredom took leave when the big op started. Operation Prairie kicked off just after our first week on the Rockpile. It was brutal, like Hastings. Most of the fighting took place just north of us on Hill 400 and, later, on 484. Hill 400 became known as Mudder Ridge. The fighting was bloody, brutal, and bad to the bone, and it went on for days as the Marines fought to take two hills in the middle of nowhere. The NVA were dug in deep, complete with bunkers built like the pillboxes of World War II. They were so well concealed in the trails that only a one-inch aperture was exposed to the world.

As the battle progressed, we directed tons of artillery and airstrikes on the retreating NVA from the Rockpile. From our site high over the valley, we commanded the valley floor, and it took the gooks a while to figure out that we lurked above. We were up there about a week when the bad guys started dropping mortars our way. We'd hear the familiar *bloop* of a mortar leaving the tube and coming our way. Then came the spine-chilling whistle of a mortar shell slicing in from the sky above. We were worried, but we knew we were a difficult target; our very tiny camp had its advantages. All the rounds fell harmlessly to the cliffs and jungle below.

About a week later, just as we were feeling better and

starting to relax, our security was again shattered. The gooks figured out that the mortars weren't working on the Rockpile. We were hanging out, observing light activity one afternoon, when I stood up to piss off the side, and *whooooosh!* The biggest fucking bullet I ever heard just passed me by! Damn! Immediately, everyone was hugging the rocks. Of course, I nearly jumped off the cliff with my dick in my hand. The lieutenant yelled, "It was a recoilless rifle."

The lieutenant ordered a spotter plane over the area ASAP. Then he told recon to stand by. He told Zulu and me to get on the binoculars and find that mother! A recoilless rifle is just a big fucking rifle. It's a giant damned rifle, 75mm or larger, that shoots straight. And it's damned accurate. That hummer they just fired buzzed right over our fucking heads. Shiiit! The next one could be right in our asses. We were all looking hard, but we had to look from behind the rocks; we wanted to be on the back side of something solid if that baby hit. Then I heard a muffled *boom*. A second or two went by and *whoooosh* . . . right overhead. That thing was so close, it stirred the hairs on my head. Then it exploded with a loud *boom!* on the mountain behind us. Another couple of shots hurled by us and into the mountain. The spotter was on station, so we relayed the coordinates to him. He called in the jets but not before the NVA lit up the leeward side of the Rockpile, one round slamming about fifty feet below us. That was a heart stopper for sure. Eventually, arty took care of the bad guys and the big rifle.

Two weeks went by, and we were still up breathing thin air on the big pile of rocks. We got our break early in week three. I spotted some bad guys to the west of the

Rockpile, in a place we hadn't seen activity before. To that point, Zulu and I had been working on the war by calling in artillery. We were getting a few gooks with the big guns but still had done no real sniping. The lieutenant came and took a look. He asked whether we could shoot that far. Why was this guy questioning us? I mean, all he had to do was to give us the word and those little assholes would be history. Well, he wasn't buying what we were selling but he was amused at our self-confidence, so he gave us the word: "Be my guest, and shoot." It looked to us like a seven-hundred-yard shot. We had to guess how the angle of shooting from so high above the target would affect our aim. We checked the wind by watching the treetops between the target and us. The wind seemed to be in our favor. It was still morning, about 1000 hours, so heat wasn't yet a factor. The three bad guys fucking around their grass hut were gonna get a surprise. They were in no-man's-land, and they didn't have a clue.

The ship's scope confirmed the uniformed and ugly guys at seven hundred meters. One had a rifle, and that's about all we could tell. I wanted their asses, and I wanted them bad. Zulu spotted for me. It was a tough shot from so high up. I couldn't lie flat, so it was a shot from a modified sitting position. I sat, twisted nearly straight up, with my rifle resting on my pack. I took my time until I had him squarely in my crosshairs. This was it, man . . . relax . . . breathe in, you can do it, be gentle . . . breathe out halfway . . . hold it . . . hold it. Rock him in your sight . . . okay. The trigger . . . you're squeezin' your girlfriend's tit . . . gentle now . . . here it comes . . . *boom!* I squeezed off a round from my 30-06. "Got his ass, Kug!" Zulu yelled. "Helluva shot."

From behind us the lieutenant says, "I second that. A

helluva shot. I wouldn't have believed it." He was looking through our binoculars, impressed as hell.

We stayed at it, watching the area for some time. We switched scoping out the dead dude. Zulu got the first guy that came out to get my dead one. *Boom!* And we struck again. We worked the west side of the Rockpile all day. Those little assholes either had orders to go someplace or they were stupid as hell. They were moving around most of the morning and into the afternoon. It was a good day for snipers after a long drought. I got three kills before it was over, and Zulu two. Hell, that isn't bad for not having shot at a distance since sniper school. Sniper school? That seemed like a lifetime ago.

By that time, Zulu and I were about ripe. It'd been three weeks, and we hadn't bathed once. None of us. It was a damned good thing we got a pretty strong breeze up there in the afternoon. But I needed to get cleaned up because, among other things, the leech bites on my ankles were infected, and life was getting strange up in the air with the apes.

A couple days later word came that the whole team, recon and snipers, would rotate off the Rockpile. They brought in a fresh recon team with two new snipers, one I'd met, but the other was new to the outfit, just having come in from the States. The guy I knew, we called Harley. He was a Hell's Angel back in California before the Corps. He was a wild looking dude who'd been around the block a time or two, or maybe three. Well, I waved him the high sign, and he could have the Rockpile. He didn't know he'd be fighting the giant flies that had somehow found us up there. As for Zulu and me and our recon buds, we were on our UH-34 headed back to base camp.

It was great to be back at Dong Ha. After three weeks

on the Rockpile, our dilapidated French compound never looked so good. The major at recon arranged it so that we could eat and drink with the flyboys in their fortress. There was a serious class difference around here; eating with the air force was like being Stateside. The little bastards had even added a swimming pool since my last visit! We went over and consumed all the real food we could get our hands on. Then we headed straight for the club. We went inside and were like fish out of water: those guys smelled like Ivory soap! We didn't last long, about an hour, before the flyboys asked us to leave because we were being too "rowdy." Weaklings! Zulu was ready to kick some ass, but they weren't worth the shit we'd get in. "Let's go where we're wanted," someone in recon said. So we left, and the Taj Mahal of Dong Ha was closed to us paupers forever.

In the northern I Corps, the war was picking up on all fronts. Dong Ha's military base was growing like a bad weed. Planeloads of supplies and troops were coming north everyday. We'd been out for a while, so Zulu and I hitched a ride to Phu Bai with a couple of the C-130 drivers. We walked into a big surprise; half our platoon was in the process of moving to Dong Ha because they were needed up north to support the work of Operation Prairie. Part of the contingent heading north was the two guys we left on the Rockpile. It would also include Zulu and me.

I needed some time to rest my legs, which were badly infected. I had six or seven sizable leech bites on each ankle. They got infected on my first patrol, and constant bush living hadn't helped any. We decided on a week's rest and drunkenness. Recon would run the next patrol without us, but we told them we'd catch up on the next round. At the time, recon was also moving, from the French "hacienda" to tents in Dong Ha. We'd still be together for more action and adventure.

Zulu and I walked into the sniper tent with our gear. The tent was empty; they'd just had mail call, and there were letters and packages lying all over the place. The racks were full of care and concern from back home. But the place was void of human life except Zulu and me, and we were questionable. Hell, I didn't know if I'd know people anymore. Lots of new guys had come in since we'd left with recon. It was mid-August already, and we'd been reconnoitering for three months. I was skinny as hell, tan as an Indian, and meaner than ever, but I still wasn't as low as a snake—like Zulu.

I look over, and he's picking up packages, shaking them, and putting a few under his arm. I said, "What the fuck are you doing, man?"

He laughed, "I'm seeing what the hell I want. I'm hungry, aren't you?"

I was appalled. I couldn't believe he was taking other people's packages. And I told him so. Then I saw the look in his eye. Oh no, not another teaching moment from my partner in crime. He was grinning that grin again. With a big package under his arm, he came over and sat down beside me on my rack. I let him have it again. "Zulu, you fuckin' lowlife. How can you take this poor bastard's stuff? He might be out there getting his young ass killed right now!"

Full of sinister enthusiasm, Zulu said, "My point exactly. Hey, my stuff is fair game when I'm gone."

I laughed. "You never get shit, Zulu!"

"Aw, that's beside the point; if I did, I wouldn't care! You need to eat this shit and not let it go to waste. They may never get back here to enjoy it." What use was it talking with him; he was a lunatic. Zulu had his own brand of Nero Wolfe psychology, and it all made perfect sense to him. I shook my head with a mixture of disgust and disbelief as he walked off to enjoy a canned ham he'd "saved" from one of the unsuspecting new guys.

I walked away to get my mail and take a look at life a world away. Mail from home was more of the same. It was nice to hear from them but I was more than a world away, and I was starting to enjoy the differences. The racing I'd loved so much seemed a thing of the past. Reading about it didn't interest me anymore. The girls of my life were long gone, and that seemed just fine. They'd either tired of hearing about Vietnam or found other directions. Mom and Dad continued to pretend I was somewhere other than Vietnam and continued their "failure to mention" anything of Vietnam in their letters. Mom was good about sending supplies, and she kept sending Care packages with lots of goodies for Zulu and me. It was good that I told her about Zulu, since he'd have taken my shit anyway. She sent enough for us both.

We stayed drunk most of our week off, but my ankles weren't making much progress. Eventually, recon called. They needed us again, and we had to go, bad ankles or not. We were going to Dong Hoi Mountain again to check it out after the grunts had swept through as part of Prairie. It was a foreboding place, but *we* hadn't hit the shit yet, so we weren't as psyched about it that time. We'd finally been getting to shoot, and that felt good. We wanted to get to where we could do some damage with our sniper training. Zulu was scheduled to leave for home in the fall, so we didn't have a lot of time to waste on snoop-and-poop specials; we wanted more chances to drop some more poor bastards in the games of Nam. We weren't sure what the latest recon assignment would

bring. And Recon had a new commander—a major—
who was getting them into some deep shit. He introduced them to the concept of "ambush at will." Now
there was a winner. Bet the commander was a Harvard
man, for sure. He wanted the five- and six-man recon patrols, out twenty or thirty miles from friendlies, to carry
out impromptu ambushes. "Ambush at will" meant that,
when the opportunity presented itself, the five recon
guys jump off the fucking trail and *bang, bang,* you're
dead! A hell of an idea if you don't ambush the point of
fifty, sixty, or a hundred bad guys. Recon had been doing
it for about a month, and they weren't impressed. They
were having some real hairy times. It wasn't a recon mission, and it was crazy as all hell, and they knew it. But
they were troopers, so they were doin' it.

We rejoined recon two days later. We worked planning and prep for a day before being inserted on the side
of Dong Hoi Mountain. It was tough country, even for us
cowboys. Our job was to find an NVA division headquarters that was believed to have been evacuated. We
weren't on the ground long when I was sure hoping like
hell it was evacuated. We were in real jungle. The weather
was hot and humid, as always, and the mountain was
steep as a barn side back home. Our first two days were
calm, eerie, and uncertain but with no action. The third
day out, we encountered a small force of gooks. Uniformed NVA! Bad motor scooters for sure.

We formed a quick line and opened fire. Damned if
"Will" didn't show up for our party. It was thicker than a
fall cornfield. The firefight boiled down to two groups of
men, deep in the woods, firing wildly at each other. I
mean, I couldn't see anything. Bullets were cracking all
around. It was all automatic-weapons work in there, no
sniper rifles allowed. I unloaded a couple of magazines

from my 14. By the third refill, it was all over. Silence regained control of the day.

Final scores, three for recon and zero for the gooks. It was midafternoon and the eerie silence gave me the heebie-jeebies. It was dark from the thick canopy overhead. The faint hint of wood smoke was hanging in the air, and the smell of black powder mixed with death hung like cheap perfume. But there wasn't time to reminisce; "Will" might have a bunch of cousins hanging out around here. We searched the bodies for documents and belongings as quickly as we could. Then we were off to put distance between the crime scene and us.

It was late afternoon when we were far enough away to look for a place to hole up. We wanted to hide until we could search again tomorrow. Our point discovered a small cave where we decided to spend the night. It was a welcome relief. The night was unusually dark and strangely quiet. There were no sounds at all. I mean none. No animals, no people . . . no nothing. I sat back and thought about the people I knew I'd killed so far, then I thought about the ones I might have aced that day. Who knows who actually killed them—bullets were flying in all directions. Somebody eventually got all three. I thought I got one, but who could tell? Were there more? There probably were. Some always seemed to slip away. I remembered seeing papers on one guy, a picture. I wasn't close enough to make it out, but it was a person. I guess one of them had a girlfriend. Looked more like a woman. It could have been a sister or wow, maybe even a mother! I wondered, could he have been married or . . . ? No . . . what the hell was I thinking? I couldn't think about that kind of shit just then. The little assholes were goddamned Communists! They didn't give a damn about people. Their whole history showed you either agreed with them or you died. They made nasty-ass booby traps that stuck bamboo spikes in your chest. And bombs, with nails and glass and debris, that ripped your young ass to shreds. Yeah, they *cared* about people. They cared about people the way Hitler cared about the Jews. Give me a fucking break. I got over my wave of giving a shit and then regained my senses. I had to have control. I was a Marine, a Marine sniper, at that. I was there to kill Communists. I realized it was my issue. I needed to control my mind. I needed to control my emotions. I'd been doing a good job, but needed to work on it more. I needed to remove all emotions from my life.

We finished our work on Dong Hoi, going three more days in, on, and around the mountain. We found the headquarters we were looking for, and walked for two whole days through a huge gook camp. It was unbelievable! Full canopy above, so thick and interwoven we couldn't even see the sun at noonday. There were bunkers everywhere. It was scary as all hell. It was perfect for an ambush on the good guys. I imagined hundreds of the little bastards charging out of the ground like rats at any fucking minute. As I walked, I thought about the history of these little guys. I'd read Bernard Fall's book on Dien Bien Phu. I knew the little assholes were ingenious. And that camp was a sight to see. It was hard to believe the primitive little bastards had constructed a place so elaborate. Two whole fucking days of snooping and pooping right through what was once home to a division. I was glad to get off the mountain. The extraction couldn't come too early for me.

I was struggling with my legs the whole patrol. The infections were getting worse, and my ankles were swelling very badly. But when our time came, there was no chopper. Elements of the 3d Battalion, 4th Marines were sweeping the area for the last remnants of the bad guys, and the choppers were all tied up supporting them. What a crock of shit. It wasn't the best place to be spending time on an overnight camp-out. Those were the badlands, where we didn't generally run into just three or four gooks the way we had at the start of the gig. Usually we found a whole mob of the bastards, complete with uniforms, AKs, and all. The recon lieutenant in charge kept the heat on for a resolution to our dilemma.

It was late afternoon when we got the word that no choppers were coming anytime soon. We were to make our way over and join up with 3/4, link up with the grunts, and fly back to Dong Ha. It sounded like a plan, even if it was a stupid one. We quickly headed out to meet up with our allies a good four grid squares away, so it was late in the day when we linked up. I knew there had to be snipers with them, and I wanted to find them and catch up. After spending the night in the perimeter with recon, Zulu and I bid them farewell and went in search of our own.

It didn't take long. A couple of guys I'd met once and two we'd never met before at all. One was called Det Cord, the other Stu. Det Cord was a really bright Midwesterner who loved explosives. Stu was a big blond dude from the Nebraska corn belt. I liked them both. We talked a while, then decided it was time to make our way to Dong Ha. I wanted to be back with our snipers at base camp. Recon was changing a lot from what it had been just a few months before. Some of the new replacements weren't as professional as the originals we knew, and I found that the confidence I'd had in recon before was no longer there. Zulu agreed with me on that.

By that time, my legs were in bad shape. Greenish-yellow pus was oozing out of my sores, which would crack open at the slightest bump. Pain was normal, and the irritation I felt with each step was incredible. I just wanted choppers to fly in. With boots up and off my feet, I'd be fine. I wasn't impressed when the word came down that there weren't enough choppers to get us all out. I needed a bath. I needed to take care of my ankles. I needed out of there.

The saving grace came in the form of the battalion commander, Colonel Masterpool. A Marine's Marine, he had led 3/4 through the worst of times. He was short, tough looking, tough talking, and seasoned. His men loved him. We got word that the colonel had promised his troops a steak dinner when they returned, and they deserved it. So when the word of "no choppers" took the place by storm, it wasn't a good scene. The men took it real hard.

Masterpool was a leader, a real one, one who wouldn't be denied. One who wouldn't let his troops down. He passed the word to saddle up; we'd be in Dong Ha that night. We were all going to march in, together, and we would have our steaks. It was seven good miles to Dong Ha, and I couldn't imagine a mess hall being open when the battalion got there. And my ankles were killing me, and I just knew they were about to grow bigger than my boots. But, I guessed if all those sick, lame, and lazy grunts could make it, I could, too. They all said they'd follow Masterpool to hell, so I guess a walk in the night to Dong Ha would be no big deal.

We saddled up for the hike of our lives. The sick were to come down and they'd arrange choppers for them. The corpsman who checked out my ankles told me to go over for the lift, but I couldn't bring myself to do it. I had done every damned thing I set out to do 'til then, so I wasn't missing the ordeal with Masterpool. Leaders like him were also as rare as hair on a frog. He'd be out there with us, soft cover on, little cigar sticking out of his mouth, walking up and down offering encouragement. No, I'd go in, step by step, with the gang of grunts and their badass leader.

We struck out into a walk that was slow but brutal. As I walked, my legs kept swelling bigger and bigger. I unlaced my jungle boots on each break. I noticed lots of grunts were hurting just like me. So, the hike to Dong Ha was certainly not a forced march. We walked for several hours, steady, with but few breaks along the way. It was about 2200 hours when we finally reached the Dong Ha Marine perimeter. The snipers were well back in the pack, but we could hear the cheers coming from the front when the first ranks made it in. The colonel led us straight to the mess hall and *damn!* . . . he was going to deliver on his promise. He'd insisted the mess hall be kept open for his troops. That was an experience I'd never forget. I'd been in the presence of real leadership. You could feel it when you were with someone like him; all your other problems went away. I agreed with his grunts—I'd go to hell and die for that guy.

But Dong Ha was a time of change for me. Zulu was getting ready to rotate home. We tried to get him to extend his tour six months, but—according to him—he had "women to bed" who missed him greatly. Recon continued to change, too. With their ambush-at-will policy, their need for us was less. That was just as well; I was ready for a change. Our platoon had lots of new people I didn't even know. And I was behind in the kill department. I didn't like that. I was grateful for my time with recon. I learned a ton. I learned how to live and survive in Nam; I learned how to fight the war with small units; I learned to call artillery and air strikes, and on that count, I was way ahead of the rest of our snipers. And my map and compass skills had been honed by three months in the bush with Force Recon. So I left knowing it was a good time for me to go. It was time to move on.

I took the next three weeks off. By the time I'd walked in with 3/4, my boots were unlaced all the way down. My ankles had swelled so big when I took off my boots that King Kong's wouldn't have fit me. The docs down at the med battalion gave me some shots to help with the infection. I had to go over every afternoon to have the wounds drained. I couldn't wear boots again for two of my three weeks off. I was in the shower shoe brigade as I prepared for life supporting the grunts.

CHAPTER FOUR

There's Gotta Be a War Somewhere Between Here and All This Walkin' Around— Just Gotta Be

The three weeks I spent nursing my ankles flew by. And the 5th Marines flew up north and into the mountains to fight the NVA. One of their units got trapped and chewed up real bad. Choppers couldn't get in for resupply or for a medevac. They'd been stuck for three days. I couldn't imagine the shit they were in. Zulu and I were at the airstrip, waiting to hitch a ride down to Phu Bai. We'd been told by one of the pilots that a late plane was supposed to come in around 2100. I don't know if I believed that shit, but I waited anyway. We wanted to go down and get a few things.

Zulu and I sat there arguing, talking, and solving world hunger. Anything to pass the time on a hot night in Nam. It wasn't quite dark, but getting there, when we heard a chopper coming our way. It was late for a single CH-46 to be out. It was coming in from the northwest. We were at the little hut that served as a command post for the airstrip, and we were the only ones there. The chopper circled to our left and was coming down hot, so we stood up to check out the action. About that time, a little military ambulance from 3d Med came flying up the dirt lane

next to the flyboys' camp. Zulu and I walked out to see
what the happening was so late at night.

It was still light out but getting dark fast as the chopper
spun around right in front of us and dropped the rear
door. The corpsmen backed their truck up to the chopper's
rear ramp, and one of the corpsmen yelled to Zulu and
me to give them a hand. As Zulu and I ran up, the crew
chief waded out the back of the chopper and motioned
us on board. Inside it was lit with eerie-looking red lights.
They cast a Halloweenlike glow over the whole inside of
the craft. We couldn't make it out at first, and then it hit
us. It was a whole load of wounded from the 5th Marines.
The pilots had just made it in, but they were the first of
many. It was the beginning of a nightmare they had been
living for three days.

The crew chief yelled, "Get in here and get 'em out . . .
we gotta go back." Zulu and I stepped up inside the
knee-high load of human misery. The corpsman had already put one guy on a stretcher and was trying to get another. Marines lay everywhere in various stages of life
and death. Bodies lay one on top of the other. You could
only tell the living from the dead when you moved them.
If they made a noise or tried to help themselves, they
were alive. If they were quiet and heavy, like a wet mattress, they were dead. The crew thought they had twenty-
six Marines on board; I never knew. It was a bunch of
meat, though. It was a terrible carnage to witness.

Outside, more Marines came to help. They brought
two mules* to load the wounded and the dead on for the
ride down to the med tent. A few walking wounded were
helped out and on board the first mule. A mule is just a
flat platform, maybe five feet by eight feet, with four

---

*The mule was no one's favorite device; it soon disappeared from use.

wheels, a little motor underneath, and a folding steering wheel. They didn't move fast, but they did move. The grunts used them to haul gear. Zulu and I worked as fast as we could, but the pilots were still yelling back for us to hurry and get them off. They wanted to be airborne ASAP. As we walked out carrying yet another dead body, I saw the skin of the chopper had holes along each side. As I was going back in the chopper, Zulu came out going the other way. He had a Marine by the feet, dragging him, feet first, down the ramp. The dead man's head was bouncing along on the deck. I yelled, "Zulu, don't drag the fuckin' guy, man!"

He turned in anger and disgust, and through gritted teeth, snarled back at me. "He's fuckin' dead, Kug, they're all fuckin' dead!"

Inside, I realized what he was saying. The bottom layer of bodies we'd finally reached was all dead. One on top of the other, all in unimaginable positions of lifelessness. All dead in an ugly moment before they got their body bags for the ride home, to ruin an unknowing loved one's life, too. Most were staring into space, with expressions much like the living we'd just helped off the bus from hell. The stench was horrible, the aroma of an instant barf. Many had been dead for some time and just now were getting off the mountain. No green body bags adorned those guys; they were real, right before our eyes, and ripe.

Between trips off to the side to vomit, we eventually emptied the chopper of its grisly cargo. I hadn't seen anything like that in *The Story of the U.S. Marines*. I wondered how a person couldn't care that it was happening. But it was so horrific, I just couldn't make sense of it. I didn't have the time or the inclination to figure it out. So we piled the dead on the mule as best we could for the few-hundred-yard ride down the dirt road. There they'd be worked on for the big ride home. The bodies looked like filthy mannequins to me as they bumped along on the mule with Marines walking next to them, holding them on. It was a bitch of a night. One or two of the dead Marines had split apart from the bouncing and the heat and the time and the decay since they'd checked out. A couple had rigor mortis. It was a sad time to be waiting for a plane. It was a sadder time to be waiting for one of those kids to come home. Hell . . . it could have been my young ass. There was something mind-numbing about the whole affair. Hell, it wasn't happening to me; I wasn't going to buy the farm. Nobody was going to be dragging my dead ass down the ramp of a Chinook.

Just a click from dark, the chopper lifted off, and I turned to see Zulu running down the dirt road behind the mule with the bodies. I looked up in time to see him hurl a rock toward the fence of the air force compound. I took off running down there in time to see him pitch another one. "You rotten, pantywaist, pogue bastards!" he screamed. "You dirty low-life sons a' bitches. Turn off the fucking cameras!" The flyboys lived in their damned fortress, but they came running out to take pictures of our dead. Fucking assholes! I thought for a minute my man was going to go right through the concertina wire after their asses.

I grabbed Zulu by the arms and wrestled him back. More Marines came, and the lily-livered bastards put down their cameras and quit eyeball-fucking the dead. REMFs! Rear echelon motherfuckers! I'd never seen Zulu so angry before. He was incensed at their lack of respect and decency. I brought him back with me to our waiting place and hoped we'd catch a plane ride out that night. Zulu was not well, and it was shaping up to be a real Budweiser night. Zulu and I sat down next to the building where it all began.

We sat in silence, along with three or four corpsmen who had their ambulance at the ready. Soon, we saw the red lights of the CH-46 and heard its familiar sound. The landing lights went on when they got near us, and the pilot came in like a man with a mission. The rear ramp dropped, and the scene was a repeat of last time. We had a few more wounded than dead this time. But it was just as ugly. Death has a way of putting life in its place. We lived in a place where the winners were those who were standing the next morning. We'd just unloaded a lot of losers, many who wouldn't be standing ever again, and a few who wouldn't be right ever again even though they'd survived. And lots more who made it, who'd spend a lifetime wondering if they'd really won.

I went around to the side door to help a kid who'd just fallen outside. It was dark, but a shadowy light came from the headlights of the meat wagon. When I reached the kid, he'd gotten himself up. He was standing, leaning really, against the side of the chopper. I couldn't believe my eyes; he was bandaged everywhere you could imagine. A big, wide, bloody bandage had been wrapped around his head. It curled down and left only one eye exposed. His neck was wrapped with bandages that were soaked in blood or just filthy with dirt. One arm was in a sling. His legs had bandages from the knees down. He looked like the poster child for bad fucking accidents. I reached out to help him as he tried to walk along the skin of the chopper. He pulled away, jerking his arm back like a rattlesnake after his strike. I said, "Come on, man, let me help you over here . . . you've had enough shit for one day," as I pointed to the ambulance. He stared straight ahead, inching himself toward the rear and to the waiting ambulance. Then, in a half-whispering, half-shrill voice, he said it all: "Fuck it . . . Just fuck it . . . Fuck you . . . fuck them fucking gooks . . . and fuck it all." With that he reached the end of the chopper and fell on his face. A corpsman rushed over to help, and I waved him off. This guy needed to finish the job he started. He shakily got to his feet and made his way to the wagon and fell in.

It was one hell of a night on our end, but it wasn't shit compared to what the guys we'd just brought in had gone through. And their brothers were still out on the mountain in some serious shit. Hell, I felt guilty for being back there. I just wanted to hitch that ride to Phu Bai, get back up, and get the hell out to the bush. Payback was a motherfucker! We needed to kick some serious ass.

It was after 2200 hours when the C-130 arrived. When the pilots climbed down from the plane, we asked for a ride. They said no problem, but they had to load some cargo for the trip south, and we'd have to wait. Zulu and I stretched out to catch some Zs while they got the plane ready.

At some point, the aircraft commander woke us up and said it was time to go. We grabbed our gear and started to climb in the side door of the plane, but the crew chief grabbed us and said, "Do you all mind flying down with all these stiffs?" What the hell? Zulu let out a loud belly laugh and said no problem. We climbed aboard and looked around. It looked like the inside of a ship, rows of bunks, or racks, stacked floor to ceiling. They told us to sit down for takeoff. I was on one side, and Zulu sat across from me. He looked over and started laughing, that same deep belly laugh all over again. His head rolled back, and he pointed all around at the racks of cargo. I looked around in the dim light and . . . I got it!

I finally got it. It was a planeload of dead bodies being transported south to Da Nang.

I got up and walked around for a closer look. It really was a planeload of stiffs. All clothed in green plastic body bags. All stacked the way we were on board ship. What an eerie, strange ride it was. I don't know if they tried to cool the planeload of meat or not, but once we were airborne, an odd steam or fog filled the hold. After a couple of minutes, we both lay back to get some rest. As the kid said back at the 5th Marine medevac, "Fuck it. Just fuck it."

Our stay at Phu Bai was real short. We didn't get to the hootch until around 0200. We quickly gathered up our gear and returned to the airstrip for the ride back in the morning. Our outfit never knew where the hell we were and, rarely, when we'd be back. If our plane ever went down, I don't think anyone would have had a clue we were on it. But then, who gave a damn? We needed supplies, and we needed mail, neither of which ever seemed to make it up our way on their own.

I needed to get back up north, but Zulu decided to stay down at Phu Bai. I didn't blame him. He was getting short and wasn't extending and he had some other things to do. I bid my main man farewell, my first partner and friend in Nam. I headed back up north; I'd need a new partner. Still based at Dong Ha, Rider was still around and handling our contingent. I needed a good guy to be with, and I decided I wanted the Pearl. He'd done well. He had a few kills, a great attitude, and a greater reputation. Rider liked Zulu and me. He also liked our work with recon. I pitched Pearl to him and got my way. He'd always taken care of me. Right after I got to Nam, he put in for and got me lance corporal, E3. I had lost that rank when I took a long weekend at LeJeune to be with my then girlfriend, Katie. Rider had just got me E4, corporal, so he was cool in my book. Anyway, Pearl readily agreed to the deal, and we were locked and loaded and ready for the bush.

On the flight back north, I rode by myself, except for a bunch of pallets of war shit sitting next to me. I sat there listening to the drone of the engines. It was a good forty-five-minute ride back to my home up north, and I was thinking about how things would be different without Zulu at my side. The thought scared me a little. I slipped into one of my reflective moods. He was always there, every time I needed him, even if he was a bonafide whack job. He'd been my teacher and coach. He helped me deal with my fears and well, yes . . . he was an asshole at times, but a good one.

I got back to Dong Ha, where life had become hot, boring, and miserable and none too exciting. Pearl and I spent some time on grunt ops out around Cam Lo. But we didn't have a lot of luck in the third-eye department. We got a kill apiece, but all in all, the hunting wasn't good. The gooks up there found strength in numbers. They only wanted to fight on their terms, which weren't too fucking favorable for us good guys. That made for some bad, bad days. And the other problem was, we were hanging out with a virtual mob. On the one hand, I loved hanging out with the grunts. On the other, like when you went out to the bush to fight those slimy little bastards, it wasn't so great. There'd be a hundred or so of you and . . . well, you just couldn't sneak up on a statue with a mob like that. Let alone the bad guys of the DMZ. I mean using large units was just no way to fight that war, and even I could see that.

So when the call came in for snipers to help the ARVN at Con Thien, I jumped at the chance. Of course, now the tables were turned. I was doing the volunteering instead of Zulu. I was speaking up, and poor Pearl got screwed. I used the "how bad can it be" argument; Pearl eventually agreed without too much whining and sniveling. We got out of our grunt assignment and headed out to Con Thien. We'd be overlooking the Ben Hai River and southern North Vietnam. It was a chance to get a close look at why we were there.

Pearl and I took a resupply chopper headed for Con Thien and got out there near evening. The type of chopper coming in was new to me, a weird contraption with two big gas engines, one on either side of the body, and they were painted to look like eyes, like a giant bug. The thing looked like a bug too big to fly and too old to try. On top of that, they were loading it down like it was the last train to Nashville. I mean they had enough cases of ammo on it to head on into Hanoi. I told Pearl, "One consolation is, if they hit us in flight, we'll be the only ones around that know what the big bang was." Of course, we wouldn't have a clue what the hell happened; we'd be little pieces falling through the air.

The crew chief was about as happy having to take us as the two of us were to get inside his bloated grasshopper. He was arguing with the pilots and just generally moaning about life in general and the load in specific. When he saw us and realized we wanted to come aboard, he threw his hands up in disgust. He, not so kindly, recommended we not go. I didn't get his drift, so I leaned down to talk with him and work it out. It was so fucking loud near this thing, we couldn't hear, so he wrote me a note. It said in his scribble, "We are 7000 pounds over max load capacity!" Hell, I didn't know about things like that, so I walked up and looked at the pilot. I motioned could we get on? He nodded yes. So what the fuck, we ignored the crew chief and got on. Pearl wasn't sure about me at that point. And neither was the crew chief.

On board with doors up, pissed off crew chief in tow, two snipers and a shitload of supplies, we start taxiing to the end of the steel-matt runway at Dong Ha. I thought it was strange he was goin' down there, but what the hell, I didn't fly those things. We spun around at the end of the runway. He started revving the engines the way a fixed-wing pilot would. The two monster engines were spitting, spewing, and roaring their awesome noise all over us. Then the flying coffin started to shake and rattle like a washing machine with its spin cycle out of control. Then I realized we were moving down the runway. It dawned on me that the pilot was trying to generate extra lift by building up his takeoff speed—the way a fixed-wing would! Next to me, Pearl was wearing one of those worried-as-all-hell looks born of second-guessing the decision you'd just made. I looked up at the crew chief. He shrugged. We were gaining speed as we rushed down the runway. Then, with a major shake, rattle, and roll, we were airborne, bobbing and weaving, just above the treetops.

The door gunners were worried as hell as we buzzed along, shaving the countryside and maintaining a slim lead over gravity. They were standing straight up with their guns waving all over like they were drawing down on flies. We didn't do any circling on the way in, just a simple, straight-in approach. I got the idea that the pilots had to get all that gear to Con Thien before nightfall. I'm sure they weren't into multiple trips into the DMZ. It worked for me, but Pearl was white as Casper on a bad night. It was early September, and he was due to go home in February. He considered himself a short-timer. So crash-landing in the DMZ wasn't a fun thing for him to be doing about now.

On landing, we boomed in and bounced a couple of times. Pearl slid sideways with the ammo, but what the hell, we walked away from it!

Pearl hopped out the side door with me right behind. I ran off and over to one side while the chopper crew started tossing supplies off. The ARVN were trying to get on to help, but they were having to jump out of the way or risk getting hit by flying ammo boxes.

The crew sure as hell didn't want to be on the ground long. And they weren't. I couldn't believe it. In minutes, they were gone, and we were alone. I looked around and damned if they hadn't dropped me in a foreign country.

I went in search of someone who spoke something other than Vietnamese. I decided I'd best find the adviser. I mean, where the hell's the adviser? They told me one was there . . . so much for faith in the system. Pearl was really pissed at me about then. My searching finally turned up a little lieutenant. At least he looked like he had a clue. He couldn't speak English very well, and we understood him even less, but it looked like it'd work.

It seems our recon buddies, who'd been working out there, had put in a good word for us. So their little buddies, these ARVN, had put in a request for a couple of snipers to come out. The little lieutenant showed us to our new home, a bunker on the corner of the perimeter guarding the compound. I found it odd that they'd give a tactically important position up to us Americans. We'd have thought they'd want it anchored by a crew-served weapon or something else heavy. As Pearl pointed out, we were just a few miles from the North, the bad part of Vietnam. I asked him if it was a good idea to have two bolt-action snipers anchoring the corner of his little base?

It was fascinating that the ARVN lieutenant could understand me for some questions but not others. I wasn't the smartest bear in the den, but I could see he was trying to screw us over.

The way it seemed to work was, if the conversation was about something he wanted, he understood us, otherwise not. Well, we'd just signed on for a couple of weeks out here, so what the hell. We're here!

Once the little guy was gone, we checked out our new digs. Our bunker had four concrete walls with a small doorway. The floors were dirt, and the top was grass, slanted, I assumed, to let rain run off. Of course, I hadn't seen any rain since my first recon patrol. I was out there in Hooterville with a pissed-off partner, a smiling ARVN lieutenant who spoke English like a preschooler, and about fifty natives dressed in U.S. uniforms, who were looking at us like we just came in from another world. Well, hell—we did! I went down into the bunker and dropped my gear. It was an oven inside. We'd intended to stay inside to get away from the gawking ARVN, who were standing around, giggling like schoolkids. Well, screw it, I thought. I lay down, my body on the dirt, blocking the doorway. I didn't know how long I could stay in there without having a heat stroke, but the rest felt good. When Pearl started to walk down the ramp, a big rat jumped out in front of him, then ran down into our bunker and across my chest. It circled, then went right back out across my chest, headed straight for Pearl, who was standing motionless, startled. Pearl spun backward as the rat raced by him into the compound with me on his ass. We decided right then and there that we'd sleep outside. I wasn't sleeping with rats!

Our first night at Con Thien was a weird one. We had to contend with all the critters and the ARVN, who for some strange reason found us amusing. It might have been the rat chase earlier, who knows? We tried sleeping out in the dirt a few feet from our bunker, but the mosquitos were king of that hill. Pearl went over to his pack and whipped out two mosquito hats that made us look like beekeepers. They looked weird as hell. But we had to get some sleep. I hadn't been down long when I sensed somebody was nearby. I opened my eyes and saw six or seven ARVN staring at us. They were bunched up in a half circle, laughing and covering their mouths, like a bunch of little girls. Pearl angrily got up and got the lieutenant. He wanted to know what was going on. The lieutenant explained that the men just found our hats funny.

The real question was not why were they laughing but why they weren't watching the perimeter. Out there, next door to all the bad guys, they didn't seem to have a care in the world. That didn't make any sense at all. Con Thien, a few miles from no-man's-land, and our hosts were just kicking back?

We decided to move inside the bunker and take our chances. It was lots better than being in the fish tank with fifty ARVN soldiers giggling at you. We survived the first night. Then we moved our sleeping arrangements to the top of the bunker. There was rarely a breeze in Nam, but if there was one, we'd catch it up there. And it was cleaner and softer up on the grass. We slept there during the night and scoped out the DMZ during the day. We spent day after day up on top of our bunker, 7×50s in hand. We rarely saw any activity during the day. Life at Con Thien started out boring and lonesome.

To break the monotony, we ran a couple of two-man daytime patrols. We came up dry, but it was scary country. The terrain was dense and rough with small rolling hills obstructing the view in all directions. Except for the hill the ARVN were on, the entire area was frightening. It rolled with deep underbrush, broken briefly by small open spaces. We had a spooky feeling about Con Thien.

We began to adjust to life with the little people, but the nights became even weirder than we first thought. Pearl and I would sit on the roof of the bunker and watch out across the perimeter with our 7×50s. We didn't have any infrared night scopes yet, but the 7×50s worked to a degree. Especially in moonlight. One night, Pearl picked up lights that seemed to sway, back and forth, in unison, like people walking along. I jumped off the bunker and ran down to the center of the compound looking for our South Vietnamese lieutenant. He laughed and blamed it on our equipment. "You no have night vision. You no see well," he said. When I pushed him to come and see for himself, he began the "I no understand you" routine. Dejectedly, I walked back to our bunker and the lights we didn't see.

The next night was more of the same, and so was the next. On the fourth night of lights, I went to the lieutenant and asked permission to call in artillery. Pearl and I wanted to put out some lights in the night. The little shit gave me a resounding no. He wasn't being quite as nice to me as when I got there either. There was something seriously wrong here.

We noticed that the good guys, the ARVN, at Con Thien didn't run perimeter patrols day or night. And they didn't run ambushes. They didn't run *anything*. They acted oblivious to the fact that there was a war going on all around. And though the NVA might be marching by them all night long, they remained very calm. How the hell could that be? Pearl said, "Kug, what if they know what's going on and just have some deal?" I couldn't imagine that, but then again I couldn't have imagined half the things I'd seen in Vietnam. Maybe he was on to something.

By then, I'd half seriously begun to think my trigger finger was going to atrophy; I needed some work. We had our own radio contact with the snipers at Dong Ha. I called back and asked permission for Pearl and me to return for a new assignment. It didn't take long to be denied. Con Thien was getting to be a drag.

We sucked it up and decided to make the most of a seriously bad situation. About the two-week mark, we got a break. I was scanning the horizon from the top of our bunker, looking east toward the South China Sea. It was just blazing out, about 1400, and Pearl was sleeping, hat over his face, next to me. I spotted movement out to the east-northeast. It was in a clearing, near a row of three grass huts. It was one helluva ways out there. I looked on the map, and the hootches were just over a grid square away. Shit, that's over a thousand meters! It looked on the map to be about thirteen hundred meters. What a shot that would be!

I shook Pearl awake and told him to watch while I got the lieutenant. He came over and Pearl handed him the 7×50s. He looked and looked, then turned laughing. He was smiling. Clearly he thought it was funny that we were interested in a shot that far out. He'd made it clear that artillery wasn't happening around Con Thien. I said, "Look, that's clearly out in no-man's-land, and you requested snipers; I want a shot at this guy." By the look on his face, I could tell he thought I was a regular comedian. But I followed after him until he told me to go ahead and "try," then walked away with a big grin.

Pearl thought I'd lost my mind when I told him we were gonna take the bad guy out. I said, "Look . . . just get the 7×50s and spot for me. There's no wind today, it's hot, this fucking bullet oughta just fly right out there. With this Model 70, we got the range." He agreed it was worth a try and took his post. I lay on the back side of the grass roof of our bunker. For support, I placed my pack just over the gable of the roof. I pushed it down, making a place for the stock of my rifle to rest. I fidgeted with it until I got it just right. Hell, that guy didn't have a care in the world the way he was acting. He was working on something, occasionally walking inside one of the huts then coming back out. Hang in there little guy, I've got one here with your name on it. We'll show the lieutenant how this shit is done.

With things looking just right, I lay down to get him sighted in. That was a major project in itself. Pearl kept pointing out landmarks he could see in the 7×50s until I picked my target up in the scope. I dialed my scope to the max of nine power. Shit, this is a long damn way. The guy was so far out that he looked like one of those little plastic soldiers I used to play with as a kid. He was damned tiny at thirteen hundred yards.

I lay down and pulled the Winchester into my shoulder . . . tight. I'm ready! I have the full five rounds loaded in my rifle. I hold tight, do my breathing, and am gentle on the trigger . . . *boom!* I'm waitin' on the dude to drop, or at least the spot from Pearl. Pearl nonchalantly says, "Nothing." Shit, he didn't pick up a sight. Okay, I've gotta hold up more. There's no wind, so I'll hold everything the same, except the up and down adjustment. I place the crosshairs about the top of his head. Okay, it's routine, hold, breathe, and squeeze . . . *boom!* In an even slower and lower tone, Pearl turns, as if bored with it all, and says, "Nothing." By now, the firing of the Winchester is starting to draw some ARVN onlookers. Pearl leans down and tells me I should pack it in and not make a fool out of both of us.

I said, "Look, I'm takin' this fuckin' guy out! Now spot!" He takes up his binoculars, and I put the 06 back in my shoulder. It takes a minute, but I pick the guy up again. He's walking back out into the open. Both of us settle in, and I'm ready. I sight in again, and the wind's still cooperating. I place my vertical crosshair right up the middle of his body, with the horizontal line just over his head. Okay, man, deep breath, no jerking, let it out, that's it, not all the way . . . now squeeze the tit gently. *Boom!* I can see the guy looking around. Pearl sits up with more excitement than I've seen for a while. I didn't hit the little mother, but I'll bet the familiar *crack* of a bullet going by got his attention. He's wondering what's up. He's eyeballing the whole area. He'll never dream it's comin' from up here.

Energized, I settle into position for round four. Damn, I'm going to nail his ass. I'm sure he's looking back at Con Thien thinking, Can't be them, they're too damn far . . . must be my imagination. Hang tough, guy, got another one for ya! I do the routine and crank off round number four. *Boom!* There's a crowd around now, and they're trying to figure out what the hell I'm shootin' at. . . . Round four missed, but it made him duck and run for cover. He didn't run aside and hide, but he ducked down on one knee and looked around some more. Pearl was becoming a believer, and sat up straight. He wanted to know what was taking me so long to get ready for number five. He didn't want the guy to get away.

I hurried as best I could and set in for round five. Each time I kept the vertical crosshair dead center of his body, and the horizontal went a little higher each time. This would work as long as the wind stayed with me. So far, so good. I continued to check the treetops for signs of wind, but we were doing okay at that point. Pearl couldn't see any signs of wind in the tall grass near the dude either, so luck was with me. It didn't hurt, either, that the guy was dumber than a truckload of garbage.

I settle in one more time. I fire off number five from Con Thien. *Boom!* The guy hits the dirt face down, and for the first time, Pearl picks up a puff, just behind him. That's it, we're on to something. He says it looks like it may have struck around knee high. Holy shit man, I'm holdin' damn near the top of the scope now. I'm wondering how much farther I can hold when the guy gets up in a crouch and runs to the hootch. Fuck! I'm screwed unless he comes back out.

Well, you gotta have faith in that business. I know I'll get his ass; it's his arrogance that tells me. I sit up to reload and turn to get some ammo. There's a crowd around me, like it's club call at the base. One grenade'll get the whole fucking ARVN company. I could see the headlines in the *Sea Tiger* already, ARVN COMPANY AND TWO MARINE SNIPERS WIPED OUT WITH ONE GRENADE.

I was ready for another round of shooting, but the bad guy wasn't. He was still in his grass hut. I turned and lay back down for just one more shot. One more, asshole, give me one more. I'll get it this time, or I'll be out of vertical height in my scope. Shiiit, this is something. I didn't know I could reach out that far. Several minutes went by and no sight of the dumb one. Pearl was afraid he'd left for good. We waited and we waited and waited. One hour, then two ... and just after two hours from shot number five, Dumber than Garbage came peeping out of his hut. The hut was at the edge of some bush, so it was hard to know if he'd stayed in there or gone back through the woods to grandmother's house.

I was back down in position and must have been living right, because the Wind God was still with me. It was nearing 1700 hours, and I knew the game would end soon. I aimed so high, his head was in the bottom half of the vertical crosshair. My rifle had to be sticking up in the air like a mortar! I relaxed, held back on that stock, breathed as right as I ever had, and *boom!* Round number six dropped the dude, in place. He fell like a rock! He didn't even squirm. Pearl was as shocked as I that I'd done it. It had taken me six shots, but hell, if he was stupid enough to stay in sight, that was his problem.

The ARVN lieutenant, Ole Smiley himself, came running. He wanted to see for himself. Pearl gave him the 7×50s and, leaning over his shoulder, guided him to the body. I said, "Lieutenant, this is a number one, right?"

"No number one, you number ten, no fucky good."

"No fucky good? My ass! That's a thirteen-hundred-meter shot, man." But the LT was not a happy camper.

Pearl and I stayed at Con Thien three weeks and a day. No one from our outfit replaced us. I think the ARVN were afraid we might actually do something warlike. We never did figure out the whole story, but we did talk to the lieutenant enough to know there was something strange going on between the good guys and the bad. Con Thien was never attacked or mortared once with the ARVN sitting on it. The flashlights continued every night and were always heading south. Pretty strange stuff if you ask me. I left there wondering which of those ARVN "paid" for letting me shoot one of their own? I hope it was Smiley.

Pearl and I were a regular pair by then. He was getting used to me, and Con Thien actually helped us work together better. Back at Dong Ha, where we now bunked with half our snipers, we went on to life supporting the grunts. There were lots of new guys in from the States who didn't know what to make of us. They were going through the stage of trying to figure out what they'd gotten themselves into. The new guys weren't into the C rats like our original bunch, so the mess hall was the thing to do. Besides, C rats were getting hard to come by. I noticed each time I came back, how much the bases were starting to look like the Stateside Marine Corps. They were starting to take all the fun out of the war.

Today was the new routine, sans C rations. Mess hall food in Vietnam had sucked serious wind since I got there. I walked over with Pearl, Zulu, and one of his friends and got in the mess line. It was going to take a damned hour. It was hot and dry as we wormed our way along until we finally reached the food. A filthy looking private was standing front and center as the first server. I knew he was a shitbird from the grunts who was sent there so he wouldn't get anybody killed. It was written all over him. I stood in front of him and held the bottom half of my mess kit. It's old, silver, and oval, with dents all over it. And it wasn't big enough for the appetite I had. I hold it out, and the dirty dude pours in some green, slimy looking liquid. He'd just scooped it from a pot full of green liquid sitting between us. I said, "What the fuck is this?" He looks at me like he's answered that question a few times and doesn't care to again. But he says, snidely, "It's pea soup!" I look at mine, and it's free of all solids except for two or three flies. I'm pissed and say so. "Man, there ain't no fuckin' peas in here. Where the hell are they?" I hit a nerve, and he stood straighter, not caring at all that I was a corporal, two heads taller than the private he was, and defiantly proclaimed, "We ran outta fuckin' peas! And we don't have any crackers either, you got a problem with that?"

Well fuck that . . . I took my "pea soup" down to the end of the line and tossed it in with the other garbage. Zulu was laughing hysterically, as usual, and drank his down. Vowing to eat C rats forever, even if I had to steal them, I took off for my hootch. I know the private was a grunt just by his attitude. You've got to love those guys; they're the real people of life. And they're hit on, shit on, tramped on, and fucked with forever.

I walked back into our hootch just as Wiener was going crazy, throwing things around and cursing. "Wiener, what's eatin' your ass?" I asked, wondering if he'd changed his mind about re-upping or if he'd also been affected by the pea soup. He'd just signed up to stay with us for six more months. He was going home for Christmas to see his honey, then come back for six more months. She was a cheerleader at one of the big Pac 10 schools. He'd been sending her all his money so they could get married when he got out of the Corps. Maybe she dumped his crazy ass and spent his money? He ignored my question, so that wasn't it. Then Zulu walked in, and it was obvious to me that *he* was the problem.

I couldn't figure it for a while; they were the best of buds. But Wiener was hot about something. He tore into Zulu with a vengeance.

"You fucking lowlife, you, Zulu!" Wiener screamed into his face, as Zulu walked into our hootch. "You fucking piece of dog shit! The fucking balls of you to bring that fucking nigger into my hootch! I told you. I warned you, Zulu. And you showed me no fucking respect!" I didn't want in the middle of what the "discussion" might become, so I went over and sat down to try and write some letters.

But the "nigger" comment was all Zulu could handle. He got in Wiener's face; they were eyeball-to-eyeball and chest to chest. They started snarling at each other, and I knew we were in trouble.

"You've always been an asshole, Wiener," Zulu said. "But now, you've gone too far! Either take that back about the nigger or I'm going to make you take it back!"

Wiener screamed, *"Nigger! Nigger!"* right into Zulu's face at a distance of zero tolerance. In about the time it took the maggots to appear in the drums of shit over at the shitter, Zulu was on top of Wiener like a junkyard dog. It was better than big-time wrestling. They were rolling all over, punching each other in the face, slobbering like a couple of pigs. It was lots better action than I remember in other fights. Those two were genuinely trying to hurt each other.

Then Det Cord sneaked in and asked if I was going to break it up! I said, "Are you fucking crazy? They'll both jump on me for bothering 'em." I knew them both, but I knew Zulu best. And when he was out there growling as they rolled by me, I knew not to play peacemaker. By then they were throwing things at each other and just generally destroying our hootch.

About that time, Corporal Tex came running in. He actually took his rank seriously, and he asked me why I hadn't stopped the battle. After all, "You are now a corporal like me," he said with all the authority of a *serious* Marine corporal.

I said, "Tex, they're both corporals like us. If you wanna stop 'em, be my guest, sucker. But they'll both jump on you like stink on shit. Besides, they're pretty damned good at this shit, and it's fun to watch." A good-size crowd had started to gather, and that didn't help Tex's attitude; he was irritated with me and left to find somebody who gave a shit. About that time, Zulu and

Wiener, clinging to each other like lovers on their honeymoon, crashed through the screened side of our tent.

Even I was getting concerned that they might end up hurting each other, so I got up to walk outside just as Zulu, both hands holding the side of Wiener's head, screams, "Wiener, my man, I love ya! What the fuck are we doing? You're a first-class asshole, but we've been through too much together. Let's get the fuck up and go have a beer!" They stood up, wrapped their arms around each other, and offered profuse apologies. I was there and it's still pretty hard to believe: they were covered with dirt from head to toe, they had cuts and bruises, and they had mucus running out of their noses. Almost made me forget that pea soup lunch.

The fight of the century behind us, we were bound for more time in the bush. Somebody besides Pearl and me must have figured out the ARVNs' deal on Con Thien. They sent in Marines to replace them, and Pearl and I were two of the six snipers who went along on the operation. We were scouring the area surrounding Con Thien for several days. There were a few firefights, nothing big, but the whole area gave us the willies. I mean, it just had the feeling of bad shit about to happen. Somebody, someday, was going to get waxed up there, and I hoped it wasn't going to be us. The gooks were all around us; it was in the air. Pearl and I came back with a kill each. We'd worked our way with the grunt company into Cam Lo, spent some time there, before catching a convoy back east to Dong Ha.

We got back to more change in snipers. Zulu and a couple of other originals had rotated home. He promised to keep in touch, and I hoped he would. There were lots of new guys coming in, and they were training at a sniper school in the States before they left. But the longer I was there, the lower the quality of the incoming recruits got, the acceptance rate being about fifty-fifty. That's not so good in the land of the bad guys. They told us the snipers in Dong Ha would soon be moving south again to rejoin the rest of the 4th Marine snipers at Phu Bai. There was an operation coming up, to the south near Quang Tri. We'd move down when that was over.

The Quang Tri show was still a couple weeks away, so I jumped at the chance for my first R & R. I chose Hong Kong and couldn't wait. I caught a C-130 to Da Nang and the Continental charter on over to Hong Kong. It felt strange to be in civilian clothes again. It felt like a world I once knew, but one far removed from life. Hong Kong was everything I thought it'd be. I can't say I remember much though; I was drunk for five days. I was like a kid in a candy store. I wanted one of everything. Zulu's famous words always echoed deep in my soul. I really didn't know how long I'd be around or if the next patrol was my last. So go for what you know now, you don't know what tomorrow will bring. I went in a restaurant my first morning there. I ordered a pizza. What to drink? Uh, a beer of course, well, oh, you have milk shakes . . . uh, give me a milk shake. Hell, give me both. And I ate the pizza and drank two beers and a chocolate shake. Hong Kong was exciting, but I found I missed my snipers back in Nam. I was surprised by my feelings. I enjoyed the partying, but five days was enough. I wondered all the while, flying back, what Pearl was doing, or if he'd figured out how best we could work as snipers.

Nam was still there when I got back. It still had all the filth, the bullshit, the heat, and the war. Pearl had run one grunt deal with no action. Soon we were heading out to be with the grunts on their op near Quang Tri. Pearl hadn't come up with a plan, but we both knew that walking along with the grunts wasn't the best use of snipers. The grunts moved around and were too big and too noisy to do much more than shoot it out when the shit hit the fan.

We convoyed down and set up along Highway 1. I'd just finished reading Bernard Fall's book, *Street Without Joy,* which covers some tragic French history along the same strip of highway, an ugly story and one you probably don't want to read just before you go there. I'd asked Mom to send me some books about the war; I wanted to learn from the French and their experiences in Vietnam. She sent me a bunch, and I kept them at the rear, and read one when I could. From Fall's *Hell in a Very Small Place* and *The Battle of Dien Bien Phu* I began to understand who I was fighting and how they thought. And the one thing I knew was, the NVA were more committed than I was: the little bastards walked down four hundred miles of ball-busting trails to fight my young ass. That was more than I could say most of us would be willing to do to fight them.

And she sent me Fall's *Last Reflections on a War* and *Mao Tse Tung on Guerrilla Warfare.* I started to recognize people, places, and things. And I started to wonder about some of the decisions I saw being implemented. I didn't understand some of the rules that were creeping in. Our "rules of engagement" for one. Nor did I get why we fought for the same hill more than once and never held the ground. Something was escaping me in that war called Vietnam.

Our trip to Quang Tri produced three kills, one for Pearl, and two for me. Pearl had gotten the 300-plus-yard shot early on the op. I knocked one dick stiff at 250 yards and the other at 400 yards. None of it came close to my record setter at Con Thien though, that was a beauty. We'd convinced the grunt lieutenant to let us go out during the day. We'd leave from their perimeter on two-man patrols. One of our biggest challenges was educating the grunt officers on how best to use snipers. They rarely wanted to use us as scouts, preferring their own point men to the unknown of an attachment; even I understood that one. There had to be a bond of trust with the people walking out front, having everyone's ass square atop your shoulders.

It was mid-November, and the rains they'd often talked about were starting to come. It was nothing real heavy or even steady yet, but enough to get you real wet. The games of Quang Tri ended, and we headed south to link up with our platoon of snipers. We'd heard there was a new base down that way, and that's where we'd now find the 4th Marines headquarters. A little north of Hue, it was called Camp Evans. I guess it was named after someone by the same name who'd bought the big one. We'd been lucky so far in snipers, only a couple of us had been wounded and sent home; to date no KIAs. I'd seen some shit up to that point, but the only casualty I'd taken was the can of C rats in my pack on my first patrol with recon. And, well, I can't forget the leech bites all over my ankles that still hadn't healed after three months.

CHAPTER FIVE

Good Fortune, Grunts, and Twenty-seven Days and Nights of Rain . . . This Is Living?

It was the Marine Corps's birthday, and I had to go out with some no-good ARVNs. Son of a bitch! Pearl wasn't any happier than I was. Even the lieutenant was apologizing about it. The one day all year you can count on the mess hall going all out, and they pull this shit. No birthday cake; worst of all, no fucking booze! We'd been going out with the grunts or on our own gigs for three weeks solid. First Quang Tri, then leading grunts all the way to the river south of Camp Evans.

The new lieutenant seemed like a decent guy. He said it was only for the day and that the ARVNs would have an American adviser with them. Now I'd heard *that* shit before, and so had Pearl. This time we were to act as scouts for an ARVN company. Lead them to an ambush site about seven clicks south of Camp Evans. Just what I wanted to do, lead the Smile Fuck Brigade on a night walk in the park.

As the story goes, after we get the ARVNs in place, in the A.M., then we go off to find an LZ. As the fairy tale continues, a chopper will then pick us up, and we'll live happily ever after. Now that's a line like Hoffa sold all

169

those Teamster retirees. The one about that beautiful land built on swamp down in Florida.

I grabbed Pearl and we headed over to meet our adviser. We had to get the details of the op so we could make our own plans. We knew the area from our two-man patrols, and knew it was booby-trapped for that Fourth of July effect. The only problem we ran into was the adviser wasn't there. They said we'd meet at the south gate of Camp Evans at midnight. The details? We'd get the details there.

Pearl and I went back and got our gear and headed over for the midnight rendezvous. But we were none too happy about it. We'd been patrolling for three straight weeks. Out snoopin' and poopin' around, day and night, the heat and the fear, well it'll just flat kick your ass, but good. And now we had to do it with those unprofessional little bastards.

We got to the perimeter gate, the one manned by the grunts, and they didn't know anything about our patrol. No one was there but the two of us and the grunts. I was supposed to lead a company of South Vietnamese infantry into position for an ambush; I hadn't yet met their fearless leader; they weren't there; it was their country; and I didn't speak their language. Something was wrong with that picture.

About 0100, a mob, and I do mean mob, approached. And the mob was led by a sharp looking young U.S. Army captain. I say "sharp looking" because the asshole was all dressed up! I mean it! Now it was dark and all, but he had gear on him that was shining in the night. Pearl was immediately on my ass over that one. While I'm not the sharpest knife in the drawer, I knew immediately that Captain Candyass wasn't going on our hike. I couldn't resist though. "Sir, I understand you'll be going along with us. Especially since we don't speak the language here." With great authority of the kind instilled only at West Point and the confidence borne of OCS survival, he said, "Why no, Corporal, I won't be going. We only go on company-size ops." Well talk about getting screwed! And we didn't even have to bend over.

The man with the shine on his uniform was gracious enough to explain that he was providing a team of three South Vietnamese soldiers. This, he said, was our personal security. They were to stay with us when we left the ambush and until the chopper picked us up. They spoke English, according to the distinguished scholar before me, and would handle any communication issues.

The good captain brought over the three dudes for an introduction. They were supposed to walk point and I could tell them where to go. The captain explained all this to them. Now walking point was a seriously big deal in Nam. Especially if you wanted to stay alive. I took one look at those ARVN, and I knew the Marx brothers would have looked better on point. And they spoke about as much English as I did gook, and that was zero.

We bid farewell to our new lieutenant, who showed up late and offered profuse and useless apologies. The cute army adviser left to go and do whatever the hell he did. Assuming these ARVNs had the same sweetheart deal their sisters at Con Thien had, I tried to place them on point. I figured Pearl and I could stay back a spell and let them do their thing. Funny thing was, their English got real bad when they heard that one word they understood, "point." I mean walking first wasn't on the ARVN agenda. They were suddenly a trio of deaf mutes, masquerading as soldiers.

Pearl and I talked it over and decided we'd wasted enough time tonight. He'd walk first; I'd take his radio and walk second. Then the three blind mice would follow us. Following the mice would come a whole gaggle of ARVNs, the ones we were leading in place for the sweep and ambush the next day. All I could say is that little patrol wasn't helping me in my quest to get Pearl to stay six more months. After that night, we both wondered what the hell we were doing over there.

Pearl took over and led the way just as it started pouring rain. As we marched, the three numb nuts behind me were asshole to belly button and right up my ass. Like how quick did they have to be to figure out that if one person hit a booby trap, they'd all get the prize? All sixty or so were following us and the formation looked like a giant wooly worm stretching down the small ravine. I stopped them for a little class on "stay off my ass!" I went back to whisper some instructions to the little folks. They were happy, smiling, looking around, just having a good old time. Not a care in the world. They might not get shot, but the NVA missed a damned good chance along the way. I explained to my three monkeys the importance of keeping distance and the basic hand and arm signals we used. That way, maybe, I could keep them off my ass and keep most of us alive for a beer and some cake when we got back. I went over all the horseshit of facing in opposite directions when you stop, of crouching down when you stop, and tough stuff like, "Shut the hell up and don't talk, assholes!" I walked back to Pearl, and the three amigos were to pass the word back to the wooly worm.

The drop-off site should have taken us three or four hours to reach, but with our mob, it'd take a bit longer. We moved again, and although noisier than I'd like, we were making a little better time, which was good since we had some obstacles along the way. We knew we had to skirt a little village to get to our ambush site. We'd done it more than once, just the two of us. We hadn't gone far when the party behind me started gaining volume once again. I stopped Pearl and turned around to reinforce the message I'd just sent. Things were deteriorating fast.

Suddenly we hear voices in the village below us. We're standing on a small knoll, maybe 150 feet from the edge of the first grass hut. It's been raining off and on, it's overcast, and things are getting pretty dark out. I decide to wait it out. Before long, quiet returns, and we move out to try and clear the village completely.

A few steps into our restart, Pearl's down on one knee, looking—his radar's picked up something serious. I crouched and motioned for Hear No Evil, the ARVN behind me, to do likewise. I make a downward motion with my free hand. Pearl and I are both carrying M-14s at the ready; our 06s are on our backs. Hear No Evil got the word and crouched down as I had done. Good job, he understood that much. But See No Evil, who was dead up Hear No Evil's ass, tripped head over heels, falling on top of his buddy. Un-fucking-believable! I stop the whole column for a good ass chewing, even if they can't understand a word I'm saying. About that time, the clouds break, and it gets brighter outside. It's almost like somebody turned on the stadium lights. I can't believe my eyes. Stretched behind me, one more fucking time, is a giant fucking wooly worm of a column. I mean asshole to belly button like they're hooked together at the navel. The little idiots either knew there was no one out there, or the NVA were about to rain-dance across my face. What assholes!

I tell Pearl to hat up. If I lose them, I lose them. We picked up the pace and hoped like hell they couldn't keep up. It was about 0400 when we reached the top of the hill where they'd break from us. They were going to

ambush anyone they saw in the morning? Yeah, right.
And Pearl and I were going to Hanoi on our next gig. And
if they set no ambush, they'd sweep the village in the A. M.
I got the ARVN lieutenant and explained to him, by
hand motions, to set his troops in a 360-degree perimeter.
I took him over and showed him the trail that led to the
village and told him what time to take off. He feigned
some English; I think he knew more. Pearl and I were
dead tired from no sleep and three weeks' running. We
just dropped in place, lay back on our packs, hats on our
faces, and just died to the world. I didn't even call COC
to tell them mission accomplished.

I don't know how long we lay there, but we were
rudely awakened by a hard driving rain. The monsoon
had to be coming, full speed. Bucketsful of rain. I was so
tired I didn't want to get up. I pushed my bush hat tighter
down over my face. Pearl kicked my leg and said, "Kug,
look, can you believe this shit?"

I pulled my bush hat from my face and put it on my
head. I was trying to get the cobwebs out of my drenched
head as I looked around. First light was trying to edge its
way into our waterlogged morning. Then I saw it!

Our distinguished allies had set up a perimeter all
right! They were one half, 180 degrees, and Pearl and I
the other half. Who the hell could do something so stupid?
I was incensed! Infuriated is more like it. They'd set up
on half of this little hilltop, and Pearl and I, out behind
the lieutenant, were literally the other half. We should
have just shot ourselves and saved the fucking battle.

I stood up, walked over, and lay into the gook lieutenant one more time. He gets deaf, dumb, and blind. I
turn to come back to Pearl, and the other ARVNs are
coming to life around "their" perimeter. These little dudes

stand up, and it's like a damned circus. They'd broken out raincoats every color of the damned rainbow. It was just unbelievable!

I needed the hell out of there. I'd had enough. I went to the gook lieutenant and told him to get his mob on the road. I got Pearl and told the three monkeys they could stay behind. The lieutenant had a fit, so Pearl and I saddled up, with Hear No Evil and his brothers in tow. It started raining like I'd never seen it rain in my life.

We took off, sloshing through the rain, making believe our chopper was coming. One look up at the sky, and we knew we were bullshitting ourselves. We called COC at Dong Ha and they confirmed our fears. They told us to "walk on in." Now who woulda thunk it?

We ditched the Hear No Evil boys by trying to make them walk point. We knew one hill was booby-trapped, so making them go first was a reasonable use of ARVNs. But they weren't buying; they knew it was booby-trapped, too. The three monkeys hatted up when it looked like real war work was coming. Pearl took point up, but after a short while, we switched, just to spread the tension around. We'd have blown it off, but after our fun night, we wanted to watch the ARVN sweep. It was 0800 when we reached the top. The hill was scrub bush and grass and nothing taller than maybe four feet. It was bare in a lot of places and was a dangerous place; we'd found booby traps there before. It was usually worth the trip; we'd get some dinks there, but only if we got in real early.

We set in on the village side of the hill. Behind the village lay another hill about the same height as ours. The village between us looked deserted. It was overgrown with huge, green vegetation. Tall palms shadowed the whole area. We couldn't see our ARVN mob anywhere so Pearl got on the 7×50s as I sat back to relax. The rain was coming down in sheets. Pearl says, "I can barely see the ARVNs on line. They're at the far right end of the village." He watched them for a while, then turned his attention to the village and hillside in front of us. I was about to doze off when Pearl suddenly whispered, "Kug, get a load of this shit." I sat up and he'd picked up first five, then six, then seven gooks moving slowly up the hillside across from us. I grab the 7×50s for a look myself. We have to be sure they aren't ARVNs headed home for the day.

These are the real bad guys, apparently headed out in front of the sweep coming in from the west. I tried to raise the ARVNs on my PRC-25. It was not happening. I called back to COC, and they told me to work with the ARVNs. No shit. I would but they're assholes. The bad guys are moving. Fuck it, it's decision time for Kug and Pearl. They're maybe three hundred yards, straight across. There are seven bad men, all in a row. I lay it out, "Pearl you take the point, I got tail-end Charlie. We'll work in from there." Pearl nods agreement, and I said, "We'll fire on three. One, two, three"—B'bang! We fired in unison. Our targets dropped dead in their tracks! Textbook shit here, man. Those guys had packs, weapons, the whole enchilada. I couldn't believe they were still up and about; it was after 0800 daylight, and our ARVN were like a marching band coming in. We were ejecting, chambering our second rounds, when they turned and filled the air with AK-47 lead. The morning began to sound like a shooting gallery full to the max. Shit was cracking and singing by our asses. Bullets were flying everywhere. It was a long-distance firefight, raging right across the village the ARVN were sweeping. I glanced down, and the ARVN were laying lower than the fucking snakes they were. The shit was getting very close. Pearl jumped up and ran down the trail and slid in. The rain was still pouring down, and the dirt had become slick, thick mud, everywhere. I rolled to the other side of the trail for a better aim and nearly got my ass shot off. A bullet or two thudded into the soaked ground right next to me. My asshole froze, then jumped right up my throat as another round broke a branch by my left foot. We had no help from the little bastards down below, and we needed to return more fire. And fast!

Now, I was a *D* student back in school, but damned if I didn't know these odds were sucking some serious wind. I saw Pearl drop his Winchester and switch to his M-14. Helluva'n idea, this bang-bang ain't gonna get us out of this one. I needed to get to my 14, and fast. But it was back on the other side of the trail. When Pearl let loose with a good blast from his 14, I jumped back across the trail. I grabbed my 14 and, crouching down, tried to turn and shoot. I couldn't spin around. My foot was caught in a bush about two feet high. What the fuck? In war timing is everything, and this sucked. Bullets were still zinging all around. I couldn't get my foot loose, so I turned and kicked hard. *Pop!* It was a heart-stopping pop, right between my fucking legs! Oh holy dogshit! Bluish white smoke was slowly rising between my legs. My life shifted into slow motion. Grenade! I dove to the right, crashing between two more bushes alongside the trail. I landed, splashing in the mud, instinctively covering my ears with my hands. Time stood still, right alongside my heart. I lay there in the muck, oblivious to the reality of the war going on all around me. I was about to be a loser in the Nam Games. Fuck!

Then there was silence. Nothing but stone cold silence, interrupted by the sound of the pouring rain. Pearl is yelling! What the hell's going on? There's no more bangs? No more shooting? Oh hell, I'm alive! The fucking thing didn't go off! I raise myself up just as he yells, "Get with it, Kug, they're getting away." The four gooks were running up the hill toward the crest. Pearl nailed another before he reached the top of the hill and lived to fuck with us another day. Shazaam! Three KIA! Not a bad day. And a faulty fucking booby trap! How lucky can you get?

I got up, gathered my senses, and checked my pants. I'm sure I shit myself on this one. Time began to move again, and I recognized I was still breathing. Pearl quit bitching at me when he realized what had happened. I walked over to where the pop and the smoke had been. It was a Chicom grenade. I'd hit the trip wire, it had pulled but been a dud. In-fucking-credible! The blasting cap had gone off but the black powder charge inside was wet. I knew where I'd been when President Kennedy got his dick knocked stiff in Dallas, and now, I'd forever remember that day as well. After carefully checking it for other wires, I took the Chicom from the bush. I wanted that one for a souvenir.

Pearl and I packed up and headed in. We'd got some more action and some more kills, even if it was a surprise from twenty-four hours ago. Lady luck had let me make it back for the beer blast. We radioed COC that we were headed for home plate. We made it about a half a mile, when they called back and said they wanted us to link back up with the ARVNs, and come in with them. That's about the last thing we wanted to hear. But you go and do what you have to go and do . . .

The ARVNs were clueless as to what had gone on. Well, at least they pretended to be. And it was some Academy Award performance on their part. I was walking along, thinking, and realized there was something seriously wrong with this picture. I certainly didn't believe in communism, but our little weasels certainly couldn't go it alone. I really wondered what we were doing here. I'd been here doin' Marine stuff for about nine months. I was getting to like what I was doing. I hadn't been wounded, or screwed up, or killed the way many people already had. They probably didn't see this as the adventure I did. I was to the point that I didn't mind being in Vietnam. But what about the others, those who did? I walked along, thinking about all the craziness and the maiming and killing. Suddenly, anger was pouring out my asshole and every orifice in my body. Who the hell was I helping? If it was the bozos around me right then, then I didn't get it. We walked in, and I left that anger outside, outside the base with the gooks, and outside of me, too.

Pearl and I came back, and things were changing everywhere. I guessed we had better get used to that; it was always changing over there. The military machine was growing and, with it, the Stateside bullshit. Wiener had come back from his re-up leave and was more screwed up than when he'd left for home. His fiancée, the looker who was his college cheerleader girlfriend, screwed him big time. And not the screwing he'd hoped for after a year in the Nam. She'd taken all the money he'd sent home for their wedding, a whole year's worth, and bought a car! The dickhead still stood by her so she slept with him. And gave him the clap! Then she drove a stake right through his heart when she told him, as he was leaving, that she was marrying somebody else! What a bitch. I said she deserved a third eye. What was happening to people? I mean that's about the cruelest thing I'd ever heard of. The guy was over here, risking his ass for his country, and the bitch couldn't be loyal for a year?

Wiener was not the same after that. And when we met

up, he was glad to be back with his snipers. I'd have just stayed there in Vietnam where life was simple for a long time. It was all straightforward there. You lived or you died. You liked someone or you didn't. You did it or you didn't do it. Simple shit.

I woke up, and it was the end of the year; 1966 was gone! I'd spent most of it in Nam. I realized I'd turned twenty that year, and I faintly remembered the occasion. August 2; seemed like a long time ago. I remembered the family sent me a card, but I didn't remember about anyone else. Who cared? For Christmas, the monsoon was in full swing, there was a truce, and it was actually kind of cold. I got sent on security detail with an adviser, a U.S. Army major, who was going to Hue. We rode down in a jeep, him, the driver, and me. He was a nice enough guy but he stayed too long, and we had to spend Christmas Eve at the army's old French headquarters, somewhere in Hue City. Even in the rain and fog, Hue was a pretty place. We passed a seriously old, but in great shape, Catholic church. I wasn't religious at all, but the building was gorgeous. I spent Christmas Eve pretty much by myself. I don't know where my major was, but the captain in my room cried as he read letters from home. I didn't understand what he was feeling or what the big deal was. I just wanted to get back up to Evans and get drunk with my guys.

Pearl went home for Christmas leave. We'd all shamed him into re-upping for six more months so we could stay together and kick some more ass. January brought in the serious weather. It just rained and rained and rained. The weather got to people, and one was Ya Ya. He'd re-upped for six more but would be going home shortly, and none too soon. He was one of only two married snipers and he was having some home problems from the decision he'd made. Fuck her if she couldn't take a joke. We had a war to fight over there. Harley was the other married guy, but he'd taken care of that right before the holidays. Harley was a Hell's Angel who carried a picture of his bike with him, not his "old lady," as he called her. One day, we were sitting at mail call when Harley went berserk. "The dirty rotten bitch. The filthy fucking worm. The whore!" Seems she had let her brother paint Harley's bike and had sent him a picture, so he walked over to me and said, "Kug, I need to borrow a piece of paper. I need to take care of the bitch once and for all." With that, he took a sheet of my paper and a pen. He put it down in front of me, and placed his right hand, middle finger extended in the universal salute, on the paper. He traced his hand, and then under it wrote "Best Wishes, Bitch." I gave him an envelope, and he went off to mail it. He was through with her.

In spite of all the rain, the COC decided to send out a big sweep. We'd go to a valley that lay to the south, and a little west, of Camp Evans. It was called Co Bi Than Tan. It lay twenty or so miles north-northwest of Hue and was maybe five grid squares wide and ten or twelve long. A hill there, Hill 51, overlooked the valley, and the grunts always had a platoon or more up there. The monsoon was really bad that year, and the entire valley was flooded. In the dry season, despite rarely seeing the bad guys, the grunts took tons of casualties there. It was known for its booby traps, and when the grunts passed through, it was like the Fourth of July done ugly.

It'd be a battalion sweep, three Marine companies sloshing around. They'd asked for three teams of snipers. That meant six of us had to go wade around for days on end. They wanted to evacuate the valley and move all the people down toward the South China Sea. I heard they'd had the Seabees build them modern versions of the standard grass shack. And of course, after being moved against their will, I'm sure everyone would live happily ever after. At least that was our government's story. The plan was to relocate all the peasants and tell them not to come back because the area was going to be a "free-fire zone." That meant anyone found inside was considered to be "the enemy."

A battalion of Marines, six snipers, and a few other poor bastards went along for the walk on the wet side. Stu, the Midwestern farm kid; Crud, the Ohio kid who could be found in the dictionary under "weird"; Harley, our new single man; Greek, a tough Italian from Brooklyn; Ya Ya; and me, that was the contingent of snipers. It was a crazy use of snipers, but not any crazier than Nam itself. Visibility was about one hundred feet, our scopes were generally fogged tight, and we were about to shoot ourselves from the rain and mud. But somewhere up the chain of command, they must have been giving points for the officer who did his ops with the correct number of "attachments." Because they were adamant that they "needed" us. We knew going in it was a walk for some serious exercise and a chance to work on our senses of humor.

And we weren't disappointed. We were out for eighteen days, and it rained constantly, day and night. One of the more unstable grunts shot himself in the leg just to get out of the madness. We passed through a bamboo thicket, and wood leeches fell down, covering us. That was creative—I'd been trying to protect my legs, so they jumped down from above. I had twenty-one leech bites on my neck and chest after that walk in the woods. At least they weren't as big as the blood suckers on my legs.

The last day of the op, the weather turned from ugly to

Author's boot camp photo, Platoon 262, Parris Island, 1964.

Author at graduation from infantry training at Camp Geiger, fall 1964.

Author boarding ship for the cruise to Santo Domingo, 1965.

At the "pagoda" lookout while taking a break at Sniper School, March 1966.

The original 9th Marine Snipers outside "The Club," April 1966.

Author after taking part in his first patrol with 3d Force Recon. A sniper sixty days, and thirty pounds lighter. May 1966.

The author, bootless because of infected leech bites, after returning from Operation Prairie on Colonel Masterpool's "hike," September 1966.

4th Marine Snipers regrouping at Phu Bai, fall 1966.

Author at home at the French-built billets, Dong Ha, September 1966.

The Greek living life in the monsoon as we knew it at Camp Evans, February 1967.

Author with the original Rogues back from the first month's patrols, 1967.

Author (right) and two Rogues returning to Camp Evans for a break, August 1967.

Author cleaning up at Camp Evans, summer 1967.

Getting ready for a Rogues patrol into the Co Bi Than Tan, summer 1967.

Author (right) and a few buds between patrols, summer 1967.

Beards and all, a weary Big Three after six weeks in the Co Bi Than Tan, October 1967. (Photo courtesy of Dan Ireland)

Building a new home at Camp Carroll, December 1967.

The morning after 140mm rockets hit the sniper tent at Camp Carroll during Tet, January 1966.

The last Rogues at Camp Carroll, February 1966.

"oh fuck." We were at the end of the valley, the choppers couldn't get in, and it was all flooded. We had people we were relocating whom we couldn't get out. The company commander, a gung ho kind of guy, ordered us to walk them out. It was late afternoon when he had that brainstorm. Everything was flooded. The nights were darker than dark, and that walk would push us into nighttime, for sure. And if night was not bad enough, the incessant rain was a serious problem. It never stopped. We couldn't walk without holding on to each other's packs. We had to stay tied in a line, and our shoulder harnesses had to be loose at all times.

We tripped around, carrying out the good captain's plan. But I'd been out there. What the hell were we going to do when we got to where the river used to be? In the dry season, that sucker had twenty-foot-deep walls in some places. By then it was about 1800 hours, and we were slogging along in the dark. The river was just ahead, and it was going to be a bitch to cross. Man, it was dark. I knew where I was, and I knew there was only one bridge.

The column came to a stop. I knew they'd reached the bridge. I couldn't see it, but the trail on the map led right to it. It was a *single* railroad rail, the metal kind trains run on. A bamboo handrail, about three feet up, was lashed to short bamboo pieces every ten feet or so. But that little footbridge was under a foot or two of water.

We were all worn out, tired, and pissed off. They'd said we had a reinforced company of grunts. I didn't know what the hell it was reinforced with, besides six snipers. It had been pretty well depleted by casualties by that point. Still, there must have been 150 of us out dancing in the monsoon rains. The valley looked like a lake, at least it had the last time we saw it, just before the lights went out. The word passed back that we were going to cross, "So be careful."

Up ahead, I heard a grunt mutter, "These little dinks are ingenious to build a bridge like that." Ingenious my ass! How smart was it to build a thirty-foot-long bridge four inches wide with a completely unstable handle that would barely hold a bird? I have to admit that it baffled me how the Vietnamese had got the heavy rail across that thirty feet. Now that was fucking ingenious!

At that point, the captain made a good decision; he called for Hill 51 to fire some mortar illumination to light up the river crossing. It wouldn't burn long in the downpour, but it was a helluva'n idea. They started firing some daylight at us as the Wallenda training began. Harley, Greek, and I were together for some reason. The rest of the snipers were farther up the column. Wherever Stu was, I'd have paid to see his crossing; he and I weren't the nimble type.

The big dog added some arty flares from Evans, and the night was getting to look like things might work out okay if they had enough to keep it up. The flares turned an awful night into an eerie, ugly day. Our column was starting to move forward, and I could see someone coming back to the column, the wrong way. It was the gunny, and he was "in charge" the way most of them are. He was looking for snipers to "help out." One of the grunt flank patrols had picked up some stragglers a ways back. Now, they'd found some more. An old lady that needed a lift. Gunny was in search of a sniper to carry her. Carry her my ass! Build a float, and we'll tie her on beside us, but carry her? In this shit? Unbelievable! But this cat was as serious as another foot of water'd be about now.

The gunny came by, looked at Harley, and said, "Come with me." He was pissed big-time for damned sure.

Harley said, "Gunny, for what?"

The gunny wasn't amused and said with great articulation, "To carry one of the fucking indigenous personnel." Harley kicked at the water and mud, but dutifully followed the gunny into the night. We followed Harley up the column about twenty or thirty yards. Laid out on a little patch of high ground was an old, old woman, who looked deader than I felt.

Harley said, "You gotta be fuckin' kidding. She's dead, Gunny!"

With the look of a man who didn't want any more shit and with a voice to match, the gunny said, "I don't know that, and you don't know that. Now shut the fuck up and carry her!" It was clear the gunny was in no mood for sniper shit just then. Harley reached down and picked her up. Greek stepped up and took his pack, I took his rifle, and Harley took the old lady in a fireman's carry. We were off on our humanitarian mission, like it or not.

As we sloshed along in the long column, getting ever closer to the river, we heard a commotion up ahead. The word had it that someone had slipped off the bridge. I hoped it was that fucking liberal and his "ingenious bridge" that had slipped off.

The hurry up and wait continued, and we finally started moving again. We moved our way to the head of the class. At last we were at the edge of the river, praying, just keep the illumination coming, folks; it was dark out there. They did keep it coming, and we saw the water, racing over the top of the tiny rail. It looked like Niagara Falls. I looked around, and people were terrified. Hell, I was one of them. It was nuts.

As we approached the bridge, I was worried about me,

but more about Harley. I'd grown to love the guy. He was
unique, but he was great in Nam. He was walking along,
cussing, bitching, like any good Hell's Angel I guess. He
reached the bridge and looked out at the water, then
said, "Why the fuck do I have to risk my ass carrying this
dead bitch across the river?" Harley was having a tough
time with this assignment. I was just ahead of him and
started across the bridge behind a grunt who was none
too happy about the arrangements either. We were
about three or four feet apart, Harley behind me, Greek
behind him. If something happened, they'd get three
snipers for the price of one.

Out on the rail, it was pure adrenaline and stark fear
right square in the jibs. The water was raging across my
feet. I was holding onto the handrail, but it was shaking,
wildly, from people all along, who were waving it all
around. My asshole was puckered tight up in my throat.
Some people were slipping and some falling, and I was
about to break the bamboo rail from squeezing it so tight.
I never raised my foot from the rail: slide . . . forward . . .
shuffle . . . oh man, this sucks. *Splash!* The grunt right in
front of me took a nasty fall, straddling the rail. Water
rushed by him on all sides, creating another rapid right in
front of me. Oh shit! Poor bastard had one leg on either
side! When he landed he let out a loud moan. At least his
balls would be cold from all the water rushing by. He
didn't have time to half step. He was surrounded with
white water. The eerie lights hanging from the sky made
it all look like a bad dream.

My palms were sweating despite all the rain. I was
holding onto the rail and reaching down for the grunt,
when I heard something behind me. Oh shit! Harley was
swearing and bitching up quite a commotion. I knew
Greek was back there to help, too, but then I heard

splash! I knew he'd slipped, and I could barely see him as I half turned while working to steady the grunt. I said, "Harley, Harley, are you back there?"

There was a commotion, and then I heard . . . "Get the fuck going, now!" It was Harley, but I was betting he wasn't packing his dead cargo. The poor grunt in front of me had nearly castrated himself, but he got up and struggled across, with the three of us close behind. Slipping and sliding our way across, we made it, on a bitch of a night.

It was a night of miracles; *all* the "reinforced" company made the crossing. Some were walking funny, from their meeting with the rail, but all were walking on land. Once on safe ground, I turned to Harley and saw he was one old lady lighter. In the light of the flares, I could also see the look on his face, and I knew not to ask any questions. We all slipped and slid along the trail heading back out of the valley for Evans. We were going in that night, and still had a few miles to go. As we walked, the rain still walked with us.

About halfway in, we finally stopped for a break. The gunny was making his rounds. Up and down the column, he sloshed along. Then I heard, "Marine! Sniper! You with the old lady. Where the hell are you?" I knew Harley wasn't in any mood for that kind of confrontation. He stood up, and I went over with him. The gunny said, "Did you get that woman like I told you to?" There was a long pause. Gunny growled, "Well?"

Harley drawled, in a Jerry Reed drawl, "Yes, I did, Gunny."

"Then where the hell is she?" And before Harley could say anything, he barked, "I'll have your ass, Marine, if you didn't do what I said! Now where the hell is she?" I was afraid Harley was about to get into it with the guy.

Harley was a wonderful guy in the bush and a great friend, but trouble had a way of catching up to him real quick. I stepped up, just in case the worst materialized.

Harley said, "Let me explain, Gunny. I went back when you told me, and I picked her up. I carried her all the way to the bridge and out onto it."

"And?" screamed the big guy with all the stripes.

"And I slipped and went down. And all that water was rushing over the fucking bridge and . . ."

The gunny couldn't take it anymore and interrupted Harley in midsentence. He gets DI-like, demanding to know where she is!

Harley defiantly said, "Well, Gunny, it was me or her . . . and here I am!" I thought we had trouble on that one. But the gunny surprised the hell out of all of us. He was a tough guy all right, but he was fair. He stared Harley down, and then stomped off, muttering something about what an asshole Harley was . . . but someday he'd be a damned good Marine.

The column moved out with all of us standing in knee-deep water, ten thousand miles from sanity and three more miles to a dry anything. We sloshed and slogged along until 0300 when we finally made it in. It was eighteen long days of pain in the rain. You had to have humor to survive. We'd slosh up hills and slide down, clawing with our hands and fingers to try to stop. We had slept in the rain and muck, and fallen facefirst in it time and time again. We played in it, and we'd seen life and death in it. If you could survive that, you could survive anything. It rained for ten more days, making it twenty-seven days and nights of rain before we got a break. I hadn't known life got as hot as it did there, and I hadn't known the world could get that wet. But it sure as hell did.

After being submerged in the valley for weeks, I

started some serious lobbying for my own sniper patrols. The valley we just swam around in would be a good place to start. With DuBay and Rider already rotated home, that gave me a problem. Fourth Marine snipers didn't have full-time leadership at that time, so politically, we didn't have much clout. We'd not had an officer in charge of us yet, so we'd wait and see. Some of our work had got the attention of the colonel, commander of the 4th Marines, so that might help down the road. On with the grunts. We'd have to work our angle through them, and keep working for the private deal when our new leaders arrived.

It was February. Last month's Tet was nothing more than a feigned cease-fire, and time was moving on, and I'd have to re-up fairly soon as I was getting on toward my year there. I walked into our tent after a little foray with the grunts, and everyone looked solemn. They weren't the snipers I'd left. "What the fuck's up with the long faces?" I asked.

It was bad news: Pearl had just been killed. I threw my shit down and raced over to COC. He'd just got back from extension leave. But it was true. Pearl had been out with the grunts, down in the sand dunes off Highway 1. They didn't expect a lot of shit, but sometime during the night, they were mortared. He took a direct fucking hit, right between the legs, and died a few hours later on the operating table of 3d Med in Phu Bai. I couldn't fucking believe my ears. I just couldn't fucking believe it!

We had a new lieutenant "officially" over snipers. He came and asked me to go over to 3d Med and ID the body. I caught a ride over right away and walked into a tent that looked like a human body-and-fender shop. Man, this is what happens to the living we toss on the choppers out there? Shit! A guy could get fucking depressed looking at that every day and not shooting back. I asked who I should see to ID someone. The guy said he'd get the corpsman in charge. I'm standing around, thinking how lucky I am, when a man walks up to me. He looked like an officer but didn't act like one. He said he was the battalion surgeon, then asked, "Marine, did you know this guy you're here to ID?"

I said, "Yes, we were actually close."

"Well, be proud of him. He should have died instantly, but had a will to live I haven't seen often. He made it four hours. We did all we could. He was literally blown in half."

I knew Pearl was a tough kid. I didn't know he was that tough. But when I realized had he lived, he would have had no legs, no family jewels, no ass, and who knows what else, I was glad he'd died. He'd wanted to be a game warden, in the worst way. He just wanted to go home and be a damned game warden. Now I'm about to say, "Yup, that's him, all half of him anyway." Fuck! And we talked him into staying for six more months. What assholes we are.

I thanked the surgeon as he left and went with the corpsman who'd just come for me. I followed him back past a long row of what looked like conex boxes, cubes about eight feet to a side. We walked along a long row of boxes, all sitting atop wooden pallets. The sun was starting to come out, the monsoon was showing signs of leaving, and it was hotter than hell again. We got to the last one, the corpsman opened it, and we stepped inside. There he was, Pearl, my man, lying there, just half of him, just half of him. Holy shit! He was clean as a new baby's ass, but nothing from the navel down. I mean, there was a leg, or part of one, on the table, and a foot. Damn! He looked like a mannequin, just like the stiffs I'd had to ID in Santo Domingo. But poor Pearl. He looked like someone I once knew, but so much older. He'd been so baby-faced before, now he looked gray, even his hair, which had been a reddish brown. Now, he looked like an older brother. He must've been through hell in those last few hours, when he was clinging to life. He'd actually aged.

I walked out of there trying to leave my morning dose of death behind, and I went for my ride back to Evans. That wasn't Pearl. That was a body that looked like Pearl. Hell, people rotated home all the time, never to be heard from again. That wasn't the same Pearl I knew. But, I wasn't the same Kug either. I could see it so plainly. Each time you had to deal in death, you had to die a little more inside, too. I don't know what the life force is and don't have any use for religion. I do know that in the war business, the light you have grows a little weaker each time you deal in death. Then one day, you'll have a brownout and eventually a blackout. That's when we'll feel nothing, nothing at all. I wondered why nice people like Pearl bought the farm when assholes like me stayed on to live and fight another day? I didn't know the answer, and didn't have time to find it out, either. When I returned to snipers, we were packing for another trip out of town.

Greek and I would be heading out with elements of the 9th Marines. They'd just been moved up from the Da Nang area. Word had it that they were a little crazy. They got cut up real bad in Da Nang. The word was ten thousand bouncing Betty mines fell into the black market, and they were used to ring the position of those guys, and it was ugly. Their daily patrols just ended up killing people with our own mines. Don't know what's true and what ain't, but Greek and I would find out. The bouncing Betty was an American-made booby trap about the size and charge of our regular hand grenades. When tripped, surprise, it bounced three to four feet in the air and went *boom!* A true ball buster for sure.

I wanted to get some letters off before I went. Over Christmas, somebody had put my address in the paper back home and I started getting letters from folks back in Ohio. One lady sent me some Christian hymns, saying that I should read one of these when they start bombing us! One I got looked like a keeper, and I started writing Sandy, a woman from California. She was out there working, but was originally from Ohio, an hour from where I called home. She was twenty-six years old, so we'd see if the relationship developed. At least she wasn't arguing that I shouldn't be fighting in the war. I got a letter off to her before we took off.

Going with Greek would be a pleasure. I'd gotten to know him when he came over from the grunts. A Brooklyn native, he was funny as hell. He looked and acted like Gene Wilder, the actor. He was meticulous and always there when you needed him. When he first came to snipers, we went our separate ways. It turned out he hated Zulu and figured I must be just like him. He hated Zulu for taking his packages from home. Greek got the best packages. It must have been the Italian deal, I don't know, but he got exotic shit in the mail. After Zulu rotated home, we got together, and he was cool.

As I was heading out, I was thinking about extending. I'd told Pearl that I would if he did, and now I would have to do it. I'd do it when we got back. We went over to link up with the grunts. We were all heading into the lower Co Bi Than Tan Valley for a sweep. It was supposed to be a ten-day deal. That was hard to believe so we planned on three weeks. When Greek and I met up with this crew, we could tell there was something different going on here.

The first thing we learned was they weren't into "sweeps." They'd be "aggressive, search and destroy, and kick some ass." Well dog my cats, was that new, or just some new way of saying the same thing? They did look like they meant it, though. Lots of grunt outfits prepared for the bush because they had to. This one looked and felt like it was heading out because it wanted to. Now that could make a hell of a difference. So what was up with this "they're here to get a rest" stuff, we were told when they sent us over?

The grunt lieutenant laid it out for us. We'd walk to our AO that night, under cover of darkness. It was maybe ten miles out. They wouldn't need us to lead them in; they had their own point men. Shit! I didn't want Greek and me sandwiched in the middle of a mob, going for a walk again. We wanted some action for the 06s. I questioned the lieutenant since we knew the area like the back of our hand. He said he felt we needed to earn their trust! The guy was new to Nam and sounded like Deputy Dawg of Saturday morning fame. What was Vietnam coming to?

At midnight we headed out, sandwiched in with a jumpy crew of grunts. They saw a spook behind every damned bush, so movement was slow. We'd stop and check the map, then off we'd go. If the asshole had just asked, I could have told him where the hell he was, all the time. Not long into our walk, the rains dropped buckets of cool liquid all over us. It felt good. The monsoon was trying to end, and the heat was trying to return, so they often clashed. It rained hard for an hour then stopped suddenly.

It was dark, one of those inside-the-ape's-ass kind of dark nights. We'd get an occasional break in the clouds and be showered with a ray of light from above. About two hours into the night, the lieutenant decided he was at his AO, and he stopped to set up a perimeter. I knew his arty plots would come next, and he could blow all of us to smithereens. I'd paid attention to where we were, and we weren't at the AO; he was a good grid square off. I needed to talk to Deputy Dawg, but I didn't know if the gunny would let it happen. I'd gotten in trouble with the gunny on the walk out. I had a watch that glowed in the dark. You'd charge up the marks with a flashlight. I don't know if I overcharged it or what, but it was shining bright that night. I kept it in my left breast pocket in my jungle jacket, tied to me with a piece of parachute cord. I tried to be careful taking it in and out, so no one would see. On one break, the gunny, who'd gotten a glimpse of it, thought it was a cigarette. Hell, I don't even smoke. He came charging back there like a Parris Island DI on the rag. I ended up showing him what happened, but he didn't buy much shit from anyone, let alone snipers.

Greek wanted me to straighten those folks out. He was getting tired of stopping and hearing the lieutenant say, "Do you knaw whaare we aaare?" We'd be laughing, under our breath of course lest the gunny shoot us. I told Greek, "Since he's from Brooklyn, buddy, you handle it." He wasn't buying my argument, so it was the Kug or no one. Right then, it was no one. We decided to relax and go with the flow. They'd made the decision and were setting the night plots for artillery. Greek and I laid back in the tall elephant grass. We were waiting for some news of what was next when we damned near shit our pants. *Swooosh!*

I didn't hear them fire from the Phu Bai arty base, but I sure as hell heard the spotter round coming in. I mean it sounded like a semi coming, when you're standing right at the edge of the road. It whistled in and slammed into

the hill just over us with a loud, deafening *kabooooom!*
The ground shook. Shit flew everywhere. I listened for
the cries of "Corpsman up," but none came. Lucky asshole the lieutenant was . . . on this one anyway.

The gunny went streaking up to the front. Greek and I
followed. He was possessed now, that I clue the lieutenant, like tell him where the fuck he is. I got there at the
start of a huddle with their star corporal, the lieutenant,
and the gunny. Covered by a poncho, they were kneeling
down with a map and a small flashlight. At least they
were doing that right. I interrupted, just as the lieutenant
was saying, "Do you knaw whare we aaare?" I felt like
saying, yes, Deputy, I do know.

The threesome turned, the gunny saying, "Snipers, go
back to the column where you were."

Greek nearly lost it at that point. "Gunny, with all due
respect, this guy here with me is an expert on this area,
and you ain't where you think you are. You're gonna
blow all our asses up if you fire again!"

The gunny stood up, but before he could say anything,
the lieutenant said, "Sniper, do you knaw whare we
aaare?"

I got down with him, laid it out, and showed him what
was wrong. I offered to go to the front and lead them to
the AO. He accepted, and this crew "cautiously" accepted us. The lieutenant turned out to be a good guy,
and so did the gunny. They'd been through the grinder
near Da Nang, and trusting others just wasn't high on
their agenda. We led them to the hill, and they set out
their perimeter. I'd gotten another glimpse of the corporal I'd seen up there, and he was weirder than a were-
wolf. I needed to see more of him.

Morning came, and they split the platoon up for some
"search and destroy," as they called it. We stayed behind

with the base camp. Two units were set up so they could check out two areas at once. Greek and I got permission from the lieutenant to go out by ourselves. We'd overlook the action of his other units. He thought that was cool, and we were off.

We went out about a grid square, just the two of us. We just had our sniper rifles as the grunts didn't want us carrying both. We broke out the 7×50s to watch the Marines, led by Corporal Crazy (as Greek and I called him), approach a village. We saw two gooks, dressed in black, making a hat out the back. I called the lieutenant, and he said shoot away. We got set and waited for just the right time. The bad guys didn't know we were there, and had their eyes glued to the village and the corporal's crew. About fifty yards behind the village, they stopped to look back. Greek and I, camouflaged with branches and leaves, sitting a couple hundred yards above them, honed in. It was a chip shot, maybe two hundred yards. We had to be careful, sometimes the short ones were tougher than the long ones. We had to hold down on these because our rifles were set with a six-hundred-yard dead center. It was as tough as holding up. Greek called the guy on the left, I took the one on the right. We did the "on three" routine, and *b'boom!* We dropped them straight out! They were history! We added two more kills to our list.

The day wore on, and eventually we were staring at a starlit sky our second night out. In tall elephant grass for the second night, I lay there thinking about what might lay ahead. I had to re-up and stay there for six more months. I knew we were getting closer on our lobby for our own sniper patrols. We could put together a great group. I looked up, and found my mirror in the sky. I realized it'd been a while since I'd thought about all that.

Life in "the World" seemed far removed. I was out doing the sniper thing and had gotten pretty good at it. Killing didn't bother me. I'd wondered if it would, but it didn't. It was all just a game, and I was one of many players. I tried to take them out of the game before they did me. Each morning for eleven months, I'd still been standing. That made me one of the winners. I didn't feel anything. I looked back up and wondered what it all would mean for me when I did go home. Hopefully, a couple other snipers would re-up, and we could go to Australia on leave together and then go back to Vietnam to kick some more ass. I drifted off looking at my mirror, which no longer seemed to stare back at me.

The mornings were getting hotter again, and the little rain we did get brought on the stifling humidity. What a fucking place to live. Strange, I thought, that I wanted to stay on there. I did want to stay, but the grunts were getting restless; they wanted some gooks to fight. Corporal Crazy was doing some lobbying of his own. He was pressing the lieutenant hard. I wasn't sure what, but he wanted to do something. But that day looked like more of the same as they sent him back to check out yet another village.

His group was about fifty yards from the edge of the ville when a shot rang out. A sniper had hit one of the Marines coming into the ville. It was a new kid, but he wasn't hit too bad. It was weird. There were some grizzled veterans in the group who'd seen some serious shit; then there were brand-new kids, fresh in from the States. There was no in-between. I guess their casualties were so heavy in Da Nang that they'd just replenished them, and sent the unit to us. Corporal Crazy called for a medevac, then searched the village. Crazy was incensed when he found nothing. What else is new? Well they surprised me when they herded the people out of town, then Corporal Crazy and a couple of his men were torching the village.

They'd gotten the villagers together and had an interpreter tell them straight up, "Don't fuck with us, don't harbor snipers, and don't set booby traps. You do, and we'll burn your fucking village." That was a first for me, but I guess it'd teach them a lesson or two. And that was the point. Fuck with us, and that is what you get. As far as the Marines were concerned, the dumbshit who cranked the round off and wounded their comrade had caused the whole thing. Maybe they were right. Who knows?

The medevac came and flew away with human cargo in need of repair. We spent another night on the same grass hill. Corporal Crazy was again lobbying hard with the lieutenant. A few Marine stragglers were standing around our hill just before dark. That attracted another dumbshit, probably out for revenge for the burning that took place. A shot rang out with a loud *crack!* and a bullet went zinging overhead. The call "Snipers up!" rang out, and Greek and I ran to the lieutenant. We checked in, and we all went to the edge of our lines to scope out the tree line. We couldn't pick up shit, but a kid on a water buffalo was sitting right at the edge of the tree line. Oh shiiit!

Another shot rang out, zinging right over our heads. The kid just sat there, eyeballing the area like nothing was happening. Crazy was incensed! "That little gook bastard is tellin' 'em where we are! Shoot his ass!" I just looked at him, and Greek was looking through the 7×50s. Crazy leaned down and spoke to the lieutenant. Then the lieutenant said, "Sniper, shoot him."

I said, "Sir, he's a kid, maybe ten or twelve. I don't see a weapon. He didn't fire that round."

Crazy angrily said, "Can you shoot the fucking thing, Sniper, or do you just carry it around lookin' bad?"

I looked at him. "I can shoot the fuckin' thing, but he ain't armed, man." He said, "Give me the fucking rifle then. If you're a fucking pantywaist, then I'll shoot his ass." I looked at the lieutenant, and he didn't say a thing. Corporal Crazy took my 06 and nailed the kid at 150 yards. He hands me back the rifle, and with a smile, says, "There. It shoots real good." That it does, that it does.

I realized as he was walking away that he had a human thighbone dangling from his cartridge belt. It was hanging down his left side, attached with a piece of black commo wire. I said, "Greek, did you see that thing?" He'd just seen the same thing. I asked around, but never could get the whole story. I'm sure there was one, a dandy. I know it had something to do with the carnage in Da Nang. But I did know one thing for sure, his was one weird outfit.

Things changed radically the next morning; the lieutenant decided to go with Corporal Thigh Bone's plan. He was a bad case of brain burn, yet he was idolized by the troops. I'm sure he was a bad dude in the bush when all the shit comes raining down, but what the hell happens to folks like that when it's all over? And there were more than a few like him in that outfit. Hell, what would happen to me?

We killed ourselves physically with the new plan; we'd sleep all day and move around all night. We'd split up in grunt squads and do "ambushes at will." Back to my recon days and poor Will. He got the shit shot out of him, that's for damned sure. It was brutal running around all night, then trying to hide during the day to sleep. The heat was unbearable, and the new routine wasn't turning out to be a whole lot of fun. And we were not finding any gooks. The place was empty, like a parking lot after the big game.

Our last night out, we ended up down at the base of the lush, green mountains I'd first seen behind the sniper range last spring, almost a year ago. They sure looked a lot scarier from close up. We were setting in on a little knoll, sticking right out in the middle of the jungle. Trees and dense vegetation were all around us. The grass was maybe three feet high, at best. Right on top of it all was a well-traveled trail intersection, probably used by the NVA when they came down out of the mountains. It headed into the valley and across, eventually, to Hue.

The crazy bastards we were with decided to set an ambush right there in the open area. They reasoned no one would ever expect it, and I bet they were right about that one. But this is bullshit, man. I guessed we'd all go out in a blaze of fuckin' glory. The Greek turned to me, and muttered, "It's just un-fucking-believable!" It was that and more.

Thigh Bone decided on two sites; that way they could run a double ambush! Down the trail and into the jungle to the west would be the second site. They split up the platoon into two teams. The plan was for the bad guys to come out through the jungle. We would let them get to our side of the site, then blast them. Then they'd run into the other ambush party, and we'd get them again. Or, it could work the other way. We'd wait until they got to the jungle side of our site, and hit them, making them run to the other ambush. The jungle group went off with Corporal Thigh Bone. He took the whacko crew, and it was a great place for them, I thought. Greek and I were with the platoon out in the open, the picnic area, as Greek called it. Our group went right out by the trail and lay prone, about twenty feet away in the grass. Greek and I were the rear guard, for our group. We were back behind the lieutenant and his radioman. With just our sniper rifles, we weren't exactly the best support for an ambush. I had to admit, the plan was crazier than hell. I was scared to death, but I was getting pumped. The adrenaline was flowing as swift as the fear that choked my asshole.

It got dark early, and that's what we were counting on to make the plan work. Around midnight, I switched off watch with the lieutenant and his radioman; it was time for Greek and me to sleep. We were beat from the un-usual routine of running every night, all night long, then trying to sleep during the hot time of the day.

I hadn't been out long when I woke up to scamper-ing . . . running . . . voices . . . then the *brrrp, brrrp, brrrp* of automatic-weapons fire! I rolled over, and people were running in front of us, and grunts were firing, but it looked too late. Then they got on the radio and called down to Corporal Thigh Bone. A couple of seconds later, all hell broke loose in the jungle below! Bullets were fly-ing everywhere and tracers lit up the night sky. Grenades provided background music for one hellacious firefight. The lieutenant tried to raise someone on his PRC-25. But no one had time for a chat . . . asshole!

Control returned to our grassy knoll, but chaos reigned in the jungle below. The lieutenant found out his whole platoon, the one lying in the grass out front, had fallen asleep. The guy that nearly flattened us, jumping in the middle, was the key to the truth. He'd woken up and heard whispering. He looked out, disoriented in the night, and saw people sitting out front. Thinking they were Marines, he got up and went out to tell them to shut up. The joke was on him, and he got the surprise of his young life. The talkers were gooks who'd apparently taken a break right in front of our sleeping ambush. The Marine ran back, jumping headlong into the middle of his platoon, while the bad guys jumped up and ran down into the jungle and the ambush below. Man, that's winning ugly.

The firefight raged in the jungle below for forty-five minutes. It seems the gooks already had spider holes dug along the trail, so they jumped in across from the ambush and hooked it out. The night brought lots of yelling and screaming, and it was awful. We prepped a team to go down, but couldn't send it until we established radio contact. As the day began to come to life, the battle below began to die. With it were bodies from both sides, dead in the night. We got down there just as reality was coming back to earth. It was ugly, real ugly. Havoc had been there, kicked ass, and left a hell of a mess. The jungle was littered with the wastes of war.

Two dead Marines lay on our side, and two dead NVA on the other. The jungle smelled of war. A corpsman was attending the wounded, of whom there were a lot more than a couple. On the bad-guy side of the street, lots of blood trails led back to the jungle. As time distanced the fight from the men, the wailing began, first as a whimper, and then it picked up. Word of the dead was taken real hard. One Marine I didn't know; he was new, just over from the States. But the other was Corporal Thigh Bone, and people mourned the loss of the guy, however weird he may have been.

He'd been their idol, their hero, their main man. He was now their dead man. They loved this guy. He died dragging a wounded gook to his side. He must have been asleep when the firefight started. He didn't have his boots on when we placed him in the green body bag for the ride home. He was one bad dude and a real combat Marine. It wasn't the spit and polish that won firefights like those . . . it was the Corporal Thigh Bones, and all the "weird" guys like him.

The dead and dying taken care of, we started the day-long march back home. It was a somber, bitter, and angry group we walked with toward Camp Evans. They hadn't got the rest they were sent there for, but then again, they hadn't looked for it either. Walking along, Greek and I agreed it'd been an interesting experience. I learned a lot. I learned how to fight this war better. And I learned what war can do to people like Corporal Thigh Bone. I learned I died a little inside each day just to stay alive. There were no real winners, and we all lost something of ourselves along the way.

We eventually reached Evans, and I was looking forward to getting good and drunk. It'd been a while, and I needed to clean it all out upstairs. I was seeing and feeling some strange things about then. I needed to forget them for the moment and head to the club for a cold one. Greek and I and a couple of the new snipers were all of our team left around. We met one of them, a relatively new guy named Hood. He was from Louisiana, and boy, was he a Rebel. I could see promise with him. We had lots of great guys in snipers, so I just had to stay. I had to stay for them, for me, and most of all for Pearl, because I'd told him I would. I went down to the CO's office and put in for an extension of six months. Fuck it! Just something I had to do. The family would just have to understand.

Another Nam morning came, and I felt so bad I just wanted to die. I hated myself for drinking that night. I don't know if there was ever "a morning after" that I didn't regret in a big way. But that time, I really hated it, and I hated me for doing it. Then we got word from COC that there was a big sweep coming with the grunts. We were going out with a huge mob again, looking for bad guys that we'd only find when they wanted us to find them. What kind of way to fight a war was that?

I picked up some mail and found out that my honey from California wanted to see me if I came home for a leave. She'd even fly home for a visit. If Australia doesn't work with any of the gang here, then maybe she's a winner. We'll see.

The op took us back to the Street, but it was to Quang Tri and east to the sand dunes. We were heading over toward the South China Sea. We were to walk straight out, starting at midnight that night. Two companies coming from one side, walking in during the night. The third inserted by chopper on the other side in the morning. What an idea! Could we keep two companies quiet long enough to sneak in and say, "Surprise!" I couldn't imagine it from my brief time there, but what the hell did I know? I'm a cynic. It was about 0930 hours, and that gave me some time to get my gear together.

Man, I hated the dunes. I couldn't get out of that patrol, though; didn't have my own thing approved just yet. The fucking dunes, man! Down there we've got to walk so light we don't leave footprints. I mean the VC booby-trap the living hell out of that place. And we couldn't see the bastards as easily as in the dirt. I can tell this won't be a good deal at all. About that time, I heard they were converting the grunts to the new M-16s. The M-14 could take a beating and still work. I heard the M-16s jam easily, don't work worth a damn in the dirt. Well, some bastard back in Washington, flying his desk, must have been driving the war. It couldn't be anybody in Vietnam, that's for sure. The poor grunts would be getting four hours training and that's it! Four hours training on a new rifle, then go shoot 'em up, cowboy! How could that be? And I'm going out with them . . . at night no less! Hell, it's probably true what they've been saying about us getting new sniper rifles. Remington 700s. Now why fuck up a good thing?

The luck of the draw had me with a new sniper. A kid from podunk Nevada. We called him Cash. He's a nice enough kid, but hell, man—the Street with somebody just two months in Nam. New guy at my side and new weapons all around, that sounded like disaster. And we were heading to the dunes, at night. Miles and miles of sand, sinister looking villages, and a bad history. Last time down there, grunts were flying everywhere, because of all the booby traps in the sand. All that made for a real bad afternoon for the Kug.

The day eased its way to night as we boarded trucks for the ride up Highway 1. At dark's first sign, we were off the trucks and heading east, to the dunes. It was hot, and we were already bone tired. We moved out, stretching the column for what seemed like miles, hoping against hope that we could secretly slither into place undetected. The officers in the COC believed there was a heavy concentration of gooks holing up around there. I hoped, as I walked, that we didn't surprise them that night. That would not be nice.

Cash and I walked along as attachments to one of the grunt companies. Stu and Crud were with another company, and Greek and Det Cord were with the third company. Six snipers on a walk into darkness and fear. The fear that night came from the uneasiness of the grunts walking all around us. The M-16 wasn't something they wanted, or should have even been given the day of their op. It was like a live field test of a weapon. Great if you're the engineer back in Washington, but a real bummer if you're the live-fire "testee" in the sand dunes!

I walked along trying to balance my anger and my

fear. I'd been in Nam a year, and I had a feel for this shit. And my feelings at that point sucked real bad. What kind of a roll-out scenario was this? I just knew some asshole back in the political world mandated an arbitrary date, a "You'll roll out this weapon to the troops or else, by God!" Probably that worthless piece of shit McNamara.

I was walking along, Cash behind me, and it was maybe 2300. We'd gone maybe four or five grid squares. I was sweating my balls off, thirsty, wanting a break. Man, could I use a . . . oh hell . . . AK rounds . . . a fucking *ambush*! *Wham!* The depths of hell rose to meet us in the sands. Evil broke out all around us as the night turned bright. Our point took a heavy hit that reached halfway back the column to Cash and me. The night was filled to overflowing with the bright streaks of tracers interrupted by the flash of grenades and mortar rounds as they exploded all around. The chatter of small arms and explosions was continuous and deafening!

The ambush cut our company in half. Just to our front, the column was split away from the point. We were regrouping to try to link back up with the point unit. The captain was near us, on the radio, screaming for help. There was none to be had as the other companies were also under attack. A last-minute change sent the chopper company on foot, so they were there already. I'm a real fucking prophet! We got the new rifles and all this shit coming at us. I didn't know if we were getting out of that one. It was going to be one mother of a night. Cash wore a face that would have made the Grim Reaper proud. He was scared stiff. We were both facedown in the sand; the incoming fire overhead was withering. Along with the bodies of young Marines, bushes around us were falling from the onslaught. The frightening noise of battle surrounded us as if we had lain down on the railroad tracks and let a train speed over us. The cries of "Corpsman up!" rang out to an evershrinking group of available corpsmen. What the fuck am I doing here, is all I could think, as I returned fire as best I could. I was seriously glad I'd lugged my M-14 along. I had my sniper rifle too. Who could tell if I'd need it?

I was low on ass and high on adrenaline, but the situation was turning ugly fast. There were bad guys on all sides, and they seemed to be winning. We were beaten back. All hell was breaking loose with no sign of how to corral it. We were having trouble holding on. We could hear gooks running around us, and there was bad news on all sides. Cries echoed in the night from wounded who couldn't be helped. The screams were haunting and tough on the mind. Concentrate, Kug. Control, man! Fucking control!

A routine patrol, huh? A possibility of some troops in the fucking area, huh? I could get better intelligence information from the kids selling Tiger Piss along the road. Somebody talked about the deal; the bastards were waiting to clean our clocks.

The captain told Cash and me to take off and defend the left flank. We took off with our asses dragging lower than our gear. Cash was seriously worried, and I wasn't far off. I was worried about him and me. We took off, with him behind me, doing that low crawl we hated so much in boot camp. I mean the shit was really flying, and the night was fast and furious. Moving was really tough. The gooks were so damned close by then that we could see the muzzle flashes from their AKs and hear them yelling to one another.

We found a spot and burrowed in like sea turtles, firing into the black hell that lay in front of us. The gooks continued putting up a withering line of fire, and we could see the main attack wasn't coming from our side of the perimeter. A good thing since there were just a few of us over there. And some of those were Marines just hanging on to their lives. The fire was still coming over here but was dropping off a little.

I dropped behind for a minute to check on some dudes we passed coming in. I was running low on ammo for the 14 and tried picking up a 16 from a wounded Marine. The thing was jammed. Cash fired another M-16 for one magazine, then it jammed. What a fucking toy! Damn it! I reached the Marine we had passed and got there in time to see him spit out his last breath. It was dark, and I couldn't see his face, but he was dead. I crawled back over to Cash, who was occupied with one muzzle flash in the darkness and was holding his own.

We took off to move closer to the Marines to our right and shore up the column. I crawled in with two other Marines I could see up ahead. But when I got there, I realized they were history. Sorrow and anguish for some unsuspecting folks back home. Dead Marines lay everywhere. Then lead started flying our way again, and we crouched down behind bodies. Moments before they were a couple of kids like me, and now, there they were, lifeless hunks lying in the sand, protecting me and Cash. What a fucking night!

Cash and I were holding our own. The fighting, the screams, the pain and horror continued through most of the night. At some point, it just seemed like things stopped. It stopped as it had started, suddenly and unexpectedly. The whiz and crack of bullets gave way to the reality of death. It was silent. So fucking silent. And it was all around. As the morning sun reared its searing head, the intensity of a night gone bad melted away with the retreating enemy. The evening warriors had disappeared with the morning sun. We were left to make sense of the carnage first light revealed.

We survivors were all clothed with a heavy coat of anxiety. The facial expression of the day was disbelief, and it was worn by almost everybody. And reality came crashing down on all us "winners." I wondered if living was a blessing today.

I told Cash to stay and watch the perimeter. He was uncomfortable with the dead Marines standing watch with him, but that didn't get to me; I'd put enough in body bags to know you should just be thankful it isn't you. I walked toward the voices of order I could hear behind me. I hoped the captain had made it. Somebody must have held the company together. As I walked, the living were venturing out and about, and I could hear choppers in the distance. I knew where they were going, that's for sure.

All around us were sand dunes, bushes, and hedgerows. We were ambushed out in the open, alongside a gook village. Squads were already searching the village. Hell, you know already they don't know shit about it. The lying bastards, we ought to burn the fucking place down, then we'll see their fucking tunnels and spider traps and shit. The dirty fucking bastards! I can't believe my fucking eyes as I walk. I thought I'd seen some serious shit but this . . . fuck these people and the fucking water buffaloes they rode in on!

All around me were bodies, dead Marine bodies. I just couldn't believe what I saw around me. Death was everywhere, on a hot morning, ten thousand miles from normal. Lots of folks back home would wake up the next day, and the war would be more than something they'd watch on TV. Their war would soon be coming home in a fucking box.

I found the captain. He asked me to get Cash and help with the dead. Cash and I located most of our gear, stashed it for later, and went to help. I knew we'd better get the show on the road; with the heat of the day racing for us, we needed to beat it to the bodies. Cash was having trouble. I said, "Man, you did cool last night, I'm glad I was with you. Be thankful you aren't being picked up." He understood, but that didn't help much with the task at hand. And it was a gruesome task. We had to hurry before these poor guys baked in the sun. We picked up body after body. A couple, three hours passed, medevacs came and went while we carried bodies to the LZ. When a chopper wasn't there, we'd line them up, ready for the last ride home. At one point, Cash got the dry heaves, so we took a break. Working with the dead never bothered me, never knew why. At twenty, I was too young to die. I just knew it wasn't going to be me, not to the Kug. Fuck, I'm a winner again; I'm still standin'. At one point, we had a row or two of dead Marines. Somebody said there were thirty-five Marine KIAs, but who really knew?

What a war . . . and for what? When the last of the dead were placed in the body bags, my overwhelming sadness gave way to outrage! Why did those guys have to buy the farm like that? We'd found Marine after dead Marine with an M-16 clutched in his hands. One or two of the poor bastards had them between their legs, apart; they were fieldstripping them in the heat of the battle. What a fucking gang bang that turned out to be! Where the hell were McNamara and his Whiz Kids? Fucking bureaucratic bullshit, that's what caused shit like this. Why didn't they properly test the weapon first? It's one thing to get your young ass killed; it's a fucking 'nother to die when you could have lived.

All the snipers survived somehow. Now, I'd never forget it, nor would I forget the piss-poor leadership, somewhere, that let this happen. Dead people, kids, just like me, dead all over the place. Just so somebody, some-where, could report how they got those new, lightweight, high-velocity rifles to the boys in Nam on time, just the way they said they would. Fucking assholes! My philoso-phizing was interrupted by word to move out! We were going on a full sweep of the village, where the heart of the ambush came from.

I walked along and into the village, with all the rest of the automatons. We didn't make it far when *boom!*, an-other booby trap went off. America's heartland took an-other one up the ass. Gook bastards! The cry of the fallen meets deaf ears. The hurt turns to a whimper and then a whisper in your mind. There, it dies and eases into your psyche as one more sign of life in the Nam. After a short wait, we got the latest guy off on his medevac when an AK-47 let loose in the hootch right next to us. Just then a Marine came flying out the front door. As he went past, I could see his face was blown away. He'd gone inside and announced himself and got his head blown off when he opened a curtain. Another Marine ran in and aced the bad guy. The Marine with no face lay dying in the dirt next to Cash. There he was, in the dirt with a face that made star billing in *Friday the 13th*.

Another medevac, more fireworks, and things were staying ugly for us again. Why we kept stupidly walking around those dunes I'll never know. It was late after-noon, walking along, when I saw a hedgerow in front of us. I was about to walk through it when a grunt staff sergeant grabbed me by the shoulder and said, "I need by, Marine!" He passed me in a hurry, got a couple yards ahead, and *booom!* he got launched like a rocket. Lucky for me, he'd hit a concussion grenade. It knocked me on my ass, showered me with sand, and gave me a headache. The sarge, though . . . whoa . . . his foot and ankle looked like raw meat. The corpsman said he'd live. Yeah, but he'd be leaning to the right for the rest of his life.

Evans looked like the Hawaiian tropics after what we'd just been through. I needed a break. And my timing couldn't have been better. My extension was approved, and I could have leave whenever I wanted it. Our joint re-up never materialized, so Australia was out. I put in for and was approved to go Stateside for thirty days. Before leaving, I went to COC and made my sniper-patrol pitch one more time. I wanted the free-fire zone in Co Bi Than Tan, so I asked for it. Who knows? I hoped they'd figure out someday that we snipers would be more effective on our own. Give me some leave, some booze, and some broads, and I'll be good as new.

And It's Time
for an Intermission

I found out flying ten thousand miles is a lot faster than floating it, but it's still one hell of a long way. My arrival in Cleveland was not much better than my departure. The family situation just never seemed to improve. I knew it was bad when I walked off the plane and met Dad for the first time in over a year and wanted to run back on and return to Nam. We didn't click at all, but then we never did.

The two-hour ride home from the airport was filled with lots of small talk and business stories I wasn't interested in hearing. At least Dad was consistent, he still didn't mention Nam. I felt as if I didn't belong but wasn't sure if I ever did. My "reentry" to the World began with a ride straight to the racetrack. After a brief reunion with Mom, everyone was off to do their jobs running the races. Welcome home, Marine!

The racetrack highlighted my need to be alone. After that great beginning, I really needed some space. I found myself lost, unable to relate to people I once lived around. I spent my days and my nights drinking, with only an occasional burst of sobriety, when I'd realize I sure didn't fit in the world we spent so much time dreaming about. My most frequent stop was my old watering hole, Poon's. I spent many a night walking home looking up at the same mirror in the sky, wondering what my fellow snipers were doing a world away in the Nam. None of this endeared me to the family, and Mom was more convinced than ever that I needed "help."

The only high spot of my visit fizzled when I met my "pen pal," my California dream girl, for Easter break. My incredibly high expectations vanished when she walked off the plane, last, following a long string of beautiful young things coming home for the holidays. I stood at parade rest in my best Hong Kong suit as she filled the passageway full to the brim. She was one B-52 of a broad. She came down the runway looking like a cross between Mama Cass and John Wayne. She walked with a swagger and wore an Easter bonnet the size of Texas. Needless to say, things weren't going the way I'd imagined a million miles before. I immediately knew I'd be in need of some serious drinking that evening. It made me wish I'd taken the United pilot I'd met earlier up on his offer of an evening with a couple of stewardesses, friends of his.

My time Stateside dragged on like a bad firefight. Outside of how bad I felt each morning, the only other excitement I had was a shot at blowing some minds, Stateside. I was flying up the highway one day when I passed a guy and a girl hitchhiking. I must have passed them at eighty miles per hour. Even at that speed, I couldn't help but notice the chick had on a skirt with no more material than it'd take to make a hanky. I mean she was showing some serious leg, and I'd been away a long time. I screeched to a halt. Turns out they were hippies and antiwar kids. But not really all that bad. We debated the war as we sped along, me checking out the great legs next to me. I took them up to town and bought them bus tickets to D.C. What the hell!

Toward the end of my time in the World I met a girl who was a novelty to me. LuAnn was nice, sweet, kind, and didn't hang out at Poon's, which was something special in Lock Seventeen. Her Dad was a former Marine. We dated hot and heavy as my time in country was coming to a close. Her mom was nice but didn't trust me, and of course, her fears were warranted. But she'd trained LuAnn well. My drinking slowed toward the end of that intermission since I wasn't permitted to show up at LuAnn's house the least bit wasted; her mom had no sense of humor and ran the place like the Corps.

I got real homesick for the snipers my last week Stateside. I got a long-awaited letter from Harley, and that made it worse. Harley and I had gotten close on some of our last patrols. He didn't have lots of mail since his "Best Regards, Bitch" letter to his "old lady." I'd written him right after coming home, so he'd at least get some mail. Then I got his letter with the news that he'd been shot upside the head. "Just like the movies," Harley said. He was knocked unconscious and had to be evacuated. He'd gotten a "graze" wound that shot his hat off. Damn! He was back on light duty now but he sounded a lot different. He said he realized you really could get killed doing that shit. Man, I had to get back to Nam. I wanted my own patrols. I wanted to be back where people gave a shit.

My time Stateside ended as it began, which wasn't saying much. The ride to Cleveland that time found me with a major hangover. Mom was driving and LuAnn was at my side. I wasn't sure about all this "in love" stuff, but our relationship was a hell of a trip to say the least.

Cleveland Airport was the same, but that's about all that was. As well as I fit in, I might just as well have been in Australia. I should have gone there instead of to the States. It probably wouldn't have been much different. They spoke the same language and things looked about the same. Stateside didn't seem like home anymore. It looked all right, but I and everyone else were different.

I was lost in thought, sitting, waiting for my journey back home to begin. I was lost in the place I'd once called home. No one wanted to hear about Nam. The girls wore skirts that brought the imagination into full view. And boys, well, they'd started looking like the girls used to. American life seemed too complicated for me. When I left it was cool to go in the Corps, or any branch of service, for that matter. But it seemed people didn't feel that way anymore.

As my plane left, LuAnn was in tears. I even thought Mom might have broken down there for a minute. I left knowing the same thing I did in the beginning: Mom cared and couldn't show it; Dad was more interested in his business than his kids; and there really was something to getting girls with that Marine uniform. I just wanted to get back to Nam, where life was real simple and the people, well, they were simply real.

Just one real long day in the air and I'd be home!

PART THREE

Making a Difference

PART THREE

Making a Difference

CHAPTER SIX

The Rogues . . .
A New Era Begins

"Who the hell are you?" whined a smartass new guy.

I looked around at the half-empty tents and said, "I'm Kug, just got back from leave. Where the hell is Wiener and Greek . . . and Crud?" I wanted to see Harley and Stu and all of the men I'd left there. But the new guys were too scared to see anything, let alone know anything. I was beat from the ride in from the other side of the world. And I was soaked, sweating my balls off from the heat. Hot, tired; who gave a big shit where everybody was? Nevertheless, I put my gear down and headed off to COC in search of my friends.

"Wiener's out with a sniper patrol in Co Bi Than Tan Valley," the lieutenant said. Damned straight! Hallelujah! Finally a chance to prove ourselves. A chance to really do what we were trained to do—wanted to do. I had to get out there. I ran back to my hootch to unpack. COC made contact with the grunts on Hill 51, then our patrol. No way to get in that night, but there was a resupply first thing in the morning.

I spent a long and restless night; I worried about Wiener leading the patrol. I loved the guy, and he was

219

tremendous in the bush, but he'd been really strange since his trip home. I wanted to stay close to him; he was a great guy, but weird as hell. He'd even taken up with an old flame from high school, was sending her money, and was said to intend to marry her when he got home again. Nobody's life made sense anymore, but his was really messed up.

Morning came, and so did the resupply chopper. I caught a Huey from Evans heading straight out to Hill 51. I loved Hueys; they were just peace of mind wrapped in a green box with a whirligig on top. We circled our way in and landed right on top of the small scrubby hill that overlooked the valley. Without all the water, it looked a lot different. There were first-class grunts everywhere, all part of a platoon guarding the place. The grunts were reinforced with a contingent of mortars and tanks, which dotted the hilltop. One look around told you the position was solidly defended.

I walked off amidst an ample supply of C rations, ammunition, and water. The hill was dotted with tiny trails running from position to position like long snakes. They wove in and out of the four- or five-foot bushes struggling for control of the hill. Everything sat on parched, dusty earth. Dirt! Lots of it was everywhere. Just then a lot of it was stirred up like a whiteout in a Wyoming winter as the chopper whooshed its way airborne once again.

I wandered off and found directions to the CO, a young but seasoned looking lieutenant. He told me the snipers were out on a day patrol. "They'll be back about 1600 hours." He gave me a little orientation to the hill and the valley, then some directions to the sniper area, nothing more than some shelter halves hung for protection against the burning sun. I lay down in somebody's hootch to wait for them to come in.

I dozed off and, about 1700 hours, woke up in one hell of a sweat. Where were they? I got up and headed out for a look. There they were ... well, they came in looking like someone had just kicked their asses. Wiener was in the two spot, Ya Ya walking point, with Stu behind Wiener, and Crud bringing up the rear. They were shocked to see me standing there. We had a good time getting caught up on all the news. Wiener was heading off in the morning for some R & R to Japan, so my timing was perfect. I'd take over the patrol in the morning. We'd finally arrived.

Wiener left on the morning chopper, just as planned. We decided to spend the day on 51, getting me up to speed. They'd been out there only two weeks as a test to see if we could get any action on our own. The valley was an interesting place. Standing on 51, looking eastward, we could see it was all foothills, somewhere between forty and seventy-five meters high, covered with scrub-grass and bushes. Small deserted villages hid between some of the hills. Most looked overgrown, absorbed by the lush, green jungle creeping in from all sides. The foothills continued, northward, but fanned to the west. There, they touched the giant mountains and rain forest that stretched from the west side of our valley to the Laotian border, thirty or so miles away. To the west, between us and the mountains, lay the valley floor, seven or eight grid squares laced with old, run-down rice paddies. They looked tired, like a football field in late fall, just after a big game. Tree lines, tall and straight, surrounded the once prosperous villages. The valley to the south was more tired paddies and run-down villages bounded by the foothills to the east and the mountains to the west.

The valley stretched for miles to the southwest in the direction of the ancient capital city of Hue, which lay twenty or so miles away.

I stood staring at the valley from Hill 51. It looked a lot different from the last night I saw it, during the monsoon. The river that had caused all the flooding ran north to south, between Hill 51 and the foothills, but it was barely flowing. The banks of the river were ten feet high on either side. The river looked as if it followed the contour of the foothills. It was muddy, thick, an ugly chocolate brown. It was all a free-fire zone, and it was made for snipers.

The guys reviewed everything with me. We had great maps of the valley with the free-fire zone clearly marked. On the east, it stretched from the top of the foothills to the mountain's edge on the west. It ran about five grid squares north and twelve to the south. All that gave us a huge area where we could work our magic. I'd never been so psyched before. I could make the idea work! I'd read the books Mom sent me on the French War there. I searched for the lessons. I wanted to take this group and do something with it. And the next day would be my first chance.

Full of raw adrenaline, I lay down for the night. I couldn't help but think of Wiener. He was gone on R & R, and did he need it. He'd been in rare form his last night. He stole a can of yellow stencil paint from the tankers and sprayed his dirty, rotten jungle boots, boots that were bleached almost white. I said, "Wiener, what the fuck are you doing with yellow boots?"

He laughed a very weird laugh, one he had developed while I was gone, and said, "Watch this, Kug." He went over and sat in a high-traffic area by the lieutenant. He got noticed all right, by an E-6, one who took life too seriously. The E-6 said, "Corporal, why are your boots yellow?" Wiener looked up at the guy, through some really wild eyes, and said, "My boots aren't yellow, sir!"

The sergeant looked at the boots for a minute and said, while walking off, "Oh, you're one of those snipers."

The guys told me that Wiener had deteriorated a lot while I was gone. At the chopper pad at Evans on the way out to Hill 51, he'd taken Crud's lighter fluid and soaked his boots with it, then waited for an officer, any officer, to walk by. At the appropriate moment, he lit his boots, let them burn a low, light blue flame, and walked out in front of a lieutenant. Of course, the lieutenant, being of sound mind and body, yelled at Wiener, "Marine, your boots are on fire!"

With that, Wiener calmly looked down, then back up at the befuddled lieutenant, and said, "Sir, my boots aren't on fire!" That just might have been what got him the R & R so quickly after coming back from leave. Whatever was happening to Wiener, it wasn't too good.

Greek came out to replace Wiener and round out our patrol. They told me we're known by the call sign Rogues, which Wiener had anointed us with. We studied the maps, and Greek and I got a fresh look at life in the valley. The grunts ran a few patrols and had gotten nothing but a bunch of one-way tickets home. The valley had booby traps growing like wild zucchini. The grunts thought we were out of our minds for wanting to work out there. Crazy or not, we were going.

I was damned glad to have Greek on board; we'd have a badass crew. Ya Ya was getting short again, and he'd be rotating home in a month. With Greek on the team, we could go on kicking ass when Ya Ya went back to the World. Ya Ya was a little dirt ball from New Orleans, but he was also great in the bush. He was forever showing us pictures of his gorgeous Cuban wife in a bikini. I had Stu, our big Nebraska farmer. He could have been a Norwegian, with all the blond hair and rosy cheeks. He was six foot four of bad motor scooter, a real no-nonsense, let's-just-do-what-needs-doing-and-get-the-fuck-out-of-here kind of guy. We were rounded out by Crud. He'd come to us from the grunts, on a bet, I think. He wanted to be a sniper in the worst damn way. But the grunts were damn glad to get rid of him; he'd actually lost the firing mechanism from his rifle while he was out on a grunt op. The whole damned thing. The trigger assembly was gone. His grunt lieutenant became so infuriated with him that he wouldn't replace it. They made Crud tape it together and walk the whole damned way with the other grunts. Fortunately, the patrol didn't see any action; if they had, the lieutenant had told him to "Beat them to death with it, the way I would like to do to you!" Crud was a real trip. He came from central Ohio, an only child, the adopted son of an older couple. He was smarter than all the books in the library, but didn't have an ounce of common sense.

We'd worked out our best plan for morning. We decided we'd stick to daylight patrols, come back each night, and see how it went until we learned the area well. For our target, we picked a village that lay to our north and east. It was overgrown with jungle and was deserted except for a few VC. They stayed in the area to plant new booby traps and fuck with Americans. I wanted in there real early to see if we could get one of those dipshits when they least expected it. The map showed that a small trail skirted the edge of the village. We'd go down in the dark, then take the trail around at first light. We'd find a place to burrow in to watch and wait.

I was excited as all hell. Everyone was psyched but Ya Ya, who said he was. But his eyes told a different story.

He was thinking of that bikini back in New Orleans. Ya Ya was my point man, and a damned good one. But I couldn't have a distracted point man. I had a chat with Ya Ya about my concern, and he assured me he was just thinking of going home because he was short, that it wouldn't impact his work on point. I trusted him, and decided to keep him on point but keep a close eye out.

We decided we'd carry M-14s and our Winchesters. There was more talk of us switching to some kind of Remington rifle, but the idea didn't make us very happy. The five of us would carry three 14s and two 06s. We'd pack the usual array of grenades and ammo. We were in pretty good shape with mortar support on 51, and artillery would support us from Evans. I decided to keep us within two to three grid squares of the grunts just in case things went to hell in a hurry.

I couldn't sleep from being so wired. I went outside and lay down, looking up at the stars. My mirror was brighter than ever. Less than a week earlier, I had been home Stateside. I was back there with booze, girls, and the whole enchilada. A week passed and I was in Vietnam again, about to go after the gooks one more time. I had my fears, and I couldn't deny that. It was mostly the fear of the unknown. I didn't know if I was afraid to die or not. Dead people were always someone else, not me. No, it couldn't happen to me. It wouldn't happen to me. My mind raced with emotions that needed reburying. Hell, the dead were just people who died and went away, never to be seen or heard from again. Hey, it's like when people rotate home. You just never see them again. I was tired and wired and needed some sleep. But I guess sleep didn't need me.

The grunt sentry woke me up at 0430. I guess I had finally dozed off. We left the grunt perimeter about 0500 hours. I could see why the guys were suckin' wind when they came in the other night. The hill was steep, hard, and scraggly. The ground was so dry, you slipped on the rock-hard crust. It was amazing to think it was the same Nam I'd seen last fall in the monsoon.

We reached the valley floor, and the moonlight helped us along. Ya Ya was focused and doing well. We crossed a paddy dike leading down to the river. It was about a hundred yards across. In the bright of the moon, just being down there scared me. If there were any gooks on the other side, in the tree line or by the river, we were dead meat. I gained courage from the team. Everyone was focused and intent on what we were doing. We crossed the paddy by spreading wide, never having more than three of us exposed at any time. We stayed far apart so no single shot could get us all at once. Across the paddy, we moved into the tree line. I could see the river shining in the moonlight. The climb down to the water was about eight feet of the same dry, crusty dirt we found on Hill 51. Crud was walking tail, with Stu in front of him. Greek was in the middle, with Ya Ya on point, and I was walking second. I had to be near the front, as patrol leader; I needed to see firsthand what was happening.

We crossed the river slowly, one at a time. The water was only about chest high. It was actually cool, compared to the morning heat, which was just stoking up. The moon was still in full view, but the sun was showing signs of life on the opposite side of the world. The sky was just trying to wake up. I made it across and climbed up the other side. Each in turn crossed then huddled with us in silence, until all five of us were safely across. The river behind us, we set out for the trail that snaked north and south along the foothills.

Our movement was slow and deliberate. We had skin

in the game and weren't about to screw it up. Ya Ya led the way toward the village. Daylight found us before we found the village. That was okay; we were learning how long the march took. Next time, surprise would be on our side. We might not get any bad guys our first day, but there'd come a day when we would own the valley. But at that moment, I wanted to get through the day, learn some things about the village, and learn some things about us.

Six or seven yards apart, the five of us lined up to move along the trail at the base of the foothills. We moved carefully, choosing each step, until we'd reached a large dike that separated us from the village. It was about 0800 hours. Plenty of time, Kug, I told myself, patience, you got to have patience. I radioed our position back to Hill 51. I didn't want them raining lead on our heads. They gave us the A-OK; they'd seen no activity in the area that morning.

It was getting noticeably hotter as I told Ya Ya to "Move it out." We hurried, moving in a half-assed run across the dike and open area. It was spook time down there. Tall palms were everywhere, stretching thirty to forty feet into the air. The ground vegetation did damned well, I thought, despite having no rain in the dry season. Everything growing there was taller than any of us. And thick. You couldn't see Jack Shit if you stepped on him.

Ya Ya found a Y in the trail up ahead. I told him to take the right; we'd save the left for another day. But we needed to get moving, I didn't like being exposed. He picked up the pace but with the deliberate caution of a great point. Before long, I was winded and sweating as if I'd just stepped out of the shower. All the "good times" back home last month were boiling out of me. The trip home had messed with my chemistry, and I was half-sick. It'd take a while to get back to fighting shape.

We were moving up along the village edge. The trail was visible from the foothills. It was open in places, and we could be seen. There was danger in the air, I could feel it. We stopped as I conferred with each of the guys, then started up again, moving deeper into the eye of the storm. At that stage, we moved very, very slowly. It was broad daylight by then, and my gut told me something was in the air.

We were about halfway by the village, where the trail was completely grown over in places. But the area was full of booby traps, and Ya Ya was moving very carefully, each step in a deliberate, catlike motion. He was raising his leg high, stepping straight down, then repeating the same, slow, cautious motion, time and time again. Going through sticks and bushes across a trail is number-one, nerve-racking shit. I could see over Ya Ya's shoulder. The trail was opening up, maybe we were out of the jungle farther ahead.

Ya Ya was about ten yards straight ahead when he froze in his tracks! He gave me the sign to be quiet, so I passed it along. Five men, frozen by fear, were motionless in the morning heat of Nam. It was a nameless village. There was a small paddy and some foothills behind it to my right. My heart was racing. Shaking, I knelt down and turned toward the village. There was a small opening, with grass about three feet high. Ya Ya's hand was cupped to his ear. He heard something. We froze in position for what seemed like hours, but then mere moments play big when the air's thick with anxiety.

I slowly stood, trying to step up to Ya Ya. Upright, I scanned the jungle to my left, into the village. I couldn't believe my eyes. A little dink bastard was crouched less than fifteen feet from me, dressed in black, rifle in hand, and ready to go. But he was looking the other way. I looked back to Greek and motioned that I have one in sight. Ya Ya saw me, and moved back for a look.

I had my M-14 at the ready and my balls in my throat. He was in open-sight range. I had Greek on one side and Ya Ya on the other. I motioned both to cover me and started creeping in for the kill. The little guy was motioning to someone back in the bush but I couldn't see them. Crud was covering one direction on the trail, and Stu moved up past Ya Ya to cover the other. Okay, motherfucker, I'm coming in! I moved one step in, then two, closing in on three. I got a bead on his head straight through the 14's sights. I had adrenaline pushing out my eyeballs. I held the 14 tight as I walked, asshole puckered tight like a vise. I wanted the little fucker to look at me . . . right before I pulled the trigger and blew his fucking head off. I was stretching out for step four . . . just then . . . he turned. Fuck! He saw me . . . there's the slow motion again. He started pulling up his rifle. I pulled the trigger on full auto! *Brrrrrrrp! Brrp! Brrp!* I emptied half a magazine into his ugly ass. Someone was running in the weeds behind him. I turned and fired again. Greek and Ya Ya were firing, too! And then it was over. There was no return fire. None.

As fast as my trigger finger ignited the chaos, it was over. A few precious seconds of terror followed by the emptiness of dead silence. With Stu and Crud as cover, Greek, Ya Ya, and I walked into the edge of the village. It was thick with underbrush. I motioned them back out to the trail. I knelt down and searched the body. It was a kid. What the hell am I saying? *I* was a fucking kid. Well, he was younger than I was. He had an M-1 carbine, a World War II–era .30-caliber weapon. Probably got it off the worthless ARVNs. I took a couple of Chicom grenades out of his backpack. The little bastard was probably going to set them as booby traps. Guaranteed! What little remorse I might have felt for a second flew right out the window. I stood up over him and looked down. Ho Chi Minh sandals, black pajamas, a real VC, right before my eyes. Well, he was a loser; I was standing, and he was not. Ya Ya led us on without incident. We returned to the hill that afternoon.

A kill at ten feet my first day out. That was exhilarating. I'd never been that close to the result of my work before. Well, now that I had been, it didn't make any difference. Maybe I was made for the work? What I knew was sniper patrols would work. We could go out and make a difference.

We ran patrols in the valley near 51 on into late June. Greek got a kill, Stu and Crud, and me, too. Ya Ya hit a dry spell. He was worried about rotating home without another kill. What the hell could I say? I got word from Evans that one of our guys had bought the big one. Dead in the head. News? There was more, Wiener, back from R & R, wanted to come back to 51 and the Rogues. And the last news was best: our dead sniper had been up for R & R and the headquarters lieutenant wanted to know if I wanted it? Hell, it didn't bother me, I'd go to Hong Kong. So Wiener came out to lead the Rogues, and I went the other direction, to Hong Kong again.

I loved Hong Kong. It cost me my savings, but what the hell. I actually found a dude I'd met on the street last time, when I'd run out of money and still had two days left on my stay. I hocked my Marine Corps ring, with a diamond in it, to the dude for five dollars. What the hell, it bought me some more booze. Then I hocked him my watch. I don't know, none of it meant a hell of a lot anymore; I guess it meant something to him, though, he remembered me and yelled at me on the street. The second time in Hong Kong, I took $650 and spent it all, double last time. I don't know what it was about the place, but I loved it.

I was half-sick from the booze and the heat. Flying back into Evans from R & R, I wondered how Wiener and the Rogues were doing. Off the chopper, I took time to barf before the long walk to our tent. I walked in and tossed my gear down on my wooden rack. It must have been about 1400, and I was dying from the heat. The booze was pouring out of me, giving me the chills. I had just sat down and in walked an even newer guy than before. He said, "Hi, did you hear about the snipers that just got messed up?" I jumped up and ran down to COC. It had to be Wiener and the Rogues.

At COC, the news wasn't good. And to top it off, the colonel was pissed about what happened and how it was handled. I just wanted the facts. Wiener had taken on a new guy, a loudmouth from Philly. Ya Ya had decided he was too short to risk himself doing what we were doing so he opted to come back to the rear. That left the point man position open, and he put Greek on point. I agreed with that decision, but not with taking the new guy on Rogue patrols. At that point, the rest of the details were sketchy. They'd taken sniper fire near Booby Trap Ville, as we'd begun to call the site of my close-in kill. Then nobody was sure what the fuck happened. Greek was in critical condition down at 3d Med, and the new guy was fucked up, too. Well, fuck the new guy, but I had to get to Greek.

I took off for 3d Med on the run. I caught a chopper just leaving the pad at Evans. I was airborne in minutes. I'd have to work with the colonel on our Rogue patrols when I got back. It was a short hop, we landed, and I raced off to 3d Med. Inside, a corpsman tried to intercept me before I got to Greek. He finally gave in; corpsmen are real people and they do take care of the troops. He took me to Greek's tent, where rows of cots were filled with the unfortunate bastards assigned the duty of clinging to life. It was a sauna in there. It was also a sad place to find yourself on an afternoon off. I find the Greek and sit down next to his cot. I take hold of his good hand. The other hand is bandaged all the way up above the elbow. He's got more tubes running in and out of him than the engine on an AA Fuel Dragster. My main man was looking bad. The corpsman had already told me he'd lost a leg.

I couldn't believe it; I left the guy for one week, and he launched his damned self. He knew better. Something happened, dammit! I sat there as he struggled to come to life. He looked like a corpse with no coffin. I knew he had to be flying higher than an F-4 with all the drugs they'd shot into him.

His right eye opened slightly, and I squeezed his hand. He tried again and again to regain consciousness. After several tries, he got both eyes to open. I don't know if they were seeing anything, but they were open. He couldn't focus well, so I just kept gently squeezing his hand. I kept saying, "It's Kug . . . you'll make it . . . it'll work out." Over and over, not believing a word of it myself, I reassured him.

He finally mustered the strength and the courage to say, "Kug, thanks for comin'." I looked him in the slits that were once his eyes and told him once again he'd be okay. He could overcome anything. He got an expression on his face that I knew would be that New York smile, if only it were a day for smiling. But his face just wouldn't cooperate, and he continued to look like certain death on an uncertain afternoon. He tried squeezing my hand but all I could feel was the strength of an old lady on the way out. He was weak and only a whisper of the guy I'd left a week before.

I started telling him what he faced, what'd happened and then he stopped me, saying, "Kug, it's okay," and with a long, long pause for a precious breath, "I'll just have a helluva time dancin' again . . . I'll be listing to the starboard side."

Fuckin'-A. He was still my main man.

I left him as he drifted back to never-never land at 3d Med. He was going to Japan in the morning. When he improved enough, he'd go on to New York. Of all things, I had to leave him with the promise to retrieve his boot. He wanted the boot Wiener had removed from his mangled leg. It was still out in the valley somewhere, and I had to find it for him.

I caught a lift back to Evans. The Rogues came back in, too. Wiener told me the story. I'd hated fucking booby traps before, and now I hated them more. They were always avoidable. I sensed the new guy had fucked this up. It took a toll on Wiener, and he didn't want to run patrols anymore. It'd be better that way, since the colonel was pissed about what just happened. Greek was gone for good, the new guy was fucked up, and we had to score one for the gooks. They'd pay.

I convinced the colonel that all was well. Snipers could be extremely effective in the valley, but we couldn't take out men just in from the States. He agreed to give me another chance to prove the concept. I was elated. I went back and lined up the team for another shot at the valley. I'd take Stu, Crud, my rebel Hood, and me. We'd go out with four. I'd just been made sergeant, and that felt good; we didn't play the rank game in the bush. But hey, it gave me a few more dollars a month to drink away or put away. And I needed some booze that day.

At the club, I sat down with Wiener to talk over what took place in the ville. Greek apparently hit a big booby trap as he was trying to stop the new guy. He said Greek flew in the air, higher than he was tall, which is over six feet. He did a backflip and came down in a twisted, crumpled heap. Wiener didn't think he'd make it for a while, or even when they flew him out for that matter. Wiener wasn't having a good day. He got up suddenly and left the club. That was unusual.

I'd had enough and walked outside a little after Wiener. I walked between the rows of hootches that led me home, and finally I spotted Wiener sitting alone in the dirt. As I walked up, he was holding a toad in his hand. It was four inches long, maybe five. He said, "Watch this, Kug, I'll blow some fuckin' minds." He sat down in the walkway and started playing with the little creature. I started to walk away when some Marines walked by from the club. "Watch this, Kug, watch," Wiener said almost childlike as they walked by and said hi. Wiener stared right at 'em. They were looking back and wondering what was up. I was too. Then Wiener took the toad, put its head in his mouth . . . then *crunch*, *slurp*, and tear! He bit its head off. The crazy bastard just sat there with a toad head in his mouth, bloody end hanging out . . . and the body in his hand. He was frozen in an empty stare aimed at the bewildered Marines.

They hightailed it out of there like NVA running from the Rogues. They didn't want any part of the guy about now, and neither did I. He was fried. He turned to me and said, "I told ya it'd blow their minds."

"Yeah, Wiener, you even blew my fuckin' mind with that one," I said with some wonder and a lot of disbelief.

I got the Rogues ready for our trip to Hill 51. Wiener needed to stay in the rear. He should only work with the grunts when he had to. Ya Ya too. They were both getting short. Wiener was trying to hold it together to get home, and Ya Ya was worried about whether his old lady would be there to meet him. She was still pissed about his six-month extension. And then there was Harley. Ever since he'd taken that hit upside the head, he'd lost some of his piss and vinegar. I realized I'd have to start over again and handpick the Rogues. It wasn't the kind of assignment for everybody.

Before going to 51, I'd picked up my mail. I got a little news from the States. There was a letter from the girl I'd met on leave. She was gaga over me. Oh man, she was a real nice girl, certainly nicer than I was used to dating. Her dad was even a former Marine. That was a plus. But I just wasn't about to get serious at that point. I wasn't serious about anything but the Rogues. I threw out her letter and picked up a postcard, a cryptic note from Zulu with a picture of a state mental hospital . . . now that fits. He said he hated the Corps Stateside. He'd already been written up and wanted to come back. He hoped to join the 26th Marines that were forming on the coast. He figured that would be his best chance to get back to Nam. Well, if he'd have listened to me, he'd have been a Rogue. Man, he'd have made one hell of a Rogue.

CHAPTER SEVEN

The Work, the Valley, and the Rogues

Hill 51 seemed like home. It was Stu, Crud, Hood, and me. The grunts we knew there had changed out; a new grunt outfit was guarding the place. They rotated like the wind. Now came the reeducation program. The biggest problem we had was that no one knew how to use us. The lieutenant said we could do whatever we wanted but that we were to keep him informed and stay out of the grunts' way. Most of them don't want to do any more than they're asked or required to do, so his request was no problem for us.

After the lieutenant cleared us for our work, it was time to rock 'n' roll. The Rogues weren't going to sit back and do the predictable. The way I figured it, the gooks wouldn't ever expect us to show up in the ville again so soon. I got the guys together, and we agreed to return to where I knocked the gook's head off. We decided to leave early, at 0300 hours, to get set in on the east side of the village before daybreak. It was risky, but we could get in.

I crowned Hood my point man. He didn't say anything, but he didn't leave footprints and had the balls of a big gorilla. He was my man. Stu was six feet four inches of pure badass. He was a great guy to have around when you needed to run through a wall or knock down a tree. Crud, he was crazy as all hell and good for laughs. That is if you could take his unending chatter about the time machine he was going to build when he got "outta here." Together we were small enough, crazy enough, and ballsy enough to pull off a Rogue patrol.

Hood led us out at 0300 sharp. It was to be just a one-day trip, but we were still loaded for bear. We all carried M-14s. Stu and Crud packed 06s on their backs. We knew where we were going and our only fear was what surprise the little assholes might have left along the trail.

We made the river in good time. Hood headed us to the trail that ran around the village. With just four of us, we learned we could move quickly and still not sound like a five-hundred-pound gorilla. Our faces shined in the night. I didn't like that, but we didn't have the face paint we needed. So we used charcoal from burned wood and smeared it on our faces. Sweat made it run, but it worked better than nothing. We made it to the east end of the village undetected. There was no sign of life anywhere. We stood at a trail junction where our trail met up with one coming from across the paddies. I could see out across the paddies to a tree line a hundred or so yards away. Behind us was a small hill, a hump maybe ten meters high. It was covered in elephant grass five feet tall. I decided we should take up position on the side of the hill behind us. They'd never believe anyone would hide in the grass on that hill.

I motioned to Hood, and he led us up the steep grade. We moved slowly and deliberately, pulling the grass back up behind us as we went. That was a trick I'd learned from Sergeant Lich in Force Recon a year ago. We sat down and camouflaged ourselves with elephant grass. Then the waiting started. Who can wait the longest? I knew if we had the patience, the bad guys would have the balls to come out and play.

By 0900, we hadn't seen shit. Stu wanted to pack it in. Crud was still asleep, and Hood and I were on the 7×50s checking out the area. I knew most of the good hunting came the first hour of daylight or the last. But I also knew to go with your gut, and my gut said this is it. Around us to the front were antique rice paddies, running left to right. Directly across was a tree line with some real dense vegetation behind it. Any shot we got from here would be two hundred yards or less. It was getting hot out. Vietnam was so hot we never got used to it. We didn't have much cover besides the tall grass. Hell, we couldn't even stand and take a piss. This could be a long afternoon.

Hood lay back to blow some Zs. Stu and I were doing the scoping out. I was walking my 7×50s down the tree line to my right . . . *bingo!* We got us a bad guy. I see him peering through the bushes. He was looking all around. I pointed Stu to his position. He was well within the free-fire zone, and he was a bad guy or he wouldn't care if anyone saw him coming. Stu got his 06 and sighted in. It'd be 175 meters when he pulled the trigger. The little gook obviously didn't know we were there or he wouldn't have even considered walking that trail.

Stu was anxious to knock the guy into tomorrow, but I wanted to wait and see if he had buddies hanging out in the weeds. I didn't want fifty of those little mothers coming out there to do a rain dance on our young asses. We waited, and it was 1030 hours and smoking outside. And damned if *we* weren't outside. Sweat was pouring off. I'd had it with that guy's eyeball-fucking the neighborhood. "Stu, ace the dude," I whispered.

Boom! I was spotting and—shiiit! Stu hit the guy dead center—right in the forehead. "Stu, you gave him a third eye, man, what a shot!" I said, louder than I should have. Crud and Hood woke up from their siesta. I immediately motioned to keep them down. The loser had been waiting an hour or so on something or someone.

Our hot morning ground on into the afternoon. The afternoon was hotter. I got some sleep, and we held tight, sitting four abreast, on the side of our little knoll. We watched the area where Stu delivered the third eye. Nobody showed up. It was getting on past 1400 hours, and I wanted one more hour to play my hunch to the finish. Stu and Crud had to piss. I told 'em they'd have to go sitting down because there was one more doofus coming our way. We waited, and 1500 came and went. Now Hood wanted us to "went." I couldn't give up, even if the vote was three to one for getting the fuck out of there. I could feel another gook.

A few more minutes passed, and I couldn't believe my eyes. A gook came out of the tree line across from us. He was on the trail that ran right at our damned position. He didn't have a care in the world. He had a small pack on his back and didn't appear to have a rifle. He was at seventy-five meters and closing. I tell Crud to get ready and shoot when I give him the signal. It was too good to be true. He was at fifty meters and Crud wants a go . . . hold . . . twenty-five meters . . . hold . . . ten meters . . . *Fire!—boom!*

Shiiit! He hit the guy in the leg. The little bastard did a flip and hit the ground. Before I could say gook, he was up and running. Stu was up chasing him, and I took off after them, bringing up dead last. The little guy was trucking down one of the old dry paddies, but Stu's six-foot-four stride was eating the guy up. I was running along behind and realized it didn't help him much that he had one leg shot up. Three or four strides later, Stu brought his 14 in a roundhouse swing coming all the way from downtown and struck right in the middle of the gook's back. The bad guy went sprawling, face first into the dirt. Stu stopped, standing over him and looking down. As I ran up, he blew the gook away. *Brrrp!* I said, "Stu, what the hell? You coulda got some R & R for bringing him in." He looks up at me with that no-bullshit look of his and says, "Kug, I just didn't think about it. Fuck 'im. Let's get the hell outta here!" We saddled up and got out of there.

Before we left, I searched the dead man's pack and took out some Chicoms and other booby-trap paraphernalia. We headed off for 51. We were so high, we nearly walked the river without getting wet. I knew that we could kick ass in small units. The bad guys never expected us to be out sneaking around like them; we'd have to do a lot of change-ups and fuck with their minds.

We continued running four-man patrols into July. Hell, I was halfway through my six-month extension, and things were just getting interesting. Det Cord re-upped again. I was glad, and lots of other folks were nervous. He was one bright dude. He'd taught himself the language and became our interpreter. He didn't have a lot of common sense, but hell, he'd have gone to Hanoi if I'd asked him.

By mid-July, blowing minds, as Wiener called it, took the Rogues by storm. One afternoon, we got a call to lead the grunts through the Booby Trap Ville. We'd been kicking back on a day off. But hell, we hadn't scouted for a while, so why not? We took off with Hood on point and the rest of us tagging along behind. When we joined up with the grunts, we put them behind us. They were worried about getting out of there by dark. Shiiit! They have a whole damned squad with them . . . who cares?

Hood got maybe twenty yards when he spotted a booby trap right on the trail, a Chicom triggered by catgut stretched across the trail. We had C4 and blasting caps, but to use all that just to detonate a grenade . . . Hood said, "Hey, let's blow some minds, Kug." I gave him the thumbs-up and took the rest of the Rogues back with the grunts. I told the grunt sergeant that it'd just be a minute. I looked up just as Hood was laying one of our hand grenades down, right on top of the Chicom. Then he ran, yelling "Fire in the hole!" He got just about to us when he dived head first and *kaboom!* Dirt and shrubs flew everywhere. The sergeant looked at me, then at Hood, with a real strange look on his face. I said, "Sarge, you wanted out of here by dark, and hey—the trail is clear." He shook his head and motioned for us to go. It was a neat trick perfected by Wiener, and it did save a lot of time. You just had to make sure you cleared the path you were running away on first!

When August came, we were doing good in the kill department. We'd jumped up into double figures, but I wanted us to reach farther out in the valley with our patrols. We found the gooks were staying away when we were in the area. So I wanted to expand the neighborhood a little. I'd kept things to single-day patrols with a couple of four-dayers that went out maybe four grid squares. I convinced the crew to head south, below the footbridge Harley had loved so well. Except I'd take us across the river upstream of that damned bridge. It was a hell of a lot harder to cross in the daytime when you could see, believe me. Our little band of merry men was finally in agreement. The tough part would be getting through a little pass in the foothills. Harley's footbridge connected to a trail that ran across the valley, over the river, and into the foothills. It eventually went to the villages along Highway 1, just above Hue. We decided on a two-day trip.

We took off at midnight to allow us enough time to cross the river near 51. We made the crossing okay and took off along the trail running at the base of the foothills. We wanted to negotiate the pass before daybreak. We'd sit in and see what was happening down that way. All went well as far as the draw, as we'd begun to call it. But the draw was scary as hell. Hood started up the trail between the two hills. It was narrow, with bushes growing on either side. When we got up into it, it reminded me of walking through tall cornstalks. You had to look up to see the light of the moon. It was perfect for an ambush on *us*. But that was not what was worrying me that night; the bad guys didn't know we were coming, I was sure of that. But I didn't want to meet up with a few of them on the trail. Hood was cautious and deliberate and got us to the top of the hill. Things opened up, and with the help of the moonlight washing the scene, we got a clue what the area was like. We were in the tops of a group of small foothills on the east side of the valley, about seven grid squares out from friendlies. It would be great hunting, but it also scared the hell out of me.

Hood stopped to check directions with me. It was 0330 hours, and we had maybe ninety minutes to get set in. The shooting was best right at dawn or just before dusk. I could feel it; it was a great place. We moved down between two foothills that I hoped overlooked the valley floor. The river should be right below us, giving us natural protection once we fired and exposed our position. When we reached the face of the hill, Hood got us down on all fours, and we crawled around the front, facing the valley. It was 0415 when he had us set in place. The grass was four feet or so high. We burrowed in as best we could, camouflaged ourselves with vegetation. They'd never, ever expect us there. I knew that. What I didn't know was how many gooks there were or how they felt about strangers.

First light showed itself around 0500 hours. Everyone was on watch until we could see what we were dealing with. Stu and I took the 7×50s to scope out the place. We hit the jackpot. The river was just below us. Along the river, a big tree line ran on either side. The river and the tree line formed a giant, backward C as we looked out in front of us. All of it was surrounded by dead rice paddies. Directly across from us, at the top of the C, it looked like there was a deserted village in the trees. To our left were more tree lines, abandoned villages, and opportunities to knock someone away. Patience would win the day.

It was about 0700 when we first got a sighting. There was movement at the very start of the backward C in the tree line. It was about four hundred meters away. We could hear chopping, and then there was a small stream of smoke coming up through the trees. Crud was out and up behind us, watching our asses. He'd lead us out if we got hit. Stu and I had our rifles at the ready. I'd take the shot. Both of us were using the 06s we carried. Hood was covering us to the front and sides. It was not quite 0720 when the bad guy came strumming out of the bush with some serious weight stacked on his shoulder. We couldn't make out what it was and didn't have time to waste trying. It was a free-fire zone, so his showing up was reason enough for us to stop his breathing.

Stu laid down his 06 and got the binoculars to spot for me. I followed the gook as he tightroped along an old paddy dike. He was apparently headed across the two hundred meters of dike that led to the trail and into the tree line on the other side. He was about thirty meters out when I lined up the crosshairs, squeezed the tit of my girl, and *boom!* Shiiit! I missed the little bastard, and he took off. My first fucking miss, and it was at only four hundred meters. Dammit! My round struck just to the right and behind the bad guy. The little dude jumped straight up into the air, turned, and sped off back into the tree line, load and all. Before I could chamber another round, he was gone!

The Kug had missed! How the hell did I do it? I'd sure as hell get some shit when I got back. But just then we were concerned that we didn't get some shit back at us. Stu watched the tree line. Nothing. We waited, knowing that the bad guy was trying to figure out where we were. I decided to call some arty on his ass. I called back to Evans and gave them the coordinates. The spotter round came in and was right on the money. I followed quickly with a "Fire for effect." It was beautiful if it was anything. I don't know if I got the bad guy, but I sure as hell killed a bunch of trees.

At around 1430 hours, we called it a day. There were no more signs of life. We low-crawled out of position just in case. Once around the side of the hill, we stood up and Hood led us on to our first night position. The remainder of the patrol was a bummer. We discovered a couple of booby traps on the way in to Hill 51; we disarmed one and brought it in as a souvenir. I let Crud practice blowing minds on the other. He about tripped and blew his own mind. We had to watch him. When he was thinking about Plato, we were all in trouble.

Back at 51, life became routine. We'd run our patrols

for a day or two, come in and kick back for a day, then do it all over again. I was planning to lengthen our stride and go out farther and longer. Stu supported me but thought I was crazy. Hood didn't give a shit, and Crud didn't know where the hell he was, so his vote didn't count. We were getting it on good with the grunts on the hill as they started tallying our results. They were sure we were crazy for going out the way we did. The four of us alone and at night no less, that didn't compute for the grunts. They feared the night. We learned to make it our ally. We tried our damnedest to keep the gooks guessing. We mixed up our directions, times of day, and how we set in. We pushed the patrols out to four days and three nights. We were bad or, as grunts say, "blown outta'r minds."

Eventually it was time to go back and check out Booby Trap Ville. Hood was leading the way when he stopped dead in his tracks. It was 0 dark 30, we were in deep underbrush, and couldn't see shit. He was standing there, frozen, and I didn't like it. I edged my way up close to him and whispered, "Hood, get the fuck going." I stepped back and waited. He was turning around, motioning. He didn't signal he heard something. He wasn't cupping his ear. I stepped back up and he grabbed my jungle shirt, pulling me toward him. I looked and he was motioning *down*. Oh shit! The man's *on* something. Can't be, not Hood. I leaned up, my ear to his mouth, and he said, "Kug, there's a trip wire caught on my foot. I can't move. I'm already leaning forward."

Could he be right? He'd not screwed me yet. I tell Hood to hold tight. I go back and tell Stu and Crud to cover us while we sort this out. It's darker than midnight in a black cave. Some son of a bitch was going to run into us, I just knew it. Stu stood behind us, facing ahead, and

Crud was facing backward behind him. I knelt down next to Hood and, with my right hand, worked my way down his leg. My hand reached his right boot top and, ever so gently, I slid my fingers down each lace. *Bingo!* Damned if there wasn't the tiniest piece of wire stretched right across his boot. How the hell did he feel that? He's like a damned cat. He'd just saved his and my ass from a body full of hot metal in the middle of the night. We stopped long enough to unhook his ass, and survived to fight another day.

With the patrol behind us, almost a week out and not a gook seen, we were just tripping our way back in. Hood was out front and a round whistled overhead! We hit the deck, looking around ... like where the hell did that come from? We were about five hundred yards to the south of Hill 51, coming through a deserted and burned-out village. It was god-awful hot. I just wanted to get back up to the hill for a break. Four days was a long time out there. Hood looked around and saw no one. None of us did. We took off, just trying to get back up on 51.

We were walking along, about thirty yards down the trail, when *crack, crack, crack* ... bullets whizzed overhead. The bastards got close enough to get our attention. Down we go, faces buried in the dirt. Without a word, we cover each other, leapfrogging our way to the edge of a village. Our nerves were riding high in the saddle. That was the third time that morning that some bastard had taken a shot at us. We didn't even pay attention to the first one.

We waited, and nothing happened. We'd no choice but to get moving. Crud makes his way to the tail end. We move out with all eyes on the tree lines around us. There was nothing there. I yell, "Quit pissing with 'em. Let's get back there before we're SOL, man!" The sniper hadn't hit anyone with three tries, so I say, "Let's take off and let the little bastard shoot."

One more time, we were up and on with our journey to Hill 51 and our booze. It was hotter than hell and showing real promise of becoming a bad afternoon. We started making good time moving along the valley trail to Hill 51. To our right front was a paddy, with an old village on our left. The village was overgrown with wild vegetation. It even had an open area with old, beaten-down paddies inside. We got another forty or fifty yards, and here came the familiar *crack*, *crack*, *crack* sounds again as a muffled *whiz* flew overhead. That time we didn't even hit the deck. I turned around and realized we were all standing defiantly, staring back into the village. The balls the little bastard had, sniping at snipers!

Hood turned and walked off toward 51, muttering, "Fuck the little bastard, I've had it." We all followed like zombies, baking in the noonday sun. Hallucinating about foaming beer as we walked. Wondering what would possess some guy to fuck with us? I mean, we'll eventually get his ass. The neighborhood was going to shit. We were making an impact, or they wouldn't have wasted the ammo on us.

As we walked in, the heart of the old village was on our left. Fences that once corralled pigs lay on their sides. The area was shaped like a U, thirty yards deep, and surrounded by twenty-foot trees. Hood stopped us to take a swig of warm water from his canteen. All four of us were standing in a row, catching our breath when . . . *crack, zing* . . . a round whizzed overhead! We were standing with maybe ten or twelve feet separating all four of us, then we were asshole to belly button down and dirty. He still missed.

It all happened so fast, no one said a word. It was sur-
real. Maybe it was the heat? I know it was weird. We
were standing there lined up like bowling pins, and the
dude missed us *again*? We glanced at each other, our
eyes met, and not a word was said. We'd had enough already. We were the Rogues, and it was *our* fucking valley.
Without a word or a signal, we looked at each other and
back at the tree line and—within seconds—we took off
running like Indians on a warpath. Charge! We were on
line, shooting, yelling, and screaming.

Under the trees at the back of the U, the shooting finally stopped. One dumb gook lay dead, apparently
falling out of a tree. Hell, none of us remembered seeing
him fall. Shit, maybe he shot himself when he saw us
coming? I stood there for a minute and realized what
we'd just done. What had happened to us? Crud thought
it was the coolest thing. Stu just wanted the fuck out of
there, and I knew it was all pretty dumb. Hood got us on
track again, and the heat helped us recover from the high
we'd just experienced. One gook sniper dead. We left
him behind, minus one ear, the one Crud always liked to
bring with him after a kill.

Back on 51, the lieutenant, King of the Grunts, called
me in. He said, "Sergeant Kugler, I was looking through
one of the scopes on the tanks when you had that skir-
mish earlier."

I said simply, "Yes, sir." I thought maybe he was pissed
about Crud's ear collection.

The lieutenant continued, with a serious, concerned
look on his face, saying, "I saw what you did out there
today. Charging that sniper. Why the hell did you tell
them to do it?"

He hadn't been around us long. He didn't know that
you didn't tell the Rogues anything. I said, "Sir, I didn't

tell 'em to do it, it just happened." He talked on, expressing his concern for our well-being. I believed he actually meant it. But he didn't understand us, and I didn't want him to. I liked to keep it all a mystery.

We took a day off and each enjoyed our two beers, the daily "standard issue" for the Corps. I spent my night off reflecting on where we were. I got a letter from Greek, and he was convinced, beyond a shadow of a doubt, that God was saving me for something. He'd lost his leg on the first patrol he'd gone on without me. He was with me on several near misses. The arty that fell between us and crapped out, a dud. The punji pit, the Chicom, and then what Hood wrote him about the other encounters. He was a good Catholic boy, and he was convinced I was saved. But religion didn't fit in my view of the world. I just couldn't buy that shit. But I loved him anyway, and what a sense of humor my main man had. He wrote his return address as, "The Philadelphia Body and Fender Shop." I hoped he kept it up and I hoped the Philly Naval Hospital could help him with the missing leg. I hoped I'd get a longer break, but I didn't.

The COC was beginning to like our work. They started to assign us places to go. Tonight, it was another trip down to "Johan's Place." "Johan" was the name I gave the little bastard I missed the first time. Since then, Stu and Crud had missed him, too. I didn't know what was up with this guy, but he had nine damned lives. We rarely missed, and we'd missed his ugly ass three times. We all voted to nominate him for the Vietnamese Olympic track team.

Hood was out front once again. He was taking us back into the foothills by Johan's. That time he wanted the shot. We had to get in before sunrise, that's for sure. It was hot and it was dark, and all we had with us was the light of the silver moon. My mirror back to the World had begun to vanish, along with my daydreams of the life I once knew. The Hood had to be point man of the century. If I'd notched my leg every time he saved my ass, it would have fallen off weeks ago. I'd follow the guy anywhere. That night we were sneaking into our favorite spot. I hated coming through the draw, but Hood threaded the needle one more time. The draw made my balls rattle with fear.

We made it up to the top of the hills and were moving down and around the front of the hill that was to be home that day. Hood was creeping catlike, poised and ever ready! I wanted him to hurry the hell up; I wanted in there before first light. Just get in and kick some gook ass in the early morning sun. And kick it on our terms, not theirs. That had been the key to our success. Then *di di* the fuck out of there. So I wanted to hurry the hell up, but Hood was not hurrying that night.

I learned long ago not to screw with the master. The Hood ruled supreme out there. I'd walked point more than once and knew the feeling. Your nerves were wired tight, adrenaline pumped your veins full to exploding. The last thing the Hood needed was an asshole sergeant pushing him. You don't screw the guy on point, he has your ass and everyone else's ass in his hands and feet. He was heading straight down the side of the hill. The grass on the face was shoulder high. It was steep, and we were going down close together. We had to be quick but quiet. But what the fuck was this shit tonight?

We hadn't found any booby traps out here. So let's hope tonight isn't a first. I'd been getting concerned lately. COC'd been wanting us down here more than we should be. We had to throw change-ups at the little bastards if we wanted to live a little longer. But Hood was slow that night. My mind started playing bad tapes. I was wired, and the night was wasting away. It was about 0400, and reveille down there at Johan's place was right close. Come on, man!

Despite my occasional whispered jabs, Hood remained unshaken. He just maintained his methodical pace. I knew we were about there, we had to be. We were almost to the bottom where we turned left. The grass was slippery with the early morning humidity. I was on Hood's ass, and Stu and Crud were up mine. I hated being so close in the bush. If one guy bought the prize, we'd all share in the winnings.

Confident we were near our position for the morning shoot, I stepped in right behind Hood. *Fuck!* Hood slipped and began to fall. I planted my right foot in the ground to hold me up. Then I reached out and grabbed Hood's pack. I was holding him up when he turned over his shoulder and said, "Don't move, Kug, I'm caught!" Caught, shit! He was leaning back with his right leg straight out and down in front of him. His left leg was doubled back, almost like he was going to sit on it. The hill was so steep that Hood was almost standing straight up, with my help.

He was saying something else to me. Something about a booby trap. A booby trap out here? Right now? I told him to shut up. Noise was a damned magnet out here. I whispered to him, "What are you saying?" Hood was cool, and he turned with, "Kug, you hold me up now. I've got a trip wire on my left foot."

"Are you sure?" I said, unable to hide either my disbelief or my terror. What the hell was I doing questioning the guy? He'd done it before, just not with me stuck up his exhaust pipe.

I was already four or five lives deep following his ugly

rebel ass. That booby trap had to be plumb-bob straight below our balls. I was holding his pack and my sex life in my own fucking hands. Hood turned to me, and he was as serious as a heart attack. I got Stu, who was behind me, to reach over and grab Hood's pack. We still had to hold Hood in place. I sat down, carefully and slowly, moving into position to get hold of the trip wire. Stu was the right guy to hold him up; he was strong as the bulls he'd left back home in Nebraska. I sat down, sliding one leg on either side of Hood. If it went off, the thing was going to blow me where the sun don't shine. "Work slow, my man," I said to myself. I needed all the encouragement I could get.

I reached down his leg one more time. I was worried about time. I needed to figure out how to take care of the damned thing. I didn't want to save our asses from the booby trap only to have daylight come and get shot by some badass down below. It was still dark, and even with the moon, I couldn't see shit. But I could still feel. Crud was up behind and trying to stay back in case the worst came. He'd have to get the three of us out. That was a scary thought all by its lonesome.

I slid my hand back down his leg to his boot to get hold of the wire. Hood leaned down, and whispered, "Kug, that feels good, turns me on." What an asshole! I found his laces and sure enough, on his left leg, the one bent back, was a trip wire. The wire was caught between the bottom lace and his toe. I whispered to Hood, "That fucking slip of yours about blew both of us a new ass." He let me know he'd never let me down, and that was a fact.

I followed the trip wire over to the right. Nothing! It was just tied off to a bush. Time was ticking. If we didn't get out of there soon, we were going to have a party on our hands. I reached to the left and, hey, there was another Chicom grenade. Just like the one I had tripped with Pearl. It was set in the Y of a bush.

I couldn't see and didn't have time to disarm it. We lifted Hood up and over the wire. We couldn't take time to blow it. First, they'd hear us, and second, we'd be sitting there in the open. Neither of those were good options about then. Once we got Hood over the wire, he got on all fours to cover the grenade. He lifted and guided each of our legs over and around the danger. He got us all over and free. I said to Hood, "I think I owe you a big kiss for that one." He drew the line on the kiss but said, "I love the way you run your hands down my legs."

That was my main man, the guy we called Hood. We'd made it by the "grace of Hood." He's the man with the magic feet. Damn he's good. But he wasn't good enough to get Johan. We registered miss number four on the dude with the rocket up his ass. This time we let him get halfway across the dike before we shot. We even got two shots off, and the guy dodged them both. The man was fast. Hell, we were starting to like him. We were getting to where we could recognize him through the 7×50s.

We got two more VC on the way back to 51. It was day three of four on the road. It was a long shot. Hood and Stu nailed the guys at about seven hundred meters. The bad guys were catching on to us. They'd been going deeper into the valley to get away from us. I needed a plan. On the way into 51, I decided to give Johan a break for a couple of weeks.

We made it back up to 51. Climbing the hill was difficult. It wasn't real big, but it was a killer on the legs. My thighs would burn like they were on fire. Inside the perimeter, a new company of grunts greeted us. The new lieutenant called me in for a chat. We hit it off right away.

He could relate to the world in the bush and the unconventional world of sniping. He was in his late twenties, older than most lieutenants. Before the Corps, he'd been a Peace Corps volunteer in Africa. My kind of guy.

Our day off was rudely interrupted by some bad news. Wiener had hit a head shot on one of the new guys in our platoon, who had only been in country maybe three months. The action was beginning to pick up again at the DMZ, and we'd sent snipers back up. But Wiener's head shot was a real freak if there ever was one. The new kid was from Minnesota. They'd been up by the Rockpile. Wiener and Cashman were with another grunt outfit in the same general area—two Marine grunt companies patrolling about seven hundred meters apart. They were in dense jungle, the weather was hot and shitty. It was Morston. He wasn't a name to me, just a face. Now, a dead one. Wiener got a head shot at seven hundred meters after asking permission to shoot. What are the chances of hitting our own guy in a group of a hundred or more? I mean there were two snipers and a hundred grunts. And he went and nailed the poor bastard. Wiener would *really* be fucked up after that. But it came down to somebody's not knowing how to read a damned map. The longer I was there, the worse the quality of Marine we received from the States. And some of the lieutenants we got . . .

I had to prepare the Rogues for another trip, a day trip. Back near the Booby Trap Ville. I kicked back to get some Zs. We were heading out at 2400 hours. I couldn't help but think of Minnesota. Hell, you didn't need a name there . . . it was a lot easier that way. I didn't really give a big shit, better him than me. That was the pact we made with each other: I love ya brother, but if one of us buys the big one today . . . better you than me. But I lay there thinking about Minnesota. He was a nice kid. I only saw him a few times. But he was nice. He prayed regularly. You can see what that got him. I remember he talked often of his mom and how much he missed her. And he went and got a third eye while an asshole like me got a bunch of dud Chicoms. Just the other day, I got another letter from Greek back in the Philly Body and Fender Shop. He's even more committed than ever to the idea that God is saving me for something. God and Vietnam in the same breath, seemed like an oxymoron to me. Sleep, that's what cured all my ills.

Morning came early those days. We spent an uneventful night and early morning snooping the edge of the ville. I was tired and bored as hell. We decided to pack it in, and started back toward 51. Our path took us across the paddies and clearing where my man, the Greek, got launched. I'd come down there before, looking for his boot. He wanted the damn thing back, but there was a frog living in it . . . and . . . well, hell, it was pretty cool. So I left it there and wrote him. He agreed to leave it. He put in a second request though. He wanted us to capture a gook for him. Then we needed to tie some det cord around his leg, the same place that he'd lost his leg, and blow the sucker off. Then of course he wanted us to leave him lying there. Man, that was a tough order. We'd have to see if we could fill it. "We'll get it," I'd written him, "we'll get it."

Nothing was happening out that day except people were melting in the heat. I saw a picture somewhere of a Vietnamese monk setting himself on fire in the street. He was said to be protesting the war; I don't think he set himself on fire, I think he just burst into flames sitting there.

We took a break to eat some canned fruit. When I sat

down, I noticed an ammo box. It was all by itself in the middle of a dried-up paddy. I got up and walked over to check it out. It was too obvious not to be something. It was an ammo box for tank rounds. There hadn't been any tanks down there for months. Curiosity could kill the Kug, but I couldn't leave the box alone any more than I could stay out of the bush.

Stu yelled, "Kug, quit fucking with the thing before you launch yourself like Greek."

"Fuck you, I'm just looking," I said. I took my K-bar out and probed the ground down around and under the box. I didn't think there was any secondary charge. Crud came over to join my ignorant exhibit of American curiosity.

Stu growled, "Now the two of you assholes, get the hell outta there. Hood and I don't want to have to pick up the pieces of your dead asses all afternoon." I looked over. Hood could give a fuck. He was sprawled out with his big bean-picker hat over his face, kicked back for the count. Crud and I agreed that we couldn't leave the box for the grunts. One of them would walk straight over there and open the damned thing.

The day was getting older, and the air was getting thicker with each passing minute. I decided to blow the sucker. No, I'd open it first. I lay down and looked in through the wooden cracks. Because of the glare of the sun, I couldn't see a thing. But I didn't think there was anything in it. For safety's sake, I put a length of parachute cord on it. I tied it onto the lid, and lay out behind it. Crud walked over with Stu. He got pissed. He came over and barked, "Asshole! You're the only sergeant I've ever liked. I'm not gonna let you blow your ass up right before my fucking eyes."

I was lying maybe ten feet from the ammo box when Stu went into his tirade. Well, it was ten feet with my arm stretched to the max anyway. Stu went into his pack and pulled out some more parachute cord. He brought it over and tied it to mine. So I was thirty feet away. Hell, that had to be plenty. Crud said, "Kug, I agree with Stu . . . I got a bad feelin' about this one. Let's get some more line." I protested like hell. It was getting late, and we needed to get back to 51. I had big plans for the next patrol, and we needed to work on them. Stu wanted me to set a charge on top of it and blow it in place.

"I'll prove you bastards wrong by opening it. It's not booby-trapped, I'm sure," I told them. By then Hood was awake, but he had no opinion on the subject.

Crud rounded up more parachute cord from Hood. With all the safety a long cord will provide, they gave me permission to pull the trigger and jerk the lid off. I lay facedown, about sixty or seventy feet away from the ammo box. The three musketeers with me lay down behind a paddy dike behind me. Hell, we were so far away we wouldn't get nuclear fallout from that distance. I lay there, quietly taking up the slack in the line of parachute cord connecting me and an errant ammo box in the middle of nowhere. When all the slack was taken up, I wrapped the cord around my right hand, leaned on my left side, and jerked hard with my right hand! *Kaaabooom!* I mean the biggest explosion I'd heard in a while went off right before my lying eyes! I mean dirt was flying up and raining down like the monsoon season turned ugly. Stu had been right! Now I'd have to listen to him all day.

Back at 51, we settled in to plan our next gig. The gooks had been moving farther out into the flatlands of the valley. We couldn't even reach 'em with our 30-06s. I was getting more and more pissed about that. I harassed the shit out of them with artillery calls, but it just wasn't the same as the eyeball-to-eyeball war we'd brought to the enemy in Co Bi Than Tan. I don't think so. I had a plan.

I sat Hood, Stu, and Crud down to lay it out. I said, "Guys, here's what I wanna do." I laid out our maps and pointed to the area where the bad guys had begun to hang out. It was about six grid squares southwest of the hill. It was flatter than a tabletop. Lots of tree lines and several deserted villages. I'd been out there with the grunts. I knew exactly where I wanted to go, and it was crazy as hell. My adrenaline was pumping.

I said, "This area, right here, is an old village. They have a couple of bunkers that save their asses when we rain arty on them. We've seen them do it but can't reach 'em with our Winchesters." I knew we were making an impact in the valley because we were disrupting the flow of things. They kept moving around us. By then they were almost out of reach.

I continued seriously, "We can sneak in here and be in place right before dawn. We know they're out doin' what a good VC does at night. They get back in here between 0630 and 0730 hours every morning." We knew that because we'd been watching them forever. "If we're in place before they get back, we'll sneak into their bunkers and wait for 'em."

"Kug, you've gone too far this time. I mean this is fucking crazy," Stu angrily yelled, jumping up and pacing the dirt floor of our squad tent.

I said, "Exactly! And that's precisely why it'll work."

Stu flew into a tirade not fit for a man his size. He was a great guy and wonderful in the bush. He was always supportive, but the new plan took him over the edge.

He said, "And, Einstein, when we get in the bunkers and they come back . . . what then? Like how the hell do we get outta there?"

I said, "Stu, we wait in the bunkers, and when they're back, we call in artillery. When they run into the bunkers, we shoot 'em."

"You are officially outta your fucking mind," Stu yelled, storming out of our hootch.

Hood thought it was a crazy idea but said, "Hey, if you think we can pull it off, I'm game." Crud, well he didn't think at all, so to him, it was just another adventure in La La Land.

It took me a good day and a half to get Stu to talk to me again about my plan. We went on a short patrol, and he still wasn't listening. "Stu, can you imagine the expressions on their faces when they first set foot in those bunkers? I mean the little bastards'll shit themselves!" I wore him down, and he finally agreed. Well, he never agreed that it was a good idea, or even something snipers—or anyone for that matter—should be doing.

But as he put it, "I think this is the dumbest fucking idea I've ever heard. But if the rest of the Rogues wanna go, then I'll do it." I got him on board and we made flight plans.

Hood and I had made plans for an R & R together in Bangkok, Thailand. He'd been wanting me to go somewhere with him for a while. When I re-upped again, they said I could have this R & R, so why not? As soon as we got the middle-of-the-valley deal in the bunkers over, we were going. I'd re-upped for three more months just the week before. The assholes said that's all they'd let me stay. There were no more six-month extensions for Kug.

Hood led us out of the 51 perimeter at 2200 hours, the earliest we'd yet left. I wanted to make sure we could take our time and be silent getting into their backyard. I walked along with the melody of the Four Seasons hit "Silence Is Golden" playing over and over in my head.

With each step, the night went even higher on the scary scale. Out in the valley, the playing field was even. I mean there weren't any rivers to put between us and the bad guys, or any hills or other natural boundaries. The four of us were stretching ourselves out into the badlands farther than we'd ever gone before.

Hood got us across the biggest open area and into a tree line. We had to skirt a deserted village surrounded by old rice paddies. Suddenly, Hood was down, crouched like a cat ready to strike. There was movement up ahead. We all froze at the ready. Hearts pumping out through our jungle jackets, assholes puckered tight, ready for whatever was making noise in the night. He had his hand cupped to his ear, forming a shell that helped to hear. There was definitely movement, lots of it. It was right out in front of us. I crept up to Hood and left Stu to cover the flanks and Crud the rear. If Crud had a brain, I'll bet it was mighty lonely back there on tail end.

I exhaled completely before talking with Hood. Another trick I learned from Sergeant Lich back in my recon days: no "lisp" sounds if done right. I hadn't been so scared for a while. I liked to have answers, and none were coming at the moment. Maybe I had been there too long? Hood and I figured we had to get off the trail and hole up for a minute or two. We needed to assess the situation better to know what we were dealing with. Hood led the four of us off into some bush. We'd sit tight and see what was coming down. That wasn't a problem for me; my asshole wouldn't be opening any time soon. With just the four of us, we couldn't take much of a hit.

The next thing I knew, I was trying to dislodge my ass from my throat. We heard noises, and here came gooks right down our trail. I didn't care what anyone said, I wasn't ambushing anybody. Twenty gooks went by within a few feet of the Rogues. I was afraid to fart for fear they'd hear me. When they'd gone, I realized the gooks had moved out there for a reason; they were there to provide cover, food, and medicine to bad guys moving somewhere south of us. There were a bunch of the assholes out there. They moved farther out in the valley to get away from us. Now we were there in the midst of them.

Stu was right all along, and he knew it. It was a bad plan. But damn, I really wanted to crawl into that bunker and call the artillery in and watch the bad guys' faces. But our problem had become how to get the hell out of there before daylight. We waited until the gooks were on their way south. Hood doubled us back, and we picked up speed getting away from there. We wanted to be able to get ourselves off the trail if another train of bad guys came chugging along. I swear Hood could see in the dark. He moved us out fast. It wasn't long, and we were back out of no-man's-land and heading back up Hill 51.

Stu berated me endlessly for nearly getting him killed. He couldn't get over my wanting to call arty in on us. Well, he'd get to run the Rogues while Hood and I went to Bangkok. There were some good guys in our sniper platoon, but there were also some idiots. With the two of us out, Stu would need some backups. He'd have to pick them because I was out of there. Hood and I caught a flight to Phu Bai and on to Da Nang for the flight out to our five days away. Stu, Crud, and his replacements caught a ride back out from Evans to Hill 51. The war went on for both of us.

Our time in Bangkok was wild and dangerous. Riding in rush-hour traffic, which was any time of the day, was a life-changing experience. A cab in front of ours hit a guy on a Vespa scooter and killed him deader than John Wilkes Booth. And what did the cops directing traffic do? They took chalk and drew an outline around him, leaving him dead right there in the street, presumably to wait on the real cops or the ambulance. Then things really picked up. Hood and I went into a bar and downed a few shooters when next thing we knew it was lights out. I woke up in the back of a bar, Hood found himself in a damned gutter. We'd been drugged and rolled. I was down a couple hundred dollars and Hood a hundred. It was all uphill from that great beginning. I can't say we left Bangkok hating it, but it sure wasn't Hong Kong. Not even close to that.

By the time we hit Da Nang on the rebound, we were two sick motor scooters. I thought for sure I had malaria. I had the shivers and the shakes, and it must've been 110 degrees outside. Hood had the dry heaves, and we both realized we were suffering from alcohol withdrawal. I realized I had stooped pretty low in life, but didn't care much. We caught the morning plane to Phu Bai, the one Zulu and I used to catch on our way home. We hit Evans in the early afternoon and ran smack dab into bad news again. Real bad news.

Stu had taken the Rogues out the way we had planned. The first night out he and Crud hit the big one. He had Crud on point, which wasn't the greatest choice, but it was his only choice at the time. Crud was out front, and Stu, as the patrol leader, was second. Then one of them tripped a booby trap. Shrapnel ripped up and down Crud's back and legs; Stu took hits in the chest and legs. It was ugly stuff. We'd avoided that for a long time. They were both going to live, but they were already evacuated and on their way home.

I couldn't believe it. We were away for five days, and I

lost half my patrol. I went over and sat down. I just wanted to be alone. I had to replace them with new snipers, and that might be tough; I only wanted the best of what 4th Marine snipers had to offer. I could choose, but what did we have left?

I grabbed my mail. A couple of letters from Mom and Dad with the usual Stateside nonsense. And Greek checked in. He was doing as well as could be expected. At least he wouldn't lose an arm along with his leg. "Damn, there went the matched set," he'd written in his letter. Then I got another cryptic note from Zulu. He'd volunteered to come back to Nam as a sniper with the 26th Marines. That old bastard wouldn't listen to me. Nooooo! He could have stayed in Vietnam and been a Rogue. But no, he wanted to go back to the World.

Lots of things were changing. Of course I'd extended again, and Ya Ya finally went home after nineteen months. Wiener was close to leaving if he didn't flip out first. One more frog's head hanging out of his mouth and he'd probably get a one-way ticket home real fast. Harley went home after getting wounded for the second time. He'd never been quite right since getting his hat shot off while I was Stateside. I picked up some new guys with little bush experience, but they'd all been trained in the Stateside sniper school. I got a rich kid from Missouri we called Raid. He had an MBA, got drafted, chose the Corps, and then chose snipers. They tried to get him to become an officer, but he turned that down. Then I got a really wild guy from California who grew up on the water. He loved waterskiing. We called him Z. Then I brought out Det Cord, a member of Mensa who'd speak perfect English in the middle of a firefight. He was brighter than the noonday sun but one weird dude. He'd already been in country eighteen months and had just signed up for six more.

The Rogues were ready once again. Hood had a few months left, and he'd walk point again. Then there was me. And I'd walk third. I put Raid in second; I wanted him to learn the point position from Hood. I put Det Cord and Z on tail end to fend for themselves. It wasn't the gooks I worried about there, it was those two killing each other. I got the new crew together and briefed them on life with the Rogues. They were good folks, and I felt we'd be okay.

I decided to go to the opposite end of the valley from Johan's. Johan deserved to have us back, but I had to find a way through the pass and another place to set up, before we ventured to the south end again. For now, we'd go north and west, to the northernmost foothills of the free-fire zone. I'd have five snipers with me, or so I thought. But at the last minute, a new lieutenant who'd been assigned to watch over our platoon decided I was moving around with too few troops. He sent me two new dudes, snipers who'd just arrived in country. The lieutenant had to be an asshole, and I hadn't even met him.

Hood took us out at midnight. I had more new guys than a DI at Parris Island. We were heading out into new territory, but I didn't expect much to happen on the patrol. But very quickly there was a commotion back in the column. Did I say fucking *column*? I was seriously pissed as I made my way back the trail. It ain't time for no fucking break, and here we are stopped. Hood's in fucking charge when we're moving out here. I got back there only to find a new sniper was asking to make an emergency head call. I swore at him under my breath; if I'da been in a safe place, I'd have killed him. It'd be a mercy killing. Do him in before he does one of us. "No, asshole . . . no emergency head calls!"

Hood led us toward the north end. As I walked, I thought of that little worm and his "emergency head call." I thought back to Parris Island when the DI in our platoon made a kid carry two buckets of water everywhere he went for two weeks. The DI did it because he stopped us from what we were doing to ask to make an "emergency head call." Now I understood why the DIs acted that way. They kicked our stupid asses unmercifully to protect our lives by instilling good combat habits. Walking along, I realized it all made perfect sense to me. Now.

Hood got us to the end of the valley. We just hung out for the next six or seven days, scoping what seemed to be the lifeless end of the valley. There wasn't anything down there, no signs of life, just us. We didn't even have any pigs to shoot. Death was absent from the Rogues' agenda.

On our last day and night out, our patience was wearing thin. And it was no thinner than with Rat Man, the guy who'd wanted to take a dump on the trail. We were set in on a knoll about fifty meters above the valley floor. I'd spread the group out so all seven of us were in a row, down in the grass.

I'd been debating with Hood and a new kid we called Ollie the merits of the Ford 427 versus the Plymouth Hemi. Hell, they didn't know anything about racing. It must have been 1400 or 1500 hours and 110 fucking degrees. I was sick of the debate. Hood stood up to take a piss and in an instant he fell to the ground as if he'd been shot, but he was still trying to button up. I started to yell at him, but he gave me the "shush" sign. "Kug, gooks, a bunch of 'em, right down there," Hood whispered, pointing out ahead and into the valley. I crept out a bit and peered through the grass. On the way, I gave Rat Man a bad look of warning. . . . There were eleven gooks! And damned if they weren't all in a row! They were coming right up a little trail that was covered by our seven snipers. I passed the word to get ready to crawl out with me. We were seven strong, packing four Winchester 06s and three M-14s. I had Hood off to one side with three of the guys, and I was off to the other side with the others. I got word out we'd fire as one. We'd aim left to right, each of us taking the guy to the right, beginning with the point man and going back through the column.

They didn't have a clue we were here. They were close enough by then that I heard them talking. When they came out of the bushes in front of us, they'd be about seventy-five meters dead ahead. They were traveling at a right angle to us. They were dressed in black, young, and I could see at least one woman. They all had rifles, but they were slung on their backs. I looked right and left and passed the word: fire when I do. I was third from our left, so I sighted in my 14 on number three, a woman. Her tough luck for wearing black and carrying that AK.

Boom! A split second later . . . it's *bbbboom, boom, bboom!* My team fired and dropped the first seven in their tracks. The four remaining bad guys took to the bush. They didn't return a shot. I got one of them on the run and Z got another. Nine kills in one setting. We could see them lying down there. What a beautiful day. I held the team in place and we used the 7×50s to scope out the area. The survivors had run into the dense jungle below us, the losers were all lying flat out in a clearing, but dense vegetation surrounded it. I wasn't taking any chances that someone would stay behind to get one of us. We waited for an hour, and there were no signs of life, so I sent two of our team out behind us to watch our rear, then I took Z and Hood and our 14s and went down to the cemetery while the two remaining snipers sat above us. We needed cover while we searched the bodies.

From down in death valley, everything looked a lot different, grass was totally out of control, and I was having a hard time locating my sense of humor, knowing Rat Man was one of the two new guys standing guard over our asses. Hood took the bodies to the left, I took the ones to the right, and Z took the two in the middle. He got the woman. I had trouble finding my runaway. I knew I had dropped him. I finally found him in some really dense underbrush. Damn we're good! I searched my bodies and found some papers, letters, and a few weapons of war. It was hard to carry it all. When I finally looked up, Hood was already sitting on a little rise just above us. It was eerie as hell down there. The grass growing around us must have been ten feet tall.

I got up on the rise and met Hood. We motioned for Rat Man to come down and make himself useful by hauling our gook gear back up the hill. I asked Hood, "Where the hell's Z?"

He pointed down toward the bodies. I could barely see Z's head. I didn't like that. "Hood, cover my ass. I'm going back down," I told him. I hurried through the heavy grass and found Z. He was just standing up over the woman as I reached him. "What the fuck are you doing?" I barked at him. He grinned, held up about a foot or so of long, black hair. I said, "Z, what the fuck are you doing?"

He stood there with the woman's locks in his hand and said, "Come on, Kug, don't give me no shit. This'll look cool on my bush hat." He held it up to demonstrate. "Come on, Kug—it'll blow some fucking minds."

Z, Hood, and I made our way up to rejoin the group.

We'd "blown some minds" on that trip all right: nine bad guys and, for sure, one Rogue, with more on the way. Hood got us home to 51. Our legend was growing with our body count: Z sewed his hairpiece onto his bush hat, and that took care of any social activity we might have been dreaming of. On 51 we were becoming a novelty act. But I learned from that trip that the gooks were becoming more active, and there seemed to be more of them wandering around my valley.

We took a short day off and then went off to run some shit by the Booby Trap Ville. Raid took off on R & R, so I was one down. Of course, with the new lieutenant, even with Raid gone, I was still one up from where I should be. The ville was a real bad place, and the grunts had been losing a lot of men there. If you operated around there, you had to have skilled point people. I had Hood, and he kept us from re-creating the 4th of July or starring in some horror flick of our own. Z was turning out to be a good point man too. That helped with Raid gone. We could tell the grunts were in the area any time we heard a big *kaboom!* followed by the *whomp, whomp, whomp* of chopper blades. We knew the medevacs were coming in to save someone's ass or start the body bag's long journey to some as yet unsuspecting loved one. I'd have loved to bring some of those desk jockeys from Washington over and take them for a walk through that park. They'd have changed their rules of engagement damned fast.

After sitting in position from dawn to near noontime, we still hadn't seen any gooks. Damn it! I knew one of the local cadres, a dealer in ugly and unsuspecting death, was in the village somewhere. We worked the 7×50s for four hours, and not a blade of grass moved. The village was maybe five hundred yards long with lots of dense underbrush and many old deserted grass shacks along the way.

I couldn't resist the temptation; I wanted one of the little bastards that day. "Patience, Kug, patience," Hood muttered under his breath.

"Fuck patience and the horse he rode in on. Let's go and get us some gooks," I said. If we went in there in broad daylight, they'd never believe it! We could sneak in on the main trail a step at a time. We'd heard the sounds of wood chopping from deep inside the village all day long. I knew the ville the way I knew my little town of Lock Seventeen.

Hood led us out and along a trail near the village. We moved along and took the Y to the right. I walked second, Z third. The new guys were behind him, with Det Cord bringing up the rear. It was about 1300 hours. I was looking for the edge of the village, and I decided to leave the new guys with Det Cord when we found it. I took Hood and Z with me, Hood first, me second, then Z. I left clear instructions with Det Cord to call Hill 51 if there was shooting and we didn't come right out.

The new guys were worried; they didn't want to go in, but they didn't want to be left behind. Well, they didn't know the ville the way I did, but the three of us had a chance to do some serious damage. It was also dangerous, but getting up in the morning was a risk around there. Those boots from the States were telling me, "This ain't what snipers are supposed to be doin'." They were as useless as the one "sniper" who came in from sniper school and said he couldn't shoot anybody! We got rid of him.

Hood, Z, and I moved deeper into the ville. The bastard was still chopping wood. The trail began with a slight bend to the right, leading us into the center of the village. I knew there'd be a junction coming up. It was electric in the air. I could smell gooks. It was thicker than wet cement in there, but we were going anyway. The bastards had the balls to fuck around in *my* valley! Putting their booby traps everywhere. That was Rogue country, and we were zeroing in on the woodchopper.

We crept, one step at a time, and finally reached the junction. It looked pretty unused. Lush vegetation was growing everywhere. It was getting dark in there, weird, scary as all hell. I shook from head to toe when I realized how alone we were. The silence was deafening. We reached another little junction. This one came in from the left and looked like it might double back. Tension began to crush out our awareness of the afternoon sun. We were focused only on the tiny patch of real estate we walked on. The woodchopper struck again! Closer that time. Hood looked like he'd got a bead on the sound. He looked like a pointer! Shivers raced up and down my spine as I tried to chase fear from the center of my being.

We were deer frozen in the headlights of fear. It was real close this time. What if the sound was a trap? We'd been picking the gooks apart around there. Could it be? No, not in the afternoon. It just couldn't be.

We crouched and decided to wait it out. Patience, Kug, patience. He who hesitates might be lost. But he who makes a noise is found dead! My gut jumped as a chop echoed out of the nearby jungle. Which way was it? My head told me to charge and take his ugly ass out. My heart told me to get out of there. We were really wired by then, riding an adrenaline high the size of Montana.

I quickly motioned Hood to take the main trail. Each step was calculated. Our nerves were exposed, our eyes reaching out, straining for the least signs of life. Man! That was living. I was scared as hell, but *this* was the real thing . . . fuck Coke. Step by silent step, we inched deeper into the village, my fingers white against the M-14's stock. Now I smelled the bastards. I comforted myself by remembering that Hood was superb on point, he'd see the bastards first. I knew he would . . . he had to! With a firefight only a few minutes—or seconds—away, I was fighting for control of my mind.

We'd reached center city. Old huts to my right, over-grown with weeds. To my left ran another trail. It would probably lead around to Det Cord and the whiners waiting outside. I look over at Hood. He was standing, finger in front of his mouth, telling us to be quiet. I motioned that I'd take the thick growth to our left, Z had the rear, and Hood the front and right. It's time for the kickoff.

Had Hood heard something? The chopping had been silent for the last few yards. I was tensed, ready, trigger finger poised on my 14. My mind racing, I was peering into the jungle darkness, ready to kill at the first sign of movement. My senses were alive and reaching out into the air around me. Then the silence spoke to me: the bastards had sucked us in big time. They'd have to dig the harpoon out of me. I'd let my alligator ego overrun my chameleon ass; I'd been there too fucking long.

It was decision time, but the battle for control of my mind was still raging. Rational wanted to know how the hell I got us into this. And irrational wanted to kick some serious ass. I looked left, peering through the greenness that was life deep in that overgrown old village. Suddenly Hood turned, kneeling, motioning, asking which way to go. I quickly motioned him to lead us out on the left trail. We needed to *di di* out of there. Hood turned to take a step just as I looked back into the jungle to my left. *Fuck me!* A hardened gook was peering right at my young ass through huge leaves. Time shifted into slow motion and fast forward all at once. He was standing, arm cocked like a quarterback ready to throw on third and long, and he gave real meaning to the word ugly. My 14 was on full auto, and I spun to meet Mr. Ugly. His arm started forward, he was going for it—his grenade was airborne and my life spun and tumbled before me as my trigger finger hit the go button and bullets ripped into his chest and neck. He screamed and his face contorted as the bullets tore into his body.

The whole place erupted around us. *"Ambush!"* Z screamed. I felt like I was standing in a pan of Jiffy Pop.

I screamed for Hood to run down the trail, then I took off after him. Z was firing and running behind me. I was trying to run as bullets, from an unseen bad guy, whizzed round my head. Seconds passed that seemed like long minutes when, *kaboom!* An incredible explosion went off right behind me! Hood, Z? Where was Z? I thought he went back, the other way? But he was right behind me, just about up my ass. Suddenly, he frantically cried out, "I'm hit!" Then passed me like I was tied down!

The freeze-frame afternoon continued as the gooks fired at Will, and Will sure as hell was us that day. What a dumbfuck I'd been. Too fucking cocky for my own damned good. I reasoned there had to be four or five, less the guy I shot. Since I'd become tail-end Charlie, I turned and laid down some protective fire behind us. Rounds were still cracking overhead and all around, and I needed an advantage of some kind. I pulled out a grenade, pulled the pin, and tossed it back at the junction. *Boom!*

I could hear voices, screaming, and all kind of noise around me. I let go with another blast of protective fire, then ran down the trail to catch up with my guys; the

Charlie Woodcutters crew ain't far behind. Hood was working on Z's right shoulder, which was bleeding from a silver-dollar-size hole. His tiger-striped jungle fatigues looked oil-soaked from the blood and sweat pouring out. It was one of those "you get some time in Japan, son, then we'll send you back to Nam when you're ready" wounds. Of course, we'd have to live until nightfall first.

I reached the two of them and went down on one knee, covering Hood as he worked on Z. I was thinking, hell, we got a couple of the little dinks, anyway, when rounds cracked and whizzed over my head. It was clear, even to me, that we needed to kill all of the bastards if we didn't want them to shoot back. I stood and let go another blast from my 14 when Hood yelled, "Look!" I glanced down to where he was pointing, and I had a three-inch sliver of shrapnel sticking straight out of my right knee. I hadn't felt a damn thing. But I sure as hell would if those bullets got any fucking closer. I saw blood on my hands and wrists. *Crack! Zing!* More AK rounds were coming my way.

There were three of us still here standing on our side. At least one of us was wounded, and there were at least two bad guys on our ass. I turned and let loose with another blast about the same time the gooks got close again. Bullets were flying everywhere, but we both missed. Z was up and started moving down the trail, but I yelled, "No, this way"; I knew where we were, so I motioned Hood to blaze a trail to the left. We were in bad trouble, but I knew Det Cord and the boys were right outside. Hood was moving, but we were in a bamboo thicket. I had the three of us bunched up, busting a trail, and I didn't even know exactly how many bad guys were breathing up my exhaust pipe. I heard voices on the other side. It was Americans!

Hood was stuck, so I told him to cover the rear. Z got behind me. I'd break through one way or the other, I thought, but it was like walking through a bag of stick pretzels. Hood suddenly let loose with a whole magazine because the two gooks coming up behind us showed their faces long enough for him to buy their lunch. Newly motivated, I put my head down and charged like a water buffalo. I crashed through and saw a trench ahead. I was still looking down at broken bamboo when I heard a loud *ping!* I'd tripped a booby trap, this time a genuine M1A1 U.S.-made hand grenade. I tripped the little mother right out of a C-rat can that some fucking numbskull like Rat Man had left behind. The grenade landed right on the top of my boot, bottom laces, and went *kerplunk!*

Life shifted gears again. I was diving forward, and life went slow-mo one more time. Z screamed from behind me as I dived forward into the trench. Hands over my ears, I landed with a thud in the bottom of the old, smelly trench. I was frozen like a mummy, my whole body one tight muscle. Then I heard someone speaking. Hood was standing above me, laughing hysterically. He was saying, "Like you ain't gonna hear the boomer that blows you a new ass?" I can't believe it! It was a dud!

I pulled myself out of the hole. Hood was angry because he didn't have any cuts or scratches from the firefight. I went over and sat down. Det Cord was there with the boys, and the grunts passed through to secure the area. The corpsman was helping Z, and the medevac was on the way. When the chopper came, I looked over and Hood was standing, pants down, naked as the day he was born, balls to the wind, looking everywhere for some sign of a scratch that might get him a Purple Heart. No cigar for the rebel.

The grunt scouts came back with news they'd left

three bodies, some blood, and some weapons. It hadn't turned out to be a bad afternoon for three lucky but stupid bastards with a sick leader and a hell of a sense of humor. Hood took our patrol back into Hill 51 and then Evans. Z and I got a ride in a Huey. I spent a day at 3d Med and two weeks in the rear. Z was off to Japan for a spell.

After my forced R & R, I gathered Hood, Raid, Det Cord, and a couple of new guys and went back to Hill 51. I missed the free-fire zone. I hadn't gotten even for Greek yet, and now there were Stu and Crud, not to mention Z and me. We were kicking their asses, and they knew it. I'd taken some casualties in the valley but hadn't used any green body bags. I decided to start working my way back down to Johan's. Fall was coming and with it the monsoon. Things were changing again, and I needed to go hunting while the season was still good. Hood had about two weeks left with us, so I needed to make it a good one.

We'd noticed woodcutters working the foothills just at the edge of the free-fire zone to our east. And after the last encounter, I considered the woodcutters dubious. We also noticed that when they were out cutting wood, our position was ambushed or mortared. What a coincidence. They'd come in surrounded by women and kids with baskets, and they'd spy on us in the valley. I had a plan. The Rogues were back in action.

I decoyed a couple of our guys in the valley at first light. During the night, I took Hood and three others and went up on the side of the foothills. We hid ourselves in grass about three feet high. Somehow, the gooks just never believed you'd do it. I positioned us right on the edge of the free-fire zone. I mean it was the edge of the map . . . this was art, not science, and there wasn't a yard marker out there. I was just tired of the rules that weighted the war in favor of the bad guys. And I was tired of the rules being used against us. I gave everyone orders before departing: no one was to shoot unless I shot first. No one was to shoot women and kids unless they shot first, under any circumstances.

First light came, and nothing happened. I'd learned over the past nineteen months that patience was a key skill of a sniper. It didn't hurt to be a little crazy either. It was about 0900 hours when the gang showed up. And yes, they came up to chop wood and pick berries. There were two or three kids, a couple of women, and three real tough looking men. I was sure *they* were berry pickers. We waited for the key sign that they were bad guys. A little bait wouldn't hurt when fishing for those damned bottom feeders. I radioed down to our decoys to make some movement down below. I wanted them to be seen. Sure enough, one of the mean looking dudes was immediately on a radio. He'd taken it out of a woman's basket. I had a guy with me we called Hoss, bigger than Stu but nobody was home upstairs. He carried my radio and could shoot the eyes out of a snake at any distance. He didn't have any kills, so I told him to take first dibs. He fired the first round about 0930 hours with a loud *boom!* The rice-paddy-daddy hat went flying off the dude as he spun to the ground. They had no idea we sat 150 meters on the side of the hill above them. Hood and the others opened fire, and hats were flying every-fucking-where. We killed four, three men and a little lady. We wounded a girl who must've been in her teens, and a little kid about eight or nine stayed at her side. I called up the decoys, and we regrouped. We all went down to search the bodies and check on the wounded. I felt bad for the first time in ages, seeing the little kid cry. The teenage girl just sat there holding her leg. A bullet flying in the melee had grazed it. I tried calling in a medevac, but the priority for evacuating "indigenous personnel," as McNamara called them, was low, and I didn't have all fucking day to sit there in the baking sun while the pilots played games. I called in another medevac, this time as if it were one of my Marines. I wanted those folks taken care of and wasn't into all the political bullshit that might accompany getting simple help for another human being who didn't share our uniform. I didn't want to hurt the villagers. They were getting used in the thing the same as the rest of us. They needed help. Escorted by two Huey gunships, the new medevac came in quickly. When the medevac landed and the pilot saw who I was bringing out to meet him, he started yelling into the radio at me, so I broke eye contact with him, turned off my radio, and walked away.

I hadn't just pissed off a Huey pilot, I'd fucked with my own life. After all the shit I'd done and been through, I got a bad call from COC. It was about an hour, maybe two, after the medevac. The colonel was calling me in to "discuss" the "incident." The new snipers from Stateside were getting all exercised about this investigation. Myself, I was pretty pissed. But I was pissed at our leaders for acting that way. We did nothing wrong. The dude called action on us from a hidden radio while hiding behind women and kids, and I called his ass on it. Fuck him! They'd about got us several times up to now, and I wanted a level playing field. The colonel sent his chopper out to pick me up that very afternoon. I had to place one of the new guys, a newly arrived staff sergeant, in charge. I was concerned; I liked Moe, he was a career Marine, but he had no combat experience.

Back at Evans, I went straight in to see the colonel, the 4th Marine CO and a good guy. I'd bought his wife things in Hong Kong when he asked me to. He was a real Marine and a gentleman. Inside the CO's tent, the lieutenant intercepted me. He said, "Sergeant Kugler, you could be in deep shit. Come with me." That was really endearing. I was excited about his possible support. The lieutenant and I hadn't exactly seen eye to eye since he came into Headquarters Company. He was a mustang officer (a former enlisted man) and I always had the feeling he wanted to be in the field rather than in the rear. I'd respected him for what I thought he was, but I found him to be a nitpicker who screwed with snipers at every turn.

He took me into his office tent and said, "Sit down. I don't want no bullshit. You talk straight with me and then see the colonel." I sensed he was clearing up an old wound. When he first came in he ordered all his troops to be clean shaven. I had a mustache that I'd had since coming across on ship. I was a sergeant E-5, with months in country, in the bush, doing crazy things, and I wanted my 'stache. He gave me a direct order to shave it. I avoided his ass for weeks while I was in the bush. Then one day he saw me and went ballistic. I requested mast to see the colonel. He granted the mast but told me if it wasn't shaved off at 0700 hours in the morning, he'd court-martial me for disobeying a direct order. I thought about it, and shaved before morning. Well, the colonel smiled, got kind of a kick out of the whole thing, and said, "Lieutenant, it's okay if the sergeant has a mustache here in Vietnam." Score one for the Kug. That was then. But I was sitting before the loser wondering what kind of support I'd get from him on a case that falls into a gray area.

Our talk was short and even kind of sweet. I was scared and pissed. But it turned out I'd be glad for that lieutenant; we had a breakthrough. The lieutenant said,

"Sergeant, you've done a helluva job here. But I need to know if you crossed the line this time. Those two kids you sent back on the medevac, they said they were unarmed and you just shot 'em right off their water buffaloes. If you want my help, you look me in the eye and tell me the truth."

I liked the guy already. I looked straight at him and said, "Sir, they had radios, no weapons, but they were calling shit on our heads in the valley. Then they'd hide over at the edge of the free-fire zone. They fucked up a lot of grunts, and I was sick of it. And—"

"Yes," he said, "what else?"

"Sir, there were no water buffaloes." He stared a dagger through me for a long minute. Then he said, "Kugler, get the hell outta my sight."

"Yes, sir!"

I didn't talk to the colonel or anyone else. I never let my people shoot anyone innocent. I never would. I wondered often why I felt that way, but I didn't know. I got back out to Hill 51 only to find out that Moe, the staff sergeant lifer, had been given my patrol. He'd run the Rogues. The lieutenant hadn't told me, but hey, I was tired, and he could have it. Another new guy we had just gotten in and I hit it off famously. I named him Tomo. He reminded me of a sumo wrestler. He'd been in country with the grunts for eighteen months already, and he'd re-upped to be a sniper. I loved the guy. He was five feet seven inches tall, meaner than a bear with a sore ass, shaved his head bald, and talked like he had a mouth full of gravel. He was one badass Marine. He weighed in about 210 and wanted no shit from no one. He was pissed at Moe for not declining the assignment. Tomo actually outranked me as a sergeant but didn't pull the rank. He wanted to learn from the others and from me. So he just became a sniper like all the others. Moe was different on that count and wanted to lead it himself. He'd been in the Corps a while and was into the rank thing.

The first patrol he planned was to take us to Don OO, an old French fort at the base of the mountains on the far west of the valley. It was way out and not a place I'd choose to take the group. It was twice as far out as where I'd wanted to go into the bunkers and blow ourselves up with arty. But he and the lieutenant had decided on the site. They also decided the patrol needed to be beefed up. I just opted to stay out of it. Tomo was thoroughly pissed at me for backing away, but there wasn't room for two chiefs. I told him I'd walk point. I hadn't done that for a while, and it would get me back in the swing of living on the edge. Walking point was adrenaline drippin' from your ears and a butt squeezed so tight you couldn't drive a tenpenny nail up it with a jackhammer. Let me at it!

Off we went to Don OO. I led the new improved version of the Rogues out at midnight. I told him I didn't think it was enough time to go as far as he wanted, but midnight it was. I was leading twelve marine snipers, a whole squad sans reinforcements. That was three of the original Rogue patrols all rolled into one. We got halfway to Don OO, and fog set in. I looked back, and eleven half bodies were walking behind me. The fog was about gut high and water heavy, and the moonlight gave it an eerie glow. I didn't like the feel of it out there. We stopped too often for map checks, we had too many people, and we were too noisy. Not to mention that over half of the patrol was greener than a cucumber.

I got us to the fort around 0500. It wasn't daylight, but it was lurking nearby. The trees were thick, and damned if everything I'd read and heard about the fort wasn't true. It had a moat around it. A real, wet moat. I was tired, bored, and half–scared silly. With that mob, if we got hit, Tomo and I had better hat up. Moe wanted me to cross the moat and get us up into the fort. Okay, the fuckin' moat is there for a reason, like to keep people out. I suggest we blow up the rubber ladies and float across. Moe didn't want to do that because it'd take too much time. Of course, if we'd left earlier, time wouldn't have been a problem. One of the fresh meat, a Stateside sniper, said he'd just been there with the grunts the week before. "The water's maybe four feet deep," he said with great authority.

Wearing my sixty-pound pack, I stepped in. It was *blub, blub, blub*, and I was sucking down water and trying to pry my ass off the bottom. The moat was well over my six feet three inches! Tomo reached down and pulled me out of the water. "Moe, can we get out the rubber air mattresses and float the fucking thing now," I asked as humanely and quietly as I could after fucking near drowning. He agreed but wanted to take time to blow up only one.

Tomo and I blew it up, then he went downstream to set up cover for me. I eased into the water and I laid my 14 across the top of the air mattress and the top half of my body on the rest of it. I eased out because they had tied the commo wire to the air nozzle of my raft. Once I was on the other side, they'd pull it back for the rest to cross. I'd set up security on the other side for them to cross. It was very scary shit being first guppy on shore. I slid off under the overhanging brush. I was hoping like hell there weren't any critters slithering along in the branches. I slid into the water and pushed the mattress back out to sea. I was wired. It wasn't long before I was being *pssssed* at from the other side. "Kug, come back over, we didn't tie the commo wire on." Nice going guys! It wasn't hairy enough doing that once; I had to do it twice! It was not as deep at that point, so I waded out to retrieve the mattress. I made it back across the moat. With the commo wire securely tied, I made my second crossing. The gooks must have been on R & R because we never saw any the whole time the mob was crossing.

There were problems with the whole patrol. And all of them were understandable; Sergeant Moe didn't have any reason to know how to conduct a sniper patrol. But then again, leaders shouldn't be putting people in a position to fail. Problem was, lots of our leaders didn't have the sense God gave a damned pig. After this patrol, the lieutenant sent Moe back to Evans and reassigned him. He came out and gave me back my patrol. That was a hell of a deal. Moe and I later became friends. He was a good guy, who spent some time with us. But, being married, with kids, leading sniper patrols into the bush was not his thing.

I had three days left on a patrol that Moe had laid out with COC. We had to take them south toward Johan's the next day. The timing wasn't right, but we'd been through enough shit with COC and the lieutenant; I wasn't changing it now. I'd figure another way into Johan's. Maybe we could surprise his ugly ass; it'd been awhile. I want to get Moe's patrol behind me. Then I want to get our style patrols going again. With fewer people.

Hood was leaving for home, so Raid led us out. We'd traverse the draw down by Johan's. I hated the place. By the time we reached the draw, I was jumpy: we should have been through here a long time ago. Damn boot from Stateside coming in here fucking up my show. The moon was long gone, and it was about 0430 hours. We need to get through the place like right now. I would have to find a new way in there, and I couldn't do it if we were late. But there was trouble in the air that night, I could feel it. The whole patrol was trouble. Raid was down on one knee like Hood used to be—that was the trouble! Did he hear something? It was darker than dark, we were rushed and hurrying, and in my math, that added up to bad. Raid was waving me forward. The mental alarms went off—adrenaline rush, adrenaline rush! I squatted next to Raid after duck-walking the final couple of yards. Raid was trying to tell me something. He was speaking so softly that my well-worn ears were having trouble picking it up. I leaned over. "Kug, I'm spooked out here tonight." What? Him spooked? I mean, he's no wallflower, even if he is light on ground experience. "Kug," he continued, "I hear noise up and above us."

"Are you sure?" I hoped like hell he was wrong.

"I know they're here tonight, man. I don't think we should go through here!"

We were sitting at a bad place, right at the mouth of the draw. It could have been worse, say, inside the draw with its fifty- to sixty-foot sides. I was worried too. Raid had antifreeze in his veins, like Hood. If he was spooked, something was up. He waited, looking around and over my shoulder. He wanted an answer, and I was still working on it. I wanted to get us through before dawn. I leaned down and told him it's time. I put my mouth to his ear and whispered, "I don't hear shit. Let's just hat up and get through this thing fast. I think you're spooked by all the new guys we got." His look in the dark told me how bad he thought that decision was. But he was a trooper. He stood, moving forward, half-crouching, and uncharacteristically hesitant. The trail moved up, getting steeper and narrower as the sides closed in. The fear of the moment took the air right out of me. I was fried.

One, two . . . maybe ten steps into my decision, I heard movement! It was up and to the left. The noise . . . was it left or was it right? Shiiit! I heard it. Raid was frozen in a crouch, ready to attack. I leaned down, and we agreed there was something out there. Then . . . *noise left!* I grabbed Raid and told him to turn us around. We were going to advance to the rear. Immediately!

There was movement . . . running, just above us. It was an ambush. They knew we were fucking coming! Z took off from the rear before Raid could get all the way back. The rest followed. I was tail-end Charlie and the joke was on me. Grenades were going off. *Boom! Boom! Boom!* In quick succession, three grenades flew through the night. Miraculously, I didn't hear any cries in the air. We were running and grenades, shrapnel, and tracer rounds were flying. Bullets and shrapnel were whirling and zinging all around us as we made our run out of there. The dark night became strobelike with the flash and firepower of a night ambush. *Crack! Crack! Crack!* went the night air around my ears. We got twenty yards down the draw, and it opened up a little. It was time to fight back. Raid turned in front of me and began firing back over my head. Shiiit, man! Now there was stuff whizzing by in both directions. I skidded in next to him, but across the trail, then I turned and pumped M-14 lead back upstream. The music of the AK-47s played in our ears as they spewed deadly projectiles our way. It was amazing that nobody'd bought the farm yet. An ambush! The dinks were waiting for the Rogues. If I didn't know better, I'd think I was losing control. *Boom!* A grenade went off to our right, showering us with dirt and debris. You bastards will pay for that! *Boom!* Another grenade showered us with debris. Our two patrols were like kids in a wild fight, swinging madly at each other, neither one landing a blow. The firing died down, and Raid and I looked up at the whitening sky of dawn. We saw the silhouettes of two bad guys making their hat over the top of the ridge. I knew there was more.

Morning was a blessing, as light showered us with the protection of a new day. Raid led us down out of there. It had been a feeble attempt to ambush the Rogues. But feeble or not, it scared the hell out of us. Everyone was okay, which was either a miracle or a testament to how inept we all were—at least in that firefight. After we called COC and let them know what was up, we holed up for the day. I got the group together, and we planned a new route to Johan's for the next morning. That day, we stayed down in the riverbed, out of sight and out of mind of the bad guys, who would never dream we'd be back in there the next morning. And we'd go in behind them, too. Payback is a motherfucker!

Most of the night was uneventful. I even had time to lie down and look up at my mirror. It'd been a while since I'd thought about the World. Mom and Dad still write, of course, and it's still the "what's happening" in their world routine. LuAnn was still writing a couple times a week. She was getting real serious, and I wasn't helping any with my bullshit. I had trouble looking up and imagining the world back home; it was removed from the one I was living in. It was something I didn't want to think about anymore. I didn't have to think long, as Raid woke me for the trip. We'd take off and take the back way down to Johan's at 0300. There'd be no time for dreaming tonight.

We moved out behind Raid and amid the fears being expressed by the boots we'd had to take along. It was a couple of them, so I'd have to deal with it when we got back. Nothing had gone right about the patrol, nothing. Why fuck yourself up worrying about it? As we walked along, the sky was dark, the way it was a lot of the time by then; the monsoon was threatening to come to life early that year. I still have nightmares of the valley from the last monsoon. I'd have to develop a plan to work the valley in the monsoon. We'd talked about that but hadn't come up with an answer yet.

We were moving pretty quickly through some fairly open terrain. Every now and then the skies opened up, showering us with moonlight. It was a catch-22. It showed us the way and the bad guys, too. We'd been on the road maybe an hour when I stumbled in a hole, tripped, and fell to one knee. I could barely see shapes in the dark. Clouds raced in and out, making our progress difficult. Raid came back and whispered, "Get up, we gotta keep moving to get in there before first light." I knew that, but something was wrong. We were walking on semiflat terrain, an old tank trail, and I hit a hole? I said to Raid, "What the hell would a hole be doing out here?" He didn't care much about it just then. He had only one focus—get us into position. Point men tended to be like that, severely potty-trained individuals.

I got on all fours and started crawling around in search of the hole, using my hands to feel the way. I found it. "Raid," I said, "I've got it." Less than enthusiastically, he joined me, kneeling at my side. I reached all around the hole, and be damned, something weird was going on there. We hadn't been down into that area before. It was a back way in to Johan's, but the hole was square. "It's almost perfectly square," I said quietly to Raid. It was maybe a foot square and about the same deep. Holes sure as hell don't grow that way. Raid agreed and went to set the patrol in a defensive position. I lay down and got wired to check on what was probably a booby trap. Raid still thought I was overreacting but agreed it was worth a look.

My blood was pumping, my heart was pounding so loud I couldn't hear me talking to myself. Which is what I usually did when I disarmed booby traps. Nothing like a potential blast in the face to wire you for sound. Okay, Kug, here we go . . . the hole is perfect. I felt the hole, one more time, just to make sure there was nothing else in there but dirt. I couldn't find anything else, so I brought my hand up and to the outside top edge. I was then lying flat on my face, head to the hole and feet farthest away. I took my fingers and slowly ran them along the edge of the hole. "Okay . . . left, okay . . . down toward me, and that's okay. You got two down, Kug, two more sides to go. Now over to the right . . . feels clear, now up and . . . uh oh, wait a minute. I can feel a bump; it's like a little trench, and it runs to the right." I ran my hand into the groove that was maybe an inch deep. I knew I was onto something. Even in Nam, holes didn't grow square.

Raid was back, wanting an update. I told him the details. He agreed that it was a booby trap. Our dilemma was whether to wait or not. If we were to wait, we'd risk exposing ourselves out in the open when daylight arrived. To not wait was to leave a potential booby trap for someone else. I carefully reached to the right, running my two fingers along the tiny groove, and it came to an end. I took a deep breath and tried it again—nothing but dirt. It was pushing daylight by that time, and our work for this morning was in jeopardy. But I was going to figure it out.

It was still dark enough that I couldn't see anything, and I was sweating a lot. I rolled back over and tried one more time. My nerves are out licking the ground like the tongue of a snake in a cage. His tongue darts and my nerves are continuous. Of course, as Hood always told me, "No sense worryin' about it when you're this close, 'cause you ain't gonna hear shit when this baby goes off." I reached my fingers along the little groove one more time. It hit me! Something was buried at the end of the groove. I took out my K-bar and carefully started to probe. I was pumped with adrenaline, excited as hell, yet scared out of my damned skin as I lay there. I angled the blade about forty-five degrees to the ground and ever so gently slid the blade in. I hit something! I changed the position and angle of the blade and repeated the slow, steady move . . . pushing the blade into the dark earth a few inches from my face. There it was! I hit it again.

I decided to wait until first light to fuck with this thing, whatever it was. Dawn came, and I'd unearthed a 105mm howitzer shell. The damned thing was booby-trapped. The square hole was just big enough for an American foot to fall in as mine had done. When I got down and took a closer look, I saw that I'd fallen in the hole and tripped the booby trap, but the wire strung across the hole had broken. I couldn't tell Greek back in Philly or I'd get his "God is saving me for something" bullshit. Det Cord wanted to lay a charge and blow the shell in place. A damned 105 could have blown our whole patrol away. Certainly Raid and I wouldn't have been around to tell about it.

I decided to hold the patrol in place. It was daylight, and I was tired and worn out from the stress of working at that 105 half the night. I set the Rogues out in a small perimeter. Raid and I went to sleep to blow some much-needed Zs. When we came to, it was near 1100 hours. Nearby, two of my new snipers were sharing their misery and fear in a pity party. I'd had it with that kind of nonsense, so I went over to set the record straight about who ran the outfit.

"Okay dudes, what's the fuckin' problem?" I asked as I walked up.

"Sarge, we just don't feel comfortable being this far out with just us." It was all I could do to talk with them. I wanted to say, "Who the fuck asked for your opinion?" I couldn't believe the kind of recruits we were starting to get in.

Tomo strolled up and said, "The only thing wrong with these two punks is that they're scared out of their minds!" They reluctantly nodded in agreement. Well, we were all scared, but that didn't stop us from going out there.

"Guys, let me show you this shit ain't dangerous. I mean, watch, I'll go out toward Johan's by my damned self." I tossed my 14 to Tomo and took off down the trail. I was furious.

Raid yelled, "Kug, get the hell back here, you're gonna fuck this up."

"I'll be back in a minute. Tomo, you're in charge." I walked for about 250 yards and looked back. Raid was trailing along about a hundred yards behind me. I couldn't see the rest. I could only imagine the hell they were going through being left with Tomo. He didn't take shit from *anybody*. I got to the front edge of the hill that led down into the valley above Johan's. It was also the hill that we were going to set in that night. I couldn't see anyone. The valley seemed dead.

I stood there for a minute and then I lost it for a second. I stood there, arms spread in the air, and just screamed at the top of my lungs, *"Fuuuuck yoooou!"* What was I doing? I was out there in no-man's-land

acting like a maniac. I turned and walked back toward
the Rogues. I could see Raid's head in the grass alongside of the trail. As I got closer, he stood and joined me
without saying a word. I approached the group and I saw
Tomo's face. As I walked past, he said, "Kug, are you
okay?"

I smiled and went to the two new guys. I was almost
kind as I said, "Guys, if I can do that, you can go out with
the rest of us. You'll be scared just like us, but you can do
it. You're fucking Marines, and you're fucking snipers!"

After my brief loss of sanity, of course we had to move
away. Raid led us right out where I'd been. We made a
brief show, looked around the valley, then took off. I
wanted us in full view of the gook cadre, who had to be
watching somewhere down below. By that time, the two
boots were doing okay, especially when I turned away
from the valley. But they about shit themselves when we
dropped into some trees alongside a deserted ville to
spend the night. We had one more night, and by God, we
were going on that hill at zero dark thirty and set in. I still
wanted Johan's ass, even if I was getting to like him.

Under cover of darkness, Raid took us in without a
hitch. When dawn came, we were all at the ready. We
were on the hill next to the one we usually used and next
to the one where I had lost it the day before. With all the
booby-trapping going on, we had to mix up the plays. The
grass we were in was about four feet tall. If someone
knew where to look, they'd have found us, but we kept
them guessing big time. We were camoed to the max. We
had the face paint Mom had sent from the archery store
back home. Recon couldn't spare any more, and supply
told us we weren't authorized to have face paint. The
charcoal we'd been using was screwing up our complex-

ions. But Mom's supply was a good one, and she was becoming a folk hero with the Rogues.

The day wore long and hot, but the sun wasn't as bad because the monsoon was trying to come to life. It was at 1300 when the natives got restless. Well, it was really my Rogues who were restless. I wanted to go back as bad as anyone, including the boots, but I knew that curiosity would get to the gooks. We waited. It was 1500 when he showed his ugly face. I was working on the 7×50s since everyone else had given up. Tomo and I were becoming fast friends. He was 100 percent up to speed on what I wanted to do. He had his 06 and knew how to shoot it. Johan himself had showed no signs of coming to our party, but I could feel somebody looking at us. I scanned the tree lines slowly, looking for any sign of life. I checked out the right, the middle, and the far portion of the tree line where Johan lived about four hundred meters away. Nothing! I looked down to our left front, just across the river and started from far out to in . . . it was about 150 meters. *Whoa!* I jerk the binoculars from my eyes. Tomo says, "Kug, what's up?" Without a word, I pull the 7×50s back up to my face and look. There was the meanest, ugliest man I'd ever seen. He was peering, glaring out between two giant leaves, his head peering right through as he leaned out into the leaves and bushes. It was as if he were looking in my bedroom window. I realized he couldn't see me. But seeing him scared the hell out of me. I mean, at 150 meters and dropping, he looks big in those 7×50 binoculars. He was tan, athletic looking, uniformed, and ugly. And he was looking right up where we were.

I pointed him out to Tomo, who handed me his rifle. I told him to go ahead, but he said, "Kug, I think you need the shot today. You'll feel better." He was right; I hadn't put anyone on ice for some time. I picked up Tomo's rifle and eased myself into the sitting position. Just like training, Kug, I told myself, bend down, feet tucked in toward your ass, rifle tight in your shoulder, knees spread wide, left elbow tucked tight against and over your left knee, and right elbow resting on your shin just below the knee. Now it's all in the head, Kug.

I had him in the crosshairs. Tomo was spotting with the 7×50s and Ugly was still trying to find us up there in the grass. Well, hello, motherfucker! I gently squeezed my girl's tit and *boom!* Ugly does a flip backward and I get another kill! Man, it was just exhilarating!

I couldn't enjoy the victory long because all hell broke loose in front of us. The gooks opened up. I mean to tell you, there was AK lead flying out of that jungle. But it wasn't whizzing overhead. What was going on? I looked at Tomo for a read, and he motioned to the hill next door. Raid said, "Kug, they're shootin' at our old hill." Now that was damned close. We regrouped, and Raid led us out and around our safe house. We crawled for a hundred meters or more. I didn't want to be detected out there so late in the day. We'd definitely be outnumbered if we got caught. And we damned near got caught. But Raid was good, and he was fast catching up with the legend of Hood. But he was also going home soon.

We got free of the bad guys and hightailed it back to Hill 51. We looked forward to a much-needed break. We wanted to catch a hop back into Evans. But the next morning, with the weather deteriorating and no choppers in sight, we walked to Evans. We all needed clothes, mail, and rid of the two boots who'd been dragging us down. I needed to regroup our team and head out for the monsoon. I also needed to solve the problem of the lake about to appear in the valley. I'd see the colonel for that, or so I thought.

We got drunk that night when we got back, and it felt good; it'd been a while. That is, it felt good until the next morning. I felt like an amtrac had run square over my damned head. Pounding or no pounding, I was off to see the lieutenant for permission to see the colonel. "Lieutenant, I have an idea." He motioned me in to sit down. Something he wouldn't have done for me before the incident. His respect for us was growing. I laid out my master plan for the coming monsoon season. I wanted a boat. If I could get a boat, I knew I could still make it off Hill 51 and over to the foothills. Then I could still annoy the folks in the valley. I wanted a rubber boat, the kind recon used. The lieutenant was impressed with our ingenuity; he said he'd take it up with the colonel. That wasn't what I wanted, but I trusted him by then, as he did me, so that's the way it would stand.

I went back to our hootch to let my head get back to normal size and get the crew ready to return to 51. Cashman was in from one of his grunt gigs. He was moaning about the shit his fiancée was giving him about being a sniper. We were ragging on him about extending, but it was clear that wasn't going to happen. But the argument his girl back home had been giving him was incredible. Sure made me glad the only chick I was writing was LuAnn. So no flack for the Kug. But Cashman got enough to go around for all of us.

I'd heard him whine about his girl before. "Cash," I yelled, "let me write her, I know how to set her straight." He laughed. "Cashman, come on, you've been whining about this bitch for months. She's giving you a major hard time, and that's just the beginning. What d'ya think you're gonna live with when you marry her? Huh?" He was actually a hell of a nice guy, but he was so pussy-whipped, it was unbelievable. But what pissed *me* off most was the hard time she gave him about Vietnam.

Tomo said, "Cash, either shut the fuck up and never bring it up again or let Kug do his thing and take care of her." That made sense to me. I'd been elected the scribe for snipers some time before. Any nonsense that came in about the war, I'd ghostwrite an answer. Any Dear Johns, and the Kug took care of it. So why should Cashman be any different?

I said, "Cash, you don't have ball one, unless you let me handle the bitch once and for all." That came on the heels of Tomo's "Not a hair on your ass" speech. Cash got into the spirit of the thing and even went so far as to confirm that he didn't want to marry her. I decided to take care of that for him. I said, "Cash, I'll just write her a note, and you rewrite it, man, and it'll be over." And it was one of my best ever. I made it short and sweet and when I ended, I did indeed wax eloquent. It read, "You, Miss Julie, have no idea whereof you speak. You tell me not to write of killing, not to speak to you of the bad people I now live with, and you tell me to get home immediately or you may not love me anymore for what I've done. How dare you criticize me for defending your right to live there and go to college, and even your right to say the things you do about my friends. You are right, I have changed. My eyes have been opened to what a spoiled, coddled, insensitive, selfish little brat you are. And for you to criticize killing . . . why you have no right to criticize the taking of a human life until you've had the exhilarating experience of doing it yourself. I hereby inform you the wedding is off!"

Man, that was beautiful. I mean it felt almost as good as giving one of the little bastards the third eye. The look on his face was speaking a greater truth than the words from his lips; he didn't want to mail that baby. But we assigned Tomo to see that it was copied the way *I* intended. Cash wrote it, and Raid insured it was mailed unchanged. She deserved it for giving us shit over here about this war. She ought to come over here and see for her-damned-self.

We were ready to leave for 51 and Cash dejectedly left for the grunts. I don't think he was too happy with the coercion applied by his fellow snipers. The lieutenant called me and gave me the word: the colonel would support us but couldn't deliver on a rubber boat. In the Marine bureaucracy, just recon had use for rubber boats, which fell into the same bullshit category as camo face paint. But the lieutenant was cutting a deal with engineers. The colonel was behind giving us "another kind of" boat, whatever the hell that meant. I didn't care, just so it held five and floated. He said they'd deliver it to Hill 51 in the next month. Shazaam! We headed off to 51 happy.

We brought along Staff Sergeant Nurial. He'd been our armorer for the past year and was getting ready to head home. He was a nice guy, a career Marine with lots of stripes and years in the Corps. He was also a member of the Marine rifle team and therein lay the problem. Sergeant Nurial didn't want to have spent a year in snipers and have to go home and tell his fellow lifers he hadn't shot anyone. What a place Vietnam was! It was sick enough to go around and shoot people, but to want to kill so you could brag to the dudes on the Marine rifle team . . . well, let's lock and load, Sarge! He came to me before we left Evans and pitched his "one patrol" idea.

Raid was out front again. We decided to go farther down the valley than we'd ever gone before. It'd take us twelve grid squares south, that's a couple past Johan's.

We'd be out a week, and my good sergeant was concerned whether he could keep the pace; he'd been working the armory for a year. If he could keep up, I'd give him something to talk about when he hit Washington on his next visit.

We left at 2200 hours the night before; it was going be quite a hike. We had to move it out since we needed to set in before first light. I was surprised at the ease with which we moved. We made the river and through the draw in great time. On top of the foothills, we took a long break to catch our wind. Raid had been moving us along, and the good sarge was sucking serious wind. It was 0300 when we reached the end of the valley, our destination for the day. We had a good hour to get in position. The only choice we had were some small hills, like the ones around Johan's. I hadn't been there before, but the tall grass was eerily familiar background for the Rogues; we got our best hunting hanging out in the grass.

We crawled into position. I didn't expect any shit for a while. Sergeant Nurial was hopped up like he was on something, so he was an easy choice to leave awake. His eyes were like saucers. I wanted some Zs; I was tired as hell. It was still dark when I dozed off against my pack. The pack and my shoulder harness loaded with the gear of war were on the ground, giving my back a much-needed rest. I don't know how long I'd been out, but the sun was up and I was hot. I rolled over and heard whispering. Trying to wake up, I couldn't figure it out.

When I looked up, Nurial's eyes were bugging out of his head. He'd locked onto something. Raid was in the weeds next to me pointing down in front of us. There in living color might well have been a poster boy for the NVA. I looked at Nurial, and he was excited, man, but he was also scared out of his tree. The dude in front of us was in full uniform, pack, rifle—and only about fifty feet away. He was eyeballing the whole neighborhood. There couldn't have been just one of them, especially the way that guy was dressed.

Nurial broke out his 7×50s, but I reached over and pushed them down. The guy'd look like Godzilla through those things. He was fifty *feet* away not even fifty yards. The guy was young, about our age. He looked angry, not mean but angry. Hell, I guess I'd be angry too, if I had to walk to the war like these poor bastards. I leaned over to Nurial and said, "Take him out, man. Adjust for the distance and aim for the chest." He looked up at me and his expression was pitiful. He was a helluva nice guy, but he was scared as hell right then. And he was shaking like a leaf. I reached over and held his barrel still. I wanted to make a point. Slow it down, man. He got ready for the shot. There were no other signs of life anywhere. But I just know this little fuck ain't alone. I'm starin' right at him, and he didn't have a clue we were there. Damn, I loved it when we got in undetected and surprised the little bastards. What a fucking hoot. Fifty fucking feet away, no less, he's still eyeball-fucking the area when . . . *Boom!* Nurial finally cranked off a round. The NVA dude went down but, dammit, he was yelling like a banshee. Det Cord said he was yelling for help. I grabbed my 14 and took off running to shut him up. Raid ran off to cover me from a finger to our left. Z went up behind us for rear cover. The rest were at the ready. I was running toward the screaming bad guy when I realized I had an M-14 with just the one twenty-round magazine. I'd left everything else back where I was sleeping!

I cut out from the grass and onto the trail the guy had been standing on. I saw him lying on his back, bleeding from the right thigh. How in the fuck can you hit a guy in the leg at fifty feet? Nurial got buck fever on his first shot. And I had to clean up his mess. I ran up at his feet. Our eyes met. I could tell he didn't like me any more than I liked him. Fuck, it's just a game, man . . . nothing personal. I have my 14 on full auto and aimed dead center on his chest. I'm standing sideways, creeping up, making each step count. I'm within a yardstick of his feet. He's lying flat on his back, legs apart, and hands at his side. His AK-47 is lying about a foot from his right hand. It's pointing my way. Our eyes are still locked on each other like lasers out of some bad sci-fi movie. He raises his head. He's no longer screaming . . . he's waiting.

I had visions of a platoon of bad guys roaring over the edge of the hill behind him. They'd ride to victory to save the little man in front of me. They'd stomp me to death with their Ho Chi Minhs. But not before I emptied my one fucking magazine of ammo. I'd been screwing up more and enjoying it less those days. I'd also been there too long. I hoped my face didn't betray the fear I felt deep inside. I was standing there exposed to the world with twenty rounds between me and a green body bag.

Oh, shit! Fuck them, I think . . . I'm fine, keep control, that's who wins . . . he who keeps control. I've got the only gun in this quick-draw contest. I'm still standing, asshole. I want his AK . . . I step toward his right and lean down, my rifle in my right hand, my finger glued to the trigger, ready for a twenty-round blast. The world around me stops, my heart races around in my chest, pounding, making the only noise I can hear for miles. I get close enough to reach out for the NVA's AK. The bad dude moves slightly up on one shoulder. I can see a big pool of blood under his right leg. I motion for him to hand me his weapon . . . time slows even more . . . what's going on, asshole? He reaches slowly for the weapon, our eyes frozen in a stare as if a line tied them together. I motion again for him to hand me the AK. I'm about a foot from his feet, bending at the knees, crouching, reaching out with my left hand. My 14 is aimed at his chest with my right hand as I reach with my left. The gook slowly reaches out and picks up his rifle in his right hand. That's a good boy . . . slow now, I'm making "gimme" signs with my fingers. All the while fighting to breathe as the tension begins to close in and suffocate me. Life's in slow motion as two gladiators meet for the first and final time. My 14 is still aimed deep in his chest. I stretch out with my right hand, finger at the ready, willing to blow him into tomorrow at the slightest sign of bullshit. No gentle squeezes this time. This little guy fucks around, he's history, right before my eyes. Fuck him and the five days R & R I'll get if I bring him in alive. Our eyes won't seem to unlock. I can see out of the corner of my eye . . . the AK's coming toward me . . . I'm reaching . . . extended . . . Oh hell! No! He's coming up to shoot! His angry little face turns haunting and evil. His mouth twists, contorting his cheeks in a harrowing smirk. His eyes are glazed with hatred as he raises the AK in front of him. He joins his left hand with his right, grabbing the stock of his rifle in the ready position. Oh fuck . . . I screwed myself! It's all happening in a split second! The barrel of the AK is inches from my gut. I raise my rifle up . . . why the fuck didn't I walk around and kick it away, I think amid the frenzy in front of me. Son of a bitch! Suddenly his face gushes with torment and revenge as he pulls the trigger in an effort to take me out! No! No! Life is a freeze-frame as two nameless kids face off, fueled by the madness of war. He pulls the trigger on the AK a split second before me. He pulls the trigger again . . . jerking angrily at his malfunctioning rifle as I let loose with a deafening blast of M-14 on full auto. *Brrrp . . . brrrp . . . brrrp!* His face travels from the terror of a kid a long way from home to the frantic fear of an asshole who just double-crossed a man with a gun.

His body jumped as the 7.62mm bullets ripped through his chest and stomach. Blood flew in the air and then pelted the ground like a heavy monsoon rain. Terror raced through my body and out the barrel of my 14 with the bullets that ripped him a new asshole. The air resounded with my revenge and anger at that little fuck doing that to me. Fuck him and all the little bastards like him. I gave the guy a break, and he tried to stick it up my ass. Now you're dead, asshole. I'm standing and you're lying on your young ass, dead.

Raid came running along my left, covering the trail the dead guy came up on. I turned and saw Nurial in the grass high above, peering down on me. A fucking leg shot at fifty fucking feet. "Kug, let's get the fuck outta here," Raid half yells and half whispers. I had to check the dude out. I straddled the dead man and flipped him over. His pack was nothing to write home about. I opened it up and pulled out a map, some papers, and a letter. I checked his trouser pockets and found a little fold-over thing . . . what the fuck? It's got pictures . . . a man and a woman, another of a cute young thing in her *ao dai* . . . a fucking regular human being this guy was . . . shiiit!

Raid came over, nervous as hell, wanting out of there. The gook nostalgia party was over. I threw my spoils in the dead man's backpack, grabbed it and his AK-47, and headed back up the hill to join the others. I looked back down one more time. There lay the loser, a dead gladiator . . . facedown, dead as fucking Pearl. Bye-bye, motherfucker. You lose; score one for the Rogues.

We regrouped after Sergeant Nurial tried giving me some shit about not taking the guy prisoner. Yeah, right! The guy got a huss from the Kug, pulled the trigger on his AK a few inches from my gut, and I was going to bring him in for a fucking Band-Aid! Sure. Nurial was sorry, though, that it hadn't worked out that way. The Pineapple was actually a good guy. I gave him the kill; I had enough. He'd get to go home with a gook story fit for the Marine rifle team. The Rogues, well, we'd just walk off into the sunset, thank you.

I took the patrol back to the hill and on into Evans. It'd been one year and one week, exactly, since I'd tripped the booby trap with Pearl. I'd held the patrol off last week to stay in and get drunk in honor of my luck the previous year. Now, on the very next patrol, I had that happen. I hoped nobody'd write the Greek; he'd be even more convinced God was saving me for something. He probably was, I thought, a five-hundred-pounder.

At Evans, it was time to get real about the monsoon. The rains were starting, and I needed a boat. The lieutenant told us to go back to Hill 51 and it'd be along "mo ricky-tick." Is this really gonna work or what? Since I'd only be able to take five of us on the boat, it was a great time to slim down the patrol again. I decided on Raid, Z, Tomo, and Det Cord. With me as the not so fearless leader, we'd have a hell of a crew.

Back at Evans, I checked out the AK I took from my dead friend. It had a round in the chamber, the hammer had come home, and the primer on the round was busted. How lucky can a guy get? I wanted the AK as a souvenir, but "the Man" said no. Now why the fuck not? I didn't know, but I took the round out of it, burned primer and all, and sent it home to be with my Chicom grenade. We headed back to 51 and the bush.

I walked along, thinking about the problems we faced. I had to do something about our continuing supply problems. By that point, I'd been three months without a change of jungle clothes. Supply could get in nothing that worked if you were bigger than a midget. It was amazing, all the REMFs were walking around in nice, new jungle fatigues, looking cool. Only problem was, they could have been serving in downtown L.A. as far as the war was from them. Mom had been sending the Rogues socks for two months. She sent us our camo face paint! But as far as I could recall, Cecilia Ann Roe Kugler ain't even an E-1 in supply for 3d Mar Div. Even I was starting not to like us, we smelled so bad.

The supply lines sucked, but being without food was the last straw. The petty Stateside Marine Corps was creeping in more everyday. We had to carry regular Marine soft cover hats with us on patrol. Why? So we could take off our bush hats at the perimeter of Evans and switch to our standard-issue M1A1 green soft covers like everyone else in the rear. So I guess it was no surprise that they screwed up on supplying us with C rats. And we had to have C rats to survive; the mess hall food was all but inedible. The fact that we hadn't gotten many packages since Greek got launched made matters even worse.

So I decided to sneak into the supply tent and steal a case of C-rat hamburgers on the way out one night. It was midnight and darker than dark out. I was tired already. I couldn't use a light inside or the guard would see me. I'd memorized where the stuff was that afternoon. I had a huge gook rucksack that I'd borrowed from one of my NVA kills; he wouldn't need the sucker anymore. I don't know how the little bastard carried the thing, it was so big. I was six foot three, and it went down to my ass. If I filled it up, I'd fall flat.

I couldn't see a thing. I stumbled through the tent, counting rows, looking for horrible food they wouldn't give us. I heard a sentry walking one of those boring shifts inside the camp. Who'd steal from there except some lowlife like me? Of course, it was bureaucratic bullshit that had me standing there, wasting time, waiting for a half-asleep grunt to stumble by. I wanted back in the bush. I couldn't take all the nonsense. They fucked with us for our meals, we got no new trousers, no fucking face paint . . . I felt my way along in the dark. Ahh, I've got it at last! I pulled it off the shelf and nearly popped a nut. The box was heavy. Did I really want those mothers that bad? Oh hell, I took it. At least it would break the monotony. I dropped it in my rucksack and headed out to meet the Rogues. I barely fit through the door of the damn tent with the NVA ruck on.

Face blackened, rucksack dragging my ass, I joined Raid and the Rogues for the trip to Co Bi Than Tan. It was hot, wet, and it was a bitch out there. My back was killing me big time. It was a five-mile walk in the rain. I was slipping and sliding along behind Z and Raid. Why the hell was I carrying that big a load? I was one dead mother. . . . About halfway out it started really pouring. Suddenly I felt like I was walking in a shower with no lights, a foot of mud, and no drain. There was little light except for an occasional illumination round off in the distance at Evans. Looking down, everything I saw looked grayish, almost like wet cement. I looked up, and Z and Raid were way out ahead. They were leaving me behind. I looked down again, and it looked like we were patrolling through a lake. The water came up out of nowhere. It was all around us.

I started edging along, doing a shuffle, sliding my feet, one behind the other. I reached down and unfastened my harness. I didn't think the water was that deep, but I remembered last monsoon when a guy could drown his ass in that shit. It got real dark again as the illumination died. I was still shuffling along in slow motion when—*zoom!* I slipped feet first, sliding with a splash, and was deep under water. Thank my lucky stars I'd unfastened my harness; it was loaded heavy with grenades and magazines. I went under and kicked off the bottom. When I popped up, I flung my harness to the bank. Between my harness and my rucksack with the case of C-rat hamburgers, I weighed a ton. I needed to jettison some weight or . . . shiiit . . . down I went again. I tried again to kick off the bottom. Where the fuck was Raid? Z? Anybody? Why didn't they slip in this shit?

I kicked with all I had to get back to the surface. I came up spitting gray, foul-tasting water. I could feel the slope of the ground under my feet. As I broke the surface, daylight was just coming to life. I could see silhouettes of people. Was it . . . Z . . . or . . . Raid . . . ? They were just standing, looking at me. As I tried to tread water, I reached out for a hand . . . it was Tomo. He was reaching for me, but he was laughing. I missed his hand and went back down. I kicked and was treading water despite the rucksack. I came up again to see my comrades laughing hysterically. Bastards! Clearly, I was on my own. I got my bearings and treaded water enough to realize I was in a big hole. I looked around as I spread my feet and realized I could touch on two sides. But I slipped and slid wherever I touched. I was in a slime hole, a water buffalo hole. I made my way to one side, carefully moving my feet in the slime and keeping my head out of the water. Raid yelled, "Kug, we'd get you out, but you're a scream thrashin' round in that buffalo shit." It was a party, and I was the main attraction. Damn! I'd been slimed in buffalo shit!

I dug, clawed, and scraped my way up and out of the slop hole. It was daylight by that time, and we were near one edge of an old rice paddy. It was gray out, but not as gray as I was; I was coated with gray slime, head to toe. And stink! Man did I stink. Where was the rain when I needed it? I'd need a typhoon to get the slime off me.

We regrouped and headed off to 51. The hysteria of the moment vanished, kicked out by the ball-busting hills along our way. Just below 51, I went down to the river and rinsed off as best I could. Up at 51, I didn't have a change of clothes, but I would have my fucking hamburgers. I flopped down in my little hootch after our six-hour walk. My shoulders were sore and bruised from humping that holstein of a pack. I was whipped! I'd crossed two rivers, countless ass-kicking hills, and about drowned in a hole filled with liquid shit. What a night!

I rested for a minute, then sat up to open my pack. I'd have some burgers. I pulled open the strings, and I couldn't believe my tired-ass, lying eyes. It just couldn't be. Lo and behold, the ton of hamburgers I'd just carried out there was none other than a case of seventy-two bottles of Louisiana Red Hot Sauce. My back was near broke, and I had no supper. Damn it! I like hot sauce, but seventy-two bottles! We'd have to use it to barter with the grunts on the hill. I'd get over it.

The monsoon was coming, but it wasn't full steam just yet. The rains came and went, but we could see a change in the making. COC sent word out that our boat was on the way. Two days later, an old UH-34 appeared off on the horizon. The bow of the boat was clearly visible sticking out the door. Man did that look weird. It landed and Tomo, Raid, and I ran out to help unload. What a trip! The valley wasn't flooded yet, and those guys were dying to know what we were going to do with it. Hell, the paddies were full, but the river was a foot away from spilling over. The three of us dragged the boat off the chopper. It was aluminum, but it was damned heavy. We dropped it, and turned to wave the chopper off when the crew chief waved me back over. He was yelling at me, "Get the motor!" The motor? What the hell was he talking about? Turned out there was a thirty-five-horse Evinrude inside. Tomo and I grabbed it and headed off. We did it! We got our boat.

We looked around the hill, and grunts were all around, staring, wondering what the hell we were up to. All my guys were there except Z. Where the hell could he be?

Tomo and I got our heads together to assess what we had: a fourteen-foot, aluminum, flat bottom swamp boat, four paddles, a thirty-five-horse Evinrude, and a small gas tank. There were only five of us and it took four of us to carry the boat. It would be tough enough climbing those hills with a big boat. And then a motor no less? The Evinrude! That was a real kick. The colonel had come through for us, but I couldn't take the Evinrude. We all knew that. Hell, they'd hear us coming in Hanoi. We'd carry the boat down and paddle that mother around. We'd hide it down in the valley and camouflage it. I was psyched.

"Where the hell's Z?" I asked Raid. He didn't know, but went in search of his red ass. He couldn't find Z, so we all looked around. No joy. Then Tomo and I heard hammering over by arty. We cut through the bushes, and there was my man, Z. He was busting up ammo boxes. Arty boxes, excited as all hell. I mean he was energized. He had two long pieces of wood that he'd tore from an arty shell box. He was trying to nail the rope box handles on the long wood, right in the damned middle. "Z, what the fuck are you doing?" I barked at him. He was like a whirling dervish. I said, "Z!"

"Kug, I'm making some water skis, man. With that boat and the Evinrude, you can take me waterskiing down at the river." I couldn't believe it, but he was serious as a gook with a hand grenade. While it would have been fun, a real kick, we couldn't risk it. So, no skiing and no Evinrude.

Now I had Z, even if he was pissed off. Tomo was with me, and I knew I'd find Det Cord off studying somewhere. So where the hell was Raid? Keeping those guys together was worse than herding chickens. I walked back over to the chopper area, and Raid was coming my way, laughing. He'd been off visiting his buds over at mortars, a bunch of black dudes from the East Coast. They thought Raid was crazy for wearing ears around his neck on commo wire, the way Crud did.

I said, "Raid, what the hell you doin'? We gotta go."

He was laughing as he said, "Aaah! They were on my ass about my ears. So I told 'em I was gonna cut the next guy's peter off and bring it to 'em." As he finished, he walked on with the rest of us.

"You assholes, we gotta go," I said as we left to prep for the midnight christening of the USS *Rogue*.

With Det Cord leading us to the river, we took off on schedule. The rest of us carried the boat down behind him, a serious ball buster. I called COC and set our route for the day. We didn't want any friendlies blowing us away. Z checked the area for booby traps before we went down and put it in, and he gave us the okay. We grabbed the boat and eased it into muddy water that looked like brown paste.

It was so hot we felt like we were paddling along under a magnifying glass. It was early morning, and we were learning to go slow and quiet. The water began to look like a bad chocolate shake and a lot thicker, and it was very piss warm. There was a thicket downstream we'd staked out for a few days. I had hopes we'd catch some dumb bad guy around there, so we paddled over and stepped out into the mud, then we hid the boat and crawled up to and inside the thicket. We took turns sacking out, but it was so hot the sweat woke me up rolling around my body. When we were up, we were usually solving world hunger, debating the issues of the day. It was very hot that day, so we couldn't sleep well.

Bizarre things began to happen when you had a mixture of rest and boredom. Z decided he wanted to take some fish back to the hill for supper. We decided to take the boat and take Z fishing. We'd just float along and chuck hand grenades in the water. The damn fish would just float to the top. Then we'd paddle Z along so he could lean out and gather his catch.

We drifted our way back toward Hill 51. Det Cord was in the bow, the point man on our little ship. Z and Raid were in the middle, with me and Tomo filling the two anchor seats. The four of us provided the power, and Det Cord pointed the way, hopefully with rifle at the ready. It was still smoking out. By late afternoon, we were maybe five miles south of the hill. The trees along the river had branches that bent lazily beneath its surface. But it was *hot*. Where was the monsoon when you needed it? It was there last week. We were debating and chucking grenades while Z had visions of fish for supper back up on 51. And Det Cord started bugging me to let him toss a couple of blasters in the mud, too.

Now Det Cord was a great guy in the bush. He was called Det Cord because he liked to blow things up, and he usually carried enough explosives into the bush to make us all disappear. The only problem was the guy was clueless when it came to common sense. And common sense kept him and me from letting him chuck a grenade so close to all of us. He could barely open a beer can without help. He set a charge once to blow a booby trap while we were all waiting on the low side of a little hill. He yelled, "Fire in the hole!" and came running down. I was lying on my back, head resting on my pack, just staring into outer space when I saw a booby trap flying through the air at about thirty feet. It cleared me and flew out about another twenty feet, then did an air burst. *Kaboom!* Man, it was beautiful for sure, Det Cord nearly killed us all! So, was I going to take a chance in the boat? No way, man; I loved the guy like a brother, but I loved living more.

We kept moving down the river, rowing along. Det Cord resorted to begging by that point, just whining. "You're not fair," he said, relentless in pursuit of the big bang. "Kug. Kug. Come on, let me drop a grenade. I'll be careful. Come on Kug. Come on!"

Well, I was bored as hell and about to burst into flames any minute, so I thought I might as well blow up as burn up. "Throw the damn thing. Just get it out and away from us," I said.

But, when Sergeant Kug relented, everybody else got angry. We were all crammed into one little boat, with everyone bitching. Frustrated, I told Det Cord to stand up and get it over with. He was standing, wobbling back and forth like a tree about ready to fall, a grenade in his hand and a smile on his face. He reared back, and stopped, looked at me for approval.

I screamed. "Throw the damn thing!" He pulled the pin and, with a grin the size of a watermelon, motioned in the direction he intended to toss it. I said, "Go, go, go, man! Throw the damn thing." Ready to throw, he turned and somehow dropped the grenade right on the nose plate at the front of the boat! The grenade hit the triangular plate that holds the front of the boat together at the bow. *Bang! Plink! Blub!* It rolled into the water.

Disbelief? Shock? No time for that shit! No pandemonium either! A real no-nonsense kind of moment. A grenade was in the water about two fucking inches from our boat. It was sinking fast but not fast enough for us. Meanwhile, Tomo and I were performing a *serious* back-paddle. Det Cord was still standing, staring into the water, wobbling back and forth. The world was back in slow motion, but we were viewing it all at double speed! What a cheap-ass way to buy the . . . *Kaboom!* Time was standing still, but we weren't! The boat rocked, water bubbled up, and Det Cord was weaving, but standing like a half-dazed fighter. The muffled boom sent a water plume up in the air beside us. The bottom of the boat took the brunt of the blast, and we heard a wave of little *tick* sounds as shrapnel hit it. We ended up with lots of dents but no holes, even though the boat did some serious rocking and rolling.

The terror of the moment gave way to the anger of four-fifths of a boatload of pissed-off Marines. Det Cord was still standing like a statue, a sick smile frozen on his face. We were still floating! But Tomo was irate. He hated Det Cord anyway. He stood straight up, grabbed his rifle by the barrel, and took a roundhouse swing. *Smack!* He caught Det Cord right in the middle of the ass. Det Cord went flying headlong into the mud of the river. Raid was crouched down, ducking the roundhouse blow. If any gooks were in the area, they must have had a heart, or we would have been dead meat by then.

Det Cord paddled around like a duck, trying to figure

out what the hell had happened to him. We got to shore and reeled him in. I wanted to *di di* before our luck ran out, so we paddled away from there while Tomo cooled his jets. For a while there, he'd been ready to take the Rogues down to four by killing Det Cord and saying he'd got lost. We eventually made it back to Hill 51.

We took a day to regroup before we headed back out to the bush. We'd yet to get Johan, and we hadn't got our revenge for Greek, Stu, and Crud—not to mention Pearl, me, and thirty or so grunts. We'd survive without it, but Greek asked us to fuck up a gook for him. So we had to try. It was near the end of 1967. I was twenty-one. I could go home and get a drink. I needed to extend. It'd be my fourth. Tomo had just extended for his second six months, as had Det Cord, which in his case may not have been a great idea. He was always wacky. We couldn't get Z or Raid to extend. They were great to have around and they lived life to the fullest, but they wanted to return to the World.

There was lots of talk about moving us north again. Khe Sanh was heating up. Even there in Co Bi Than Tan, we were seeing more gooks than ever before. Hunting was as good as it had been, but hunting in general wasn't what interested me; I wanted Johan. And it was time to make our hit. After the holidays, I knew from all the scuttlebutt, they'd be moving us north one more time, so I put plans in place to go down to Johan's again. Then we'd go to the far reaches of the valley where dumbshit tried to put the AK round in my stomach. That one would be the better part of seven days, and we'd take the boat in part of the way, stash it, then move in by night. Johan's luck was about to run out.

Our last few patrols had been wild. Raid got his kill

and got to blow the minds of the mortarmen of Hill 51. He went down to search the body and cut off an index finger. He stuffed it in his jungle-jacket pocket for the trip back to 51. We all hid in the bushes by mortars when Raid made his triumphant return. He took the finger and held the nail end in the palm of his hand with the bloody stub sticking out. He approached the mortar crew from back east like he was sneaking up on a squad of gooks. They were playing cards on an ammo-box table when Raid walked up and stuck that bloody stump out of his hand right in the middle of them. He said, "Hey, Willie, look what I brought ya!" Those dudes were screaming like coeds at a frat party. In their haste to avoid the fickle finger, they flipped the table upside down, and cards flew everywhere. Threatening Raid's life, they ran away. That provided us some comic relief, and they were glad to see the Rogues leave the hill one more time.

We loaded down for the big one, and off we went. We were still running on the same clothes and Mom's socks, but we were back to homemade charcoal face paint. I hadn't shaved or had a haircut in two months. We went down and picked up the USS *Rogue* from where we'd hidden it in the bushes. Raid and Z checked it for booby traps, said it was A-OK, and we were off. It was dark, hot, and wet, and raining again, but nothing like last year. We paddled along to the south and to the footbridge, where we hid the boat before dawn. Then the five of us made our way inland. We hid out for two days, just eyeballing the area. Activity was higher than I'd seen before. I called in some air strikes, a little arty, but we continued to play our trump card—patience. We'd outwait the little bastards; I wanted Johan. No Johan, no shots with the sniper rifles.

On night three, we went into position from the valley

side, something we'd never done before. We made it and were on the south knoll in the usual four feet of grass. We worked hard at insuring we were camouflaged as well as we'd ever been. First light came, and there was activity on the top of the U, across from us. The tree line had movement. With arty and all just a phone call away, there wasn't a gook safe within two miles if I was calling in. I decided to drop arty on the tree line.

We phoned back to Evans and laid out the coordinates. The call was for a "fire for effect" with airbursts right out of the blocks. I knew exactly where we were. Arty knew my call sign and let it rip. It was beautiful! It walked down that tree line like I knew what I was doing. There was no more movement. Tomo leaned over and whispered, "Kug, you shoulda got that on film."

Mom had sent me over a Super-8 camera for Christmas but I never had it out when something cinematic hit the fan. Hell! I said to Tomo, "You're right, I gotta do it over." I went to my rucksack and pulled out the trusty Kodak, then called COC back and ordered another fire for effect. Pretty soon an instant replay raged across the tree line. *Boom! Boom! Baboom!* I got it all, alive and in color. I could relive that Kodak moment forever. Raid reminded me that my film cost the taxpayers about $50,000. Who cared? It wasn't even a rounding error in that war. Hell, McNamara and his Whiz Kids wasted that much in paper, playing what-if games with themselves.

The day ground on with unsteady rain and steady heat. The monsoon was quite different from last year's. It was hotter, and the valley still was not a lake. It was midafternoon, and there was still no more activity. I knew we hadn't got all those bastards; I was lucky, but not that damned lucky. By that time, my gang was getting fidgety; we'd been in place for over eight hours; we were cramped, tired, and sick of burning up. Still, something told me to hold tight. Tomo agreed with my hunch. No motion, no movement, just hours of sitting and lying in the grass.

By 1600 hours, we decided we'd stay there into the night if we had to. I didn't want to go north without knocking Johan stiff. I hadn't even seen him that day. From that distance, four hundred yards, we could pick his ugly ass out of the lineup with the 7×50s. Patience. At 1630, along came our break. There was activity in the tree line on the set of my movie. It was tempting, but I knew it was coming, and we had to hold tight. I knew we were going to get some good action. Everybody was wired and on edge from waiting. The movement picked up again, and we saw bad guys in the tree line. There were seven bad guys that we could count. I passed the word to stand tight and be ready but do nothing. Tomo and I were on the 7×50s. I called COC to put them at the ready with more arty. My preplots were set, and the race was about to begin.

Then ... *What the fuck?* I couldn't believe my eyes! Along came a gook, marching out of the tree line on a beeline for our hill. He was looking like he'd been on a forced march across the paddy. His arms were swinging, and he was almost goose-stepping. There was a river and a tree line between us and them. What was he doing? Tomo dropped his 7×50s and said, "It's Johan." I was watching the guys in the tree line. Something was up for damned sure. Johan was out there to draw fire. A kamikaze mission for damned sure. He must have been a VC private or a screwup like Crud ... he'd sure drawn the short straw.

I tell Tomo it's his turn, and Johan's the winner. I felt bad that they fucked him like that, but that was war in

Nam. I passed the word to the other three to pick a target in the tree line. Det Cord finds another one peering through the tree line down below us along the river where I'd knocked "mean and ugly" out of the game last time out there. There was a bunch of gooks that day. I guess they wanted our asses, too. Johan was marching ankle deep in water, but he wasn't missing a step. He was a hell of a soldier. He started four hundred yards away and was closing in on two hundred. Tomo said he'd sighted in and was ready. "No, hold tight, man, a little closer," I whispered. He was stomping now, angry and defiant, as I gave Tomo the sign to take his ass out. *Boom!*

The guy is fucking amazing. I mean the shot knocked him flat on his ass. He went straight down, and then he was up and running. He's hobbled but trying to get out of there. We knock people dead at seven hundred meters every day of the fucking week, and we miss a clean close-in shot on Johan. He had more lives than me! Tomo was shooting, I was shooting, and suddenly the whole place was shooting. The day erupted in every direction. Holy shiiit! They were fucking everywhere!

Johan zigged and zagged and finally fell in the water near the tree line. He was down and out, but there was no time to celebrate. Lead was landing all around us. The bastards had sent Johan to smoke us out. They sacrificed the poor bastard. The air was full of bullets streaking back and forth. We needed to get out. I had a flashback to Santo Domingo. A man could get killed doing that shit. I got on the hook and called COC for my arty, and none too soon either. The little bastards were filling the hill with hot lead. I got Det Cord and started crawling away around the hill. The other three kept returning fire. We had made about two or three crawls when the arty arrived. No Kodak for that round. But, oh was it beautiful!

I wouldn't want to fight a war without those guys and the jet jockeys.

The arty ripped down through two tree lines right on the mark. What a trip. Everything just stopped. In-fucking-credible! The bad guys either bought the farm or ran away. The silence that followed was deafening. I wasn't sure if it was for real. We crawled away on fast-forward, then regrouped. Z checked in with me; he wanted to get us the hell out of the foothills. No way man! I get Raid going, and he takes us out the draw and down into the riverbed. We agreed to hide until dark and then make our way back up into the foothills for the last leg of our journey. Z wasn't happy, but he'd do it. I could always count on him.

In the early hours of the morning. Raid worked us down to the end of the valley and the farthest foothills. We'd hold up until near first light when we'd move into position. I left two people on watch. We'd rotate hourly. I lay back and looked up as the monsoon sky smothered the moon. There was no magical mirror for me to stare into that night, nothing to magically transport me back to the World the way I used to go. The World? It was so far away, I couldn't imagine it anymore. I really couldn't relate. The girlfriends were long gone, except LuAnn. And she was way too serious for me. Nothing and no one made sense anymore. I wasn't sure I wanted to go back to that World. Why should I? I was good at being a sniper. They might as well have had somebody there who wanted to be there. It would be better than the new ones we were getting in who did more whining and sniveling than anything else. I couldn't connect that night, all I could do was think about tomorrow.

Raid moved us into place just before first light. Our position was on the tip of a long finger that ran out from the hills behind us. It was our favorite, tall grass! We were about four grid squares south of the shoot-out the day before. That put us way, way south of the friendlies at Hill 51. The day was an off-and-on battle between driving rain and blazing sunshine. The river lay to our front and protected us from the bad guys playing the valley floor. About six hundred yards to our right was a tree line. Running to the left were rice paddies, half-filled with dirty water from the monsoon rains. To the far left, another tree line was eight hundred to nine hundred meters out. It was all like a big open playing field.

It was year-end, and we were about to move north. Lots of gooks were on the move, and so were we. Things were changing big-time, so we needed to get the work in the valley done while we could. They were about to make us change rifles, and we all hated the thought of giving up our Winchesters, but the brainchildren were going to get their way, and we'd all have new Remington 700s soon. I just hoped they weren't anything like the M-16.

The day wore long and hard. Noontime brought monsoon rains that were chased away by the searing afternoon heat. We hung tight . . . patience would win, the way it always did. Det Cord was on the 7×50s late in the day. I was pondering extending for another six months, which would take me right to the end of my enlistment.

"Kug, Kug, look!" Det Cord's excited chant came my way. He was rarely excited. I crawled over for a look. "Oh my aching ass!" I couldn't believe my eyes. Coming out of the tree line to my right was a column of NVA. It was broad daylight, and they were truckin' across the paddies like it was I-70.

I get on the hook to COC . . . this is big. The bastards were in full uniform with packs so big and so heavy that the guys were doubled over forward. They were moving out in a forced march like they were possessed. They had a mission. The lieutenant calls out asking why we ain't taken a shot. Now that fucking question deserved a prize. We were counting as they went ... ten ... twenty ... thirty ... forty ... the colonel was on the radio for an update. Tomo had all the Rogues at the ready. The shot'd be long, and the targets were moving ... seventy ... eighty. We set the arty plots in the tree lines. I'd have to try and walk them where the army of bad guys was. By then, the NVA column stretched from tree line to tree line. I couldn't believe it, a whole company and more.

The colonel wanted the straight scoop. He wanted to rally a Sparrow Hawk to come in and go after them. I gave the coordinates on the arty plots, then called for a fire for effect! The little guys were asshole to belly button and moving out. They were packing more weight than a grain train in Kansas.

The strange encounter the day before suddenly made sense. Somebody wanted us the hell out of there. They were motoring south toward Hue. When I got to a hundred and thirty, the colonel told me to quit counting and start shooting. I'm crazy as a fucking loon, but not crazy enough to take five snipers and fire off a round against a couple of hundred bad guys armed to the teeth. The arty took longer than usual, but when it arrived, it was a beautiful sight. I picked the plot in the far-left tree line and walked it over, left to right. The little bastards were disciplined; they went down with the ship, without breaking ranks. I was damned impressed. The rounds were singing in and exploding all around and on the now frantic column of gooks.

It amazed me that the little guys didn't break ranks; they just split in the middle, with half running forward to the left and the other half to the right, during a real "bombs bursting in air" moment. All the guns in Evans must have been aimed our way. I sat watching through the 7×50s during one of the most beautiful moments I'd had in a while. That arty was just beeeautiful.

With the arty in the air, Tomo and the gang were firing away. Raid got one closer in, Tomo one, and Det Cord, too. But the shells were blowing away several at a time. I was calling more arty and more arty on fewer and fewer visible targets. I was getting off on just watching this one.

One poor bastard was in the middle of the paddy, about two hundred yards across the no-man's-land where all the hot metal had been flying around. He was doubled up beneath a pack the size of a water buffalo. Shells were exploding in front of him and to the left. He turned and started running to the right, back the way he came. The arty wasn't lettin' up, they were getting off on it back at Evans. *Boom. Boom. Boom!* Arty was coming in everywhere out there. "Oh shit, man . . . move . . . go . . . go," I heard myself saying. Then I realized I wasn't hearing any shooting. I looked over to see that the Rogues had stopped firing; they were all up on their knees watching the war below. *Boom! Boom! B'boom!* More artillery exploded in front and beside that poor gook with the VW on his shoulders. The right wasn't working, so he turned again and started running toward the left. "Go, motherfucker, go!" Tomo was yelling. What the fuck? He hated the bastards. What the hell was going on? More arty, and the poor sucker turned around again. That pack was going to crush the little bastard if he tripped. It was like watching a ball game from up there. "Go . . . go . . . go." He was chugging by then, heading back to the right, back to go.

"Run, run!" Raid was in the swing of the game, too.

Our lone gook was getting into a rhythm. He was kind of bouncing along.

He's got fifty yards left, forty yards . . . we're up in a crouch . . . we're cheering him on. "Go man, go!" Raid's hands in the air, waving him on . . . Oh man, don't buy the big one now, I thought. He's running . . . twenty yards to freedom. He's gonna make it, we thought. "Go, asshole, go!" Det Cord is up smiling his ass off. He was never into cheering. "Come on man, you can do it," he said. I hear more arty from Evans. It's coming, man. "Come on, you're slowin' down, asshole," I said. Oh shit.

B'b'boom, boom, boom . . . kaaaaboom! Dirt and muck fly everywhere, shower the area all around. Suddenly, the bad guy was gone. He went up in smoke, got vaporized. I've heard it said but never saw it happen before. The dust settled around a new hole in the ground where our hunchback sprinter had stood just a minute earlier. He'd nearly made it.

"Son of a bitch," Z yelled. "The son of a bitch should have made it. Fuckin' war anyway!" That guy was okay.

With the sudden disappearance of our distant friend, the battlefield grew quiet except for the drone of the Bird Dog spotter flying overhead. Bodies lay everywhere amid the holes strewn about the dilapidated paddies. The grunt Sparrow Hawk reaction force was on the way. The Bird Dog took over the spotting duties from us, and we went down to the river, picked up our boat, and paddled to 51. It had been a hell of a trip. We'd rained death on a whole circus load of bad dudes. One of us got Johan, but we didn't know who'd done it. I got another one along with Det Cord. On the big hurrah, a total of thirty-five dead NVA was confirmed by the spotter plane. We knew Tomo, Z, and Raid each got one. That left thirty-two for me and the arty machine.

On 51, we got a couple days' rest before word came down that we were moving north. And they gave us the Remington 700s, too. They didn't shoot near as far as the 30-06s. We packed up and boarded a small convoy heading north to the DMZ. The ride was hours long but seemed like days. We left Evans and headed north on Highway 1, through Quang Tri and on into Dong Ha. After a brief stop, we made a left and headed out to Camp Carroll. We set a tighter security and headed out Highway 9 past Cam Lo toward the Rockpile. It was still scary as hell up there. The underbrush on both sides of Highway 9 was ten or twelve feet high. Out there you could get a serious case of the heebie-jeebies in a heartbeat.

We made a left near the Rockpile and headed up the mountain to the east of Highway 9. Boy, they'd built that up since my walk through there the previous year with Colonel Masterpool. We headed to a mountaintop base, Camp Carroll, which was named after Captain Carroll, a KIA on Operation Prairie. We had a new home with lots of new snipers and lots of gooks out in the mountains. New Year's was just around the corner. I guess we'd be in our new home for the holidays.

CHAPTER EIGHT

The DMZ, It Ain't
What It Used to Be

The convoy came to a stop atop the high mountain base, which looked like something out of World War II. It was shrouded in clouds, and a heavy mist hung in the air. It was muddy, and puddles stood everywhere amid rows of tired green tents. I was just about to jump down from the back of my six-by when an earsplitting roar raced in with a thundering *boooom!* It was followed closely by screams of "Incoming!" Welcome to the new and improved DMZ.

Before I could scream or shit my pants, I was following all the other elbows and assholes looking for a bunker or a trench or *anything* that was below ground level. Five more rounds came roaring in, followed by the cries of the wounded. The second truck in the convoy took a direct hit. The incoming turned out to be a welcome to us 4th Marines; the NVA called the COC on the radio to welcome us to their turf. It was my first encounter with 140mm gook rockets, and they were frightening. Life at the DMZ was never good, but just then, it was downright horrible. As Greek would have said, "There goes the fuckin' neighborhood."

The colonel ordered an underground COC be built. For two days, every available swinging dick was digging the colonel's new house. We filled sandbags nearly twenty-four hours a day. I was so tired and so sick of those sandbags, I could have slit my wrists. That was real work; I needed to get us to the bush and fast. It was also dangerous as hell sitting there, waiting to get blown halfway home. I didn't want to go out with the grunts either, not in that damned country. But our digging and filling seemed like they would never end. I'd never seen so many sandbags. Dig and fill and pile them up . . . then do it all over again and again. We got just enough incoming to give me a taste of what Zulu was getting in Khe Sanh. And I didn't like it at all.

Christmas on Carroll came and went, and so did Raid. He was headed home. A hell of a guy and one I'd miss. I extended but the lieutenant would only let me sign on for three months. He said it had to be my last. Tomo and Det Cord extended, too. Things were quiet over the holidays, and we used the time to dig our own bunkers once we finished the COC. The big guys were sure that we were going to get hit with some heavy shit from the north. The DMZ was always a tough place, but I had no idea what to expect anymore.

Everything seemed different up there. It wasn't the Wild West anymore; it was Washington, Far East version. The fucking bureaucracy was thicker than the monsoon mist covering up Carroll. The first casualties of the modern Vietnam Marine Corps were my hair, beard, and demeanor. I had to cut my hair for the first time in three months, shave, and take a good bath. The clothes I'd worn for the previous three-plus months without a change went into the trash so I wouldn't smell like Co Bi Than Tan anymore. I wouldn't be the Rogue of the valley, so I'd have to be King of the fucking mountain. But first I had to fly right and keep the Rogues intact and out of trouble.

We finished building a large bunker next to our squad tent. It was about four feet deep and twenty feet long, divided in the middle with sandbags. The roof was six layers of sandbags, lying flat with a latticework of metal tent stakes between the layers. The work was done and the cease-fire was keeping things cool, and it was New Year's. Our new hootch was adorned with a game Mom sent over, a life-size poster of a nude woman where we played pin the tits on the broad. Now *that* was a game for the Rogues. We got good and drunk, and hell, with any luck, we'd miss the New Year.

I got totally drunk and went to lie down on my rack. I wanted to trip out. Three months left. What was I going to do back in the World? I'd just take it all one day at a time. Just make sure I was the one standing in the morning. I had to be the winner. It was all just a game, just a fucking game. I was trying to cool my jets and lay back, but I couldn't trip out because Hoss was outside complaining about something he'd bought from an ARVN lieutenant. I wished he'd just shut up.

I hated the ARVN worse than the I did the NVA. Did I say worse than the NVA? Hell, I liked the NVA, at least they had balls! At least they had honor! At least they'd die for what the hell they believed in. At least they didn't run like rabbits when the shit hit the fan.

I couldn't sleep. I had a headache the size of Texas. It was hotter than blue blazes on an oil fire. Everybody was partying, I was drunk, and Hoss was still moaning. My last clear memory was of attempting to light a cigarette that had been doused in a liquid that was "absofuckinlutely" guaranteed to give me a buzz. . . .

* * *

The bright morning sun beat down on me. I hadn't moved yet. Just lying there moving one eyelid was about the best I could hope for. I was in bad shape. Did somebody drive a spike in my ear sideways? No matter; I had to rise from the dead to get me and the Rogues ready for the patrol we'd planned. Of course, in my condition I couldn't have led my way to the local pisser. So the patrol lead would have to go to Tomo; I was in deep shit.

By noontime, we were long gone. I had some bruised brains, and even the bush hat hurt my forehead. I just wanted to go out into the bush and sleep my hurt away. Whew! What a day. New Year's? Somebody said it was New Year's.

Tomo took us out, and the terrain there was rugged and dangerous. It was a lot worse the way I was feeling. I shouldn't have been there, but I was not letting these guys go without me. I know my time here is finally limited; I don't want to reenlist in the Corps. I've grown to love being a sniper and especially a Rogue. But the peacetime Corps wasn't for me. I'd slit my wrists, or they'd have me in the brig.

Tomo was doing okay, and I knew he was cool. There was an old village in a high valley, east of Carroll, and he was taking us in there. It was a scary place as we approached near dusk. We were out to fulfill Tomo's dream and answer Greek's request, finally. We were going to capture a live gook. That's why we'd brought Hoss. He'd been absent when they handed out smarts, but he was strong as an ox with an attitude. He carried my radio. He reminded me of Jethro on *The Beverly Hillbillies*, but he looked like he'd been hit upside the head one too many times. I'll remember the big dude forever because of his sense of humor. Sick? None sicker. He got his Purple Heart with some shrapnel to the knee. Well, when those telegrams were sent home, they were general, mentioning things like "wounds to the lower extremities." When Hoss got hit in the knee, it was just three or four weeks off, nothing terrible. So he writes his mom, and in the first paragraph says, "Mom, I've been wounded. Everything's going to be okay but you need to cut off all my right trouser legs at the knee!" Well his dad wrote back and said she passed out before she read the "Ha, ha, I'm kidding" note he put in the next paragraph. His dad wanted to kill him. I knew the feeling well; I wanted to kill him half the time.

We got set in early, and Hoss was the only one of us who could sleep. His brain was already fried. The rest of us kicked back, leaving Z on watch. Most of us were philosophizing about life back in the "fuckin' World." Night at least made the heat bearable. It was monsoon time, but the heat and humidity were like sitting inside a dog's mouth. But we were ready to kick some ass just on general principles. I didn't like it up there at the DMZ anymore. Between all the bad guys roaming around, the 140mm rockets, and the mixed-up monsoon with its heat, well, we were hot enough to explode.

Tomo had a fantasy about wrestling a gook to the ground with his bare hands and beating the life out of his ugly ass. None of the rest of us shared that particular vision, but hey, to each his own. For me, I just assumed the NVA must all be karate experts.

Nightfall was nearby. Patience was long gone, and it was time for the first bell of the wrestling match. I was afraid the patrol would prove to be one of my dumber moves in the Nam. How did ever I agree to that bullshit? I got impatient and moved us out a little sooner than I should have. I knew we had some real bad boys in the neighborhood. I knew what we could do, but the DMZ felt different, scary. We quickly found a trail. Trail, hell, it was a superhighway. It led from the east, where the active villages were, and on across the paddies into "our" ville, where the cadres lived who dealt with the travelers from the North, providing them with food and whatnot for the journey on south. Or so I guessed.

We moved in quickly. I worried, maybe too quickly. When we reached our site, it was nearly pitch black. We didn't know the area as well as the valley, and we were taking some chances. If we came in too early and were spotted, it could be a deadly mistake. All this so Tomo could jump a gook. The Rogue mentality had taken over my life. Hell . . . it *was* my life. The girls back home were long gone. I had no mind space left, but for Nam. We stopped, and I called in to the grunt platoon up on Carroll, some three thousand meters to our west. I set out protective preplots for mortars. If needed, they'd protect us where we sat and cover our most obvious escape routes. But I didn't like what I felt at all. After nearly two years in country, I could almost taste trouble; I could feel it deep inside!

The five of us set in with an old village to our rear. We crawled into the dense brush at trail's edge. The grass and bush were real tall all around, perhaps five or five and a half feet high. It didn't take a brain surgeon to figure out that what we were doing wasn't sniper work. Our sniper rifles were packed away, but our full-auto M-14s were at the ready. Up in the DMZ, the bad dudes moved all night; they gave up the days to U.S. airpower. Well, that night, we planned to take it to them.

Sitting in the thick bush, the five of us were maybe four feet back from the trail. The four shooters were ready. Tomo was curled down at the trail's edge. We were counting on hitting three, four, maybe five gooks who'd slip in from the east where they lived as real-life citizens during the day.

The plan was simple. Regardless of which direction they came from, when the gook crew came by, we'd let 'em go by, almost. When the last one passed, Tomo would spring from hiding and roll his little dude into the bushes on the other side and hold him down while the rest of us would level the others in a heartbeat.

While visions of sugarplums were dancing in my head, I was startled by rustling in the brush up and to my left rear! Oh fuck. There was a small rise of dirt at the south edge of the village just behind us. Bursting with yet another adrenaline rush, I whirled around. I couldn't see a thing, but I knew what I'd heard. I froze. The others tensed up like me. They heard it. We're in here close. I motioned for the rest to stay still, and partially turned to look again. Wired, ready to kill, run, or both, I tried not to shit my pants. It was 0 dark 30 and real lonely. I saw a silhouette on the rise behind me. The night sky was clear, and the silhouette I could see didn't look like a good guy. I carefully and quietly took out my starlight scope. We didn't normally use them mounted on the rifle; for our work they were too clumsy and heavy.

I raised the scope to my right eye and scanned the horizon. It lit up for me like a silver tunnel. It was eerie looking out through this baby. As I looked, I was startled by a scraping noise from my left again. Boosted by another adrenaline rush, I turned as quickly as I could. A megarush this time. Fuck! It was coming, man, it was coming! I could taste it. Gooks crouched! Coming around behind us, I knew it. I was counting gooks: two, three, four—shit! I was up to ten! Bad odds at two-to-

one and dark. Damn! The bastards had to have seen us
come in. Patience is a virtue, and I wasn't any too virtuous that night. I knew we shouldn't have gone in there
before it was pitch-black. No time for a committee meeting that night! We needed to hat up.

I reached out and pulled four heads next to mine. I
told them what I'd decided. They said, "Do it!" I got Z
out front, going fast, running down the trail. We were
moving out fast because Z knew the trail wasn't boobytrapped. We'd come in that way last night. I could hear
the bastards running around behind us. Z was out front,
ready to mow down any resistance he ran into, and Hoss
was in front of me with my radio. I was trying to keep up
with him; he had a stride big enough for the Kentucky
Derby. All the time, I was talking to the grunts up at Carroll on the radio. I had a new kid behind me. It was his
first time with us. Still hoping to grab a gook by the ears,
Tomo was bringing up the tail end.

At the edge of the village, Z was about to make a left
up through the brush when the *brrrp, brrrp, brrrp* of
Tomo's M-14 broke the otherwise still starlit night.
Shivers of fear raced up my spine. Why the fuck did I let
us get in here? With Tomo's blast, the whole field behind
us opened up. Small-arms fire filled the night air. Crouching on the sides of the trail, we returned fire. Z took off,
trying to lead us up and out of there. I'd seen ten NVA in
the starlight scope, but the level of lead flying our way
said there were probably more. Tomo passed word up to
"get the fuck outta here, we're in deep shit." Now that
was brilliant, and what, you don't want your fuckin' gook
now, I wanted to say. Nearly running by that time, we
cleared the brush and were into some knee-high grass.
The gooks were close enough that we could hear them
yelling. My lungs and legs were burning as we pushed

our way past the gooks and through the night humidity. I was gasping for air as I yelled into the radio for mortars to fire our preplots. "Hit Alpha and Romeo now!" I gasped. I thanked my lucky stars for the feeling I'd had earlier to set those babies up. We needed desperately to even the odds. The NVA were gaining on us, and it was about three-to-one, gooks up, at that point.

The mortars weren't there, and I was dead from running in that oven. The NVA were outstepping us and the whizbang of AK-47 ammo cracking overhead was getting old fast. Oh *shiiiit!* We stopped, spread out in a five-man line, and dropped into the prone position just as the bad guys cleared the top of the rise behind us. Surprise, motherfuckers! We were slightly above them looking down in the dark of night. We needed to slow them down long enough to run on up the hill. We had to fight! It was a bad time to pick a fight, but what choice did we have? I wasn't fast enough to run away, and I was tired, pissed, and still hungover. Where the *fuck* were the mortars? We heard the gooks below, so we opened up with all we had to give, five 14s doing what they do best! We rained lead and confusion down on our pursuers. It was fucking wild! Cries rang out in the night, a gook chorus but none too together at that point. There was little return fire, and we must have slowed them up. "Move out," I yelled into the night.

Z took off, the rest of us close on his ass. We were scared bloody shitless and adrenaline was rushing through our veins quicker than blood. I was worried I'd shit my pants as I ran. It must have been twenty or thirty yards to the top of the rise, and we were halfway up when I saw movement off to our right. They were trying to flank us. Shiiit! What the fuck, are all these bastards track stars? In unison, we turned and cut loose with another blast of hot lead. I was down on one knee, Tomo was chucking grenades, and Hoss was trying desperately to get mortars. We laid down our barrage and headed off to the races again.

"Where the hell are the mortars?" I yelled at Hoss. I grabbed the radio and called again, but they couldn't hear me. It's tough trying to talk when you're running for your life and out of breath, too. Bastards! We were near the top when lead started flying every-fucking-where, and the clouds rolled in overhead making it darker. We couldn't see Jack Shit if we'd bumped into him. Things were looking bleak, but there had to be a way. I called for illumination off to the southeast. When it came, we could see the glow it cast without exposing ourselves. I was still trying to get a new plan when I realized again how stupid the old one had been. We started running again while I bitched at Carroll about the lack of mortar support. All of a sudden, a blast from an AK-47 stitched the ground, inches from Hoss and me. Then Hoss and my radio were flat gone! *Whoosh!* I mean, he like turned on his afterburners. He took off so fast; he took the handset right out of my hand as I was talking to the mortar platoon.

It was looking bleak about then, and we were on the move again. The only good news? By some miracle, we hadn't taken any casualties yet. We cleared the top of the hill and that was a goodness. It was flat, fifty meters long, but had no damn grass. I knew if we could get across here, it dropped off and down to some paddies and then back up to Carroll. I catch Hoss and my radio. I get back on and . . . fuck . . . the grunts are sending a patrol out to meet us. I *hate* being rescued. There must have been five hundred meters to go. I was dead, physically, burning everywhere—lungs, legs, head, hell, I was already burned out. So it was, *Suck it up, asshole! Do it, man! Run!*

It was the fifty-yard dash, and we had the ball. *Go!* About halfway across the plateau, mortars start landing behind us. No fucking shit! About time I'd say. Too far back I thought. I'd caught Hoss by then and got the rest of the Rogues laid out prone once again, waiting for the gooks to clear the top of the hill and get on the plateau with us. It'd be a thirty-yard shot, if that. We'll make it, man, we'll make it, I told myself. The first mortars were a little off, falling just behind the dead meat chasing us, but I got on the hook and started walking the mortars toward us. When the first gooks cleared the hill, we let them have it. All five of us blasting with M-14s on full auto. Fucking beautiful, man! Some went down in pain, but others to the prone. They started hooking it out with us. A bitch of a time that was, all for Tomo to get his ugly ass a gook.

For a few seconds, our little plateau was like a full-blown shooting gallery—flat out of control! It was wild as hell! Adrenaline was still in good supply. The illumination came in on target. It was hanging behind their backs, and we could see pretty well. Even so, we needed to get out of there. I walked the mortars up the backside of the hill, then I called in for them to dump rounds across the top. They did, and we ran like hell! We ran over and down to the tree line at the edge of the paddies. But we still had to cross the paddies to get to Carroll. We stopped briefly to catch our breath, and I called to stop the illumination so we could cross the paddy dike without silhouetting ourselves. We'll make it, man. I know it. We'll be safe. They'll never follow us that close to the grunts. The mortars were working their stuff, and we could feel the tide turning. Death was working for us again that night. We were about to run the punt back for a touchdown. I could see the end zone in sight. The mortars were nailing the gooks.

The last illumination canister went out, and we were gone—racing across the dike in the black of a bad night. We were about halfway across when some fool shot off another illumination. How the fuck could they? Maybe it was for the grunts? Down we went, face first and belly button flat in the paddies; the gooks might still be in rifle range. Fuck! The mortars were still raining death behind us, and atop the bald hill to our rear, we could see the shapes of two or three crouched gooks silhouetted. They appeared to be looking in our direction. It was weird— they stood still on the hill for maybe a minute as if to let us know we didn't get them all, then they vanished as the illumination dropped out of the night sky.

Finally we stood up on the paddy and made our way back to Carroll. We didn't encounter the grunts because they hadn't left yet. It was probably better they hadn't. I was glad to be back in one piece and safe. Tomo and I decided to chuck his idea of jumping a gook. Things were really fucked up over here anyway. If we were winning the war, then how come there were so many of the cocky little bastards out there?

It was January '68, and Camp Carroll turned out to be one hell of a place to call home. The pigs we replaced there hadn't burned trash for weeks. And we came back to a change of command; the rats controlled the joint. I needed sleep, but the fucking rats in my tent made sleeping scary as hell. Chief, our Navajo sniper, got bit and had to get the rabies shots. Send me to the bush, man.

And then life on Carroll became real depressing. We got three squares at a bad mess hall every day, and shells fell in constantly from our buddies up north. Every few hours, they bombed us. It was Russian roulette with somebody else's gun. And they were shooting some big bullets. After a few days, I needed desperately to get back out to the bush. Tomo and I had had all we could take of the good life. Calls were coming in from grunts in the area for sniper support. By then, I'd been doing my own thing too long to want to go back to that. There was lots of grunt activity below Carroll on Highway 9. I knew the surrounding area from my recon days back in '66. What seemed a lifetime ago.

The lieutenant reluctantly gave me the green light to take the Rogues north of Highway 9. We'd go down to the grunts and leave from there. We caught a ride down from Carroll on the daily resupply convoy, then hopped off with the 9th Marines on Highway 9. It was spooky down there, or maybe I was just getting short. Thick, clumpy bushes, standing taller than us, were growing everywhere. The line of sight was, well, there wasn't one.

We spent the night with the grunts near Mike's Hill. After bumming some Cs, we lay back for some rest before venturing out into no-man's-land. There wasn't a sky to look at that night; everything was black.

It was midnight and time to take off. We left the grunts and headed for the river, about two miles north of Mike's Hill. It was serious bush most of the way. Five of us, loaded to the gills, were looking for a long-distance encounter with the NVA. Our mission? Set in above the river and "harass" any NVA coming for water in the early morning. I walked along, thinking about how we abuse the language in war. Maybe that makes it all seem better? Made it easier. It sure dehumanized the enemy. Just ambush the shit out of "Will" and "put 'im on ice!" "Giv'em a third eye!" Gooks, dinks, bastards, who knows why we did that? More important, who cared?

We were five Rogues strong. My point man, Z, was

shorter than me. He'd picked up after Raid took off. He had the usual array of skills. Nerves of steel, cool as the morning dew, regardless of the heat, and a bonafide nutcase. Crazy as hell! He'd saved my ugly ass like the other two, but none like Hood. But Z was good and carried on the point man tradition of being the best. But that night, even he was spooked going into this place. Me? I was what you could describe as "concerned"! It was one of those serious nights, where every step was magnified a thousand times, where a twig sounded like a Douglas fir crashing in the forest. It was time for nothing but serious work.

Z got us into position above the river, through the black of the DMZ night. The morning sun revealed we were in our favorite cover—grass. We had learned to love the grass. You could get in, hide, see out, and the enemy never suspected we were there. And for all the close calls we'd had, we always got out. To one side, our hill had a steep cliff overlooking the river that signaled the border between the good guys and the bad. The grass was only about four feet high. The cliff was real steep, but it gave us a helluva view. It was a perfect position. Z had done good. I couldn't wait for the party to start. Anticipation ran higher than Dong Ha Mountain to our north.

In a few hours dawn came, but the action didn't. The day wore on like a real bad movie; there was no action to be found anywhere. We knew from experience that good sniping happened in the hours, minutes, and seconds right at dawn as the night became day; or right before dusk, before darkness took control for good. But that day, things were calm, too calm for me. I knew something was going to start cooking any minute. "Get the fuck ready," I passed the word along. But the Rogues were bored and simply looked at me in disbelief.

As the sun rose and it got hotter, we continued to hold tight, snuggled together in the tall grass above the river. Patience, we had to have patience. But nothing was happening. Eventually, I decided to get some Zs. We all crawled in a tight small little circle, and I left Det Cord on watch. Tomo and I lay back for some rest before the fast-rising sun made it impossible to do anything. Our sweet dreams hadn't got to first base when we heard a clanking noise. Startled, we woke up. Det Cord was pointing down the cliff below us. This wasn't just a clanking noise; it was a *serious* clanking noise. It was loud. Tomo sprang to action on hands and knees, crawling to the edge of the cliff. He had a serious face on when he turned and motioned me over. We were all up and on edge. I told Hoss, my radioman, to sit tight. And went to take a look.

Tomo met me, turned, and led the way; both of us were on hands and knees, slithering through the grass to the edge of what seemed like nowhere. About fifty feet straight down the cliff and along the riverbank, going left to right, was a *long* column of NVA solders. No ordinary bunch of bears, they were from the first team: full uniforms, all slicked up, AK-47s, the whole bit. The clanking? A .50-caliber machine gun they were carrying along like they didn't have a care in the world. A .50-caliber? There must have been forty or fifty of the little gook bastards. My first thought was, these are bad odds. And like, where in the hell are these cats heading at 0930 hours?

Tomo was concerned, and that was a real bad sign. The possibilities even had Det Cord raising his eyebrows. What the hell? No meetings, philosophizing, or bullshitting; it was lights, camera, and action time. Tomo and I fixed on their direction. They were going to the hill next to ours. It was like Twin Peaks; we were maybe two hundred meters apart, east to west. We did a backward shuffle, a low crawl to the rear, to reach our three comrades. Three and two make five. Let's see: fifty of them, five of us; ten-to-one in favor of a group of slopes brazen enough to be dancing around in broad daylight while a reinforced company of Marines sat a mile or so to the south, along Highway 9.

I couldn't help but think that if the NVA didn't care about 150 or so troops down by Highway 9, they sure as hell weren't going to worry about five snipers. We'd be breakfast! Adrenaline was pumping so hard I thought I'd blow up. I quietly regrouped. Using our four-foot grass for cover, we got right and ready as our new neighbors continued to move in. Det Cord said the lieutenant was on the hook. The lieutenant? Who the hell wanted the lieutenant? What did he know? He'd never been to the bush yet in six fucking months. I wanted the colonel! I'd done my tricks for him the previous six months in Co Bi Than Tan. He was the 4th Marines regimental CO! He had a clue!

Then I remembered that with the move to the DMZ and Camp Carroll, we were all mixed up. The 9th Marines were up there. I didn't even know the CO there! What the hell was I thinking? And what a time for a daydream to stop by. We could see them. They were setting up the big gun. They had two of them, the .50-calibers next door. It was a sobering experience seeing them in broad daylight in such numbers. The one .50-caliber was down in the grass, and the other they set up on a tripod in broad *daylight*! It was out there, the barrel glistening in the morning sun like the chrome on my brother's 396 Chevy. I took the handset from Det Cord. I wasn't stupid; I needed the lieutenant's or someone's help. I keyed the radio and called, "Birdseye One, Birdseye One, this is Rogue One."

The brains of the outfit comes in all right. The next couple of minutes I listen with unfuckingbelieving ears! This brilliant college boy, who has yet to be on patrol in Nam, tells me to open fire! "Just pick as many off as you can!" he said to me. Now ain't that the brightest human being you've ever laid eyes on! Well, Rogue One hadn't stayed alive that long by being a dumb shit like the lieutenant! I called the lieutenant back to confirm his insane instruction. And as the lieutenant was repeating his brilliant orders, Z picked up more movement, that time between us and Highway 9. More gooks?

I shut down the lieutenant's babbling and checked it out. Gooks? Worse! The 7×50s showed a Marine patrol out from the base camp by Mike's Hill. They were not supposed to be there; they were probably lost. And they were about to get nailed.

I called back to the base and informed the lieutenant to pass the word to the grunts and get them pulled back. Then he was to get on the hook to the arty battery up at Carroll! What a deal! I was giving the lieutenant orders.

The stupid lieutenant was back on the hook. "Rogue One, Rogue One, listen to me." Listen to you? Why would I do that, asshole? "Rogue One, you can have the arty, but I want you to open fire." Say what? We're talking a numero uno asshole. A fucking clueless human being we got here. By now it's pandemonium. A few seconds passed, and the arty was coming in, and the lieutenant was still on my case. Then the .50-caliber started its all too familiar *whomp*, *whomp*, *whomp*ing into the valley. We were hoping that the Marines were warned and ready.

We started our low-crawl, centipede-high about-face. I wanted the hell out of there; I mean the *sound* of a .50'd do you in. We were five snipers, assholes puckered tight and peckers dragging. But even as I was moving out, staring dirt in the eye, that persistent little bastard on the radio was still saying we should open fire? Not being given to courts-martial and the like, as I crawled along, and the lieutenant continued his ridiculous attempt to pull rank on the airways, I started keying the handset, saying things like "I can't hear ya, sir. It's comin' in garbled." Click, click. "We're on the move, and we're goin' on radio silence." We were still belly down, inch high, and dicks to the ground. This was a big-time low crawl, boot camp kind of race! In boot camp when we'd practiced the low crawl, I'd thought, "What the hell? You'll never do this!" And it was not the first time I'd done it in combat. All the while, we were making a real effort not to disturb the tops of the tall grass, lest the bastards next door catch on. All we could do was slither along, moving west. We began to breathe easier as we got on the downside of the hill, then our hot morning got hotter as the damned .50-caliber erupted again overhead and across the top of our hill. We looked around, not wanting to blow our cover but needing to see what was up. We quickly realized the machine-gun fire was aimed at some Marines out in front of us who'd thought they were on a routine morning patrol until then. There was something different about how the bad guys were acting from back in '66 and '67. They were leaving no doubts about who they thought owned the territory in mid-January '68.

The artillery whistled in right on target about the time we got to the bottom of the hill. Knowing we had to distance ourselves from the area, we regrouped. Arty continued to rain down as we put distance between us and them. The .50-caliber soon stopped. I could only guess that they'd moved back, the way we did. We continued to work our way through the scrub and, by noon, made Highway 9 and the grunts. We caught an afternoon convoy back to the top of the mountain. Home again to Camp Carroll. And home sweet home it was. I sat down thinking of what might have been. Hey, I was a little short for this kind of bullshit.

Back home, lying on my cot, it started making sense. It was Tet, and the cease-fire wasn't working up at Carroll. We were getting hammered as never before. We couldn't sleep; we could hardly eat. The rockets were frightening.

The lieutenant came by and told us the bad guys had attacked everywhere. Word had it they took Hue. Well, that explained why the valley and everywhere else was so damn hot. Why didn't the brass see that one? What the hell was I doing there? I just entered my last extension. The way things were, I could use a break, so Tomo and I worked hard on getting another patrol. But the lieutenant finally came to me and officially said that I was to stay back at Carroll and take care of things in the rear. But, what the hell could I take care of there? And with arty flying in from the north every hour, it was nerve-racking as all hell. Between the incoming artillery and the rockets, life around there was pretty damned dismal.

They'd moved the army's 175mm artillery into Carroll to provide fire support for Khe Sanh. I guess they were the only pieces with the range to reach the besieged combat base. It may have been good for Zulu and the boys at the Khe Sanh, but it sucked wind for us. Those 175s were artillery and rocket magnets. The guys at COC claimed we'd been getting 150 rounds of incoming a day, which to me was like living in a mine being dynamited. *Boom! Boom! Boom!* Explosions were everywhere. And people were freaking out from their new life underground. What I wanted to know was which one of the REMFs was sitting out there counting?

Tomo'd get some action soon. Me, I was in charge of

the rear. But while we were in the rear, we had to devise a way to get some sleep. Most of us had gotten good at hearing the gooks fire the arty somewhere across the DMZ. We could hear a muffled *boom, boom, boom*. And when we did, we had six seconds to get our asses "downstairs." Of course, we couldn't get from our racks to the bunker outside in six seconds. In a dead sleep, we'd hear the muffled sound, roll off our cots, and hold onto our asses. *After* the incoming barrage, we'd jump up and run like hell to the bunker.

After about two weeks I told Tomo we had to do something about our sleeping arrangements, so we got the group together for some serious thinking; the rounds were getting too close for me. I had confidence in the bush with the Rogues, but sitting there and hoping some bad guy twenty miles away didn't get lucky was just too much. I had to find me a safer home. By then, word had it that—I don't know who the fuck counts—the incoming was up to three hundred rounds a day.

We decided to dig trenches under the tent. Our tent hung on a wooden frame and had a plywood floor. Our tent had twelve wooden cots, six on each side. If we dug a separate trench under each cot and a path down the middle, we could sleep down there when the nights got too loud because of the incoming. Most of the guys weren't convinced the work justified the safe sleep. Digging six feet down was a daunting task in the hard clay of Camp Carroll. But things were about to change, and so was everyone's mind.

I was asleep, lightly, but asleep, when I heard the muffled *boom, boom, boom* of fire in the night. Used to the six seconds' lead we'd been enjoying, I rolled out of my rack, just as a deafening roar rifled overhead, followed by a tremendous explosion that ripped through our tent.

Dirt, dust, and debris showered us in the night. Ten harried, tired, and frightened snipers battled their way into the bunker. We were barely inside when a new round of death rained down from the sky. The whirl of white-hot shrapnel made a sickening sound as it screamed through the door of our bunker. Outside, screams of "Corpsman up!" rang through the long, long night. I thought, Man, if Khe Sanh's getting one thousand rounds of incoming a day, their minds must be jelly. I didn't know if staying here was one of my better decisions. *Boom, Boom!* The arty kept whistling in. *Boom!* An earthquake, the ground shook. It was blacker than black in there. It was hot, sweaty, and ugly . . . then . . . stone cold silence. It was over. That time. We had no way of knowing if it was safe, but we couldn't stay down there forever. Morning wasn't long off, and that was good.

The sniper tent next to ours had been nailed good. It looked like giant rats had chewed ragged holes all through it. One of the newer snipers had bought the big one, and two were wounded. The COC narrowly escaped, but the colonel's jeep didn't. I guess they knew what they were going for that night. That was one time it didn't pay to be near the headquarters pukes. The NVA were after their asses. Damn near got them too.

After that surprise, we realized they'd moved their guns closer, and it would mean much less time between *boom* and *crash!* But at least everybody was suddenly motivated to build a better house. We started digging our own new underground kingdom, COC commissioned a new sandbag drill, and they brought in a machine to dig zigzag trenches at the mess hall. They even wanted us to be able to jump into trenches when we lined up to eat. Life had become a real bummer up at Camp Carroll.

Tomo and I led the charge as we all pitched in to dig

our new kingdom. It was hell digging, but for three days, we hadn't had any incoming. That was a record. Life above ground was a dream. It's funny how the longer you got from the incoming, the less you wanted to dig in the heat, the clay, and the fog of the mountains of the DMZ. Even so, we dug and dug and were making headway. The trenches we'd originally built on both ends turned right or left, then angled down into a common bunker. The bunker was divided in the middle by sand-bags and metal poles. We'd added two more layers of sandbags on the top of it, too. The NVA were throwing some heavy artillery at us, and we needed the illusion that what we built would take a direct hit. We all had to have fantasies.

I was beat, we were all beat from working on our own system and the COC for three days. We knew our day would come and it would have to be soon. They didn't just shut down after kicking the shit out of us. Anytime they hit Khe Sanh, they'd hit us if we supported it. Carroll was getting bigger with the addition of the 175s, and it was becoming an easier target. We'd finished some of the digging underneath our wooden floor, and our ramps had been dug out to a depth of six feet. With a little luck, in another day, we'd finish the project completely. We lay down for some much needed rest and a couple of beers.

Boom, boom! Oh shit, it's back!

Kaboom! BOOM! Kaboom! Incoming! I was up running for the tent door. Debris was flying, whirling through the air. *Boom!* I reached the door first. It was dark. I turned right, and I fell with a thud into the trench we'd just dug. I was sandwiched into the bottom sideways, with my feet bent up, and *ugh!* Somebody fell on me. Damn, *another*! I couldn't breathe. I was stuck. I didn't know how many people were on top of me. I couldn't move. Then I heard the laugh. It was Tomo. "Get the fuck off of me," I had to strain to yell. He couldn't stop laughing. Who else was up there? One by one they got up and then dragged my crushed ass out with them. The other end of the bunker was damaged. Oh man, did I hurt from all the guys who were on me. And now we'd have to fix the damned bunker in the morning.

Morning came and with it reports of more dead and wounded and, of course, more incoming. The big difference was they had shifted targets to shoot at the 175s, which were set in across the base from us. We'd heard the same slight *boom, boom, boom* and the immediate whiz-bang of the shit flying in everywhere. But the big explosions were a hundred yards away. We were all still moles, but when the NVA were shooting over there, they didn't have enough of those big devils to hit our side, too. At least, that's what we chose to believe.

We were still grounded—going on two weeks. All time, energy, and available bodies were tied up building more fortifications. Word had it that the bad guys had dealt us a hell of a blow with Tet. All I knew was that Vietnam wasn't a safe place to find your damned self anymore. Between Washington's bullshit and Hanoi's attitude, they were taking all the fun out of the war.

The Rogues continued to spend their days digging the underground fortress. We added another "feel good" layer to our bunker and tried to stay sober. Life was dark, with monsoon hanging overhead and gook artillery visiting three hundred times a day. Tomo was taking over the Rogues because I was due to rotate home in less than a month. There'd be no more extensions for the Kug. It was time! Well, I only had a few months left in the Corps;

I was not going to re-up, so I might as well go back and party.

It was hard to believe when we got our first day of partial sun: there was no water raining down and no incoming raining in. What a day! We were about done digging, and I needed to take a dump. Hell, they were even sprucing up the shitters by now. The one I chose was made of nice new plywood, with a corrugated metal roof, screened vents, and three holes. The Cadillac of shitters! I sat down and saw that underneath were the same sawed-off fifty-five-gallon drums. I looked down. Hell, I do believe there are fewer maggots in that nice new headquarters shitter than there were in the old grunt shitters we used.

I was sitting there enjoying myself, pondering the world's problems when, *ping, zing, rump, rump, rump!* Machine gun bullets ripped holes in the screen around the top of the shitter. I rolled to the floor, jungle pants around my ankles, no shirt, no rifle, and asshole exposed to the world. People were running and yelling. The perimeter on our side opened up . . .

There was a minor firefight going on out there while I was in the shitter trying to get my pants up without getting myself higher than the seat on the shitter. Which, I might add, is no small task. I had a two- or three-foot-by-six-foot space to work with. Now who would attack at 0900 in the morning? I mean what was Nam coming to, anyway? I got my ass covered with my jungle pants, all while still lying on the filthy floor of the new toilet. I slid over and opened the door for a peek. It was already like normal out there. The firing had stopped, and people were coming out of their holes again like worms after a rain. Life . . . is moving. I got up before anyone saw me and wondered what the hell I'd been doing kissing ass down on the shitter floor. I stepped outside, dusted myself off, and noticed the shitter had been riddled with about a dozen holes. Damn! Obviously, that shitter just happened to be in the line of fire.

I started walking back to my bunker when the faint *boom*s echoed from beyond the DMZ. I dropped face first into the dirt, right where I stood. The shells whistled in, detonating loudly across the base at the 175 battery. As I stood up, I heard pieces of shrapnel falling. Back at the bunker, everyone had had it with all the digging and the constant shelling, but we couldn't quit until guys in the sky took care of the big guns over the border. They'd started building thirty-five-foot-high observation towers at the edge of our perimeter.

I was down to a few weeks left in country. I didn't want to go home, but I couldn't stay. If I had to go, which I did, then I'd need to get into the same line of work again. I still had the names and contacts for mercenary work that a British Marine had given me in Hong Kong. It all seemed to work through Brussels. Hell, I didn't even know where Belgium was, but I guessed I could find it. I thought I'd go home to party away the summer, then take off to find Brussels.

One night the mess hall was advertising steaks. Now that'd be a real treat if it were true. We were still stealing C rats most of the time because I still couldn't stand most of the shit they called food at that mess hall. Tomo was in charge by then, and he was working his snipers hard, getting them ready to be Rogues again. Rogues at the DMZ . . . now that'd be cool.

One new kid was Dickie Welborne. Dickie was something else. Nice as nice could be. The kid would do anything for anyone. How could anyone not like Dickie? Tomo liked him but felt that he needed to toughen him up if he was going on Rogue patrols—and, if all went well, he'd start the patrols again in another week. The times were changing, and I was finally accepting the fact that I was not responsible for the snipers anymore. I didn't like it, but I had to deal with it. I didn't think I'd have taken Dickie with me on patrol, but that was Tomo's choice. I liked the guy, but I didn't know what the hell he was doing in the Corps.

Steaks! Damn, that'd be good. They said a line was forming already. Tomo stopped digging long enough to bark orders at Dickie. "Dickie, run up to the mess hall and see if there's a line." Like a newly trained puppy aiming to please, Dickie was off on the double. Then Tomo was telling me of his concern about the Rogues. "I can't even get Dickie to fight me," he said in disgust.

Now that was not a surprise. "I wouldn't wanna fight you either, man. You're fuckin' crazy," I replied. Tomo was five-foot-seven and 210 pounds of 100 percent bad dude. I loved the guy but, like me, he was on the strange side. And he loved to fight. But I did agree with him on his concern over the team he had. I'd had the best in Co Bi Than Tan; he had the B team lined up behind him. And at the DMZ, it was always the A team that was needed. When you were bumping into folks with .50-calibers and brass balls the size of watermelons, you needed the best.

"Tomo, Tomo, they're here. They're here." Dickie was running between two rows of seriously bunkered tents.

"Who the fuck's here?" Tomo growled. Dickie said that four or five people were already in line at the mess hall. Man, that was an hour early. Faced with the choice of leaving early or possibly being left without steak,

Tomo shut down his work party, and we headed off to take our place in the chow line. But instead of the five or so people in line, there must have been twenty. Damn! I started for the end of the line, but Tomo walked up and told Dickie to point out the last man who'd been in the line when he was just there. Then Tomo pardoned himself and stepped in place behind that dude. Well shit, what's this? I followed Tomo when the guy behind us, a corporal, got in Tomo's face. Well, I knew better than to fuck with him after he'd been filling sandbags all day.

I said, "Come on, Tomo, let's just go back in the line and—" He interrupted me with "Kug, *this* is our place." He turned to the corporal behind us and said, "Corporal, that's right, isn't it? Corporal?" The kid wisecracked that yes, he was a corporal, at which point Tomo unloaded with full auto. "Well, Corporal, I'm a sergeant and so is he," he said pointing to me. "That's two sergeants and one corporal. We're cuttin' line right where we were supposed to be." Corporal Wiseass started arguing, and the next thing I knew, Tomo was in his face. "Corporal, I'm pullin' rank! And unless you shut the fuck up, I'll run you up and . . ." *Boom! . . . kaboom! baboom!*

Incoming! We didn't even hear the firing from across the DMZ. They were hitting the 175 battery again. Tomo and I were down on one knee, Dickie was in the zigzag trench with all the rest of the mob that had been in line for steaks. Suddenly I heard, "Kug, Kug! Tomo! Here." Kneeling, I turned to see Tree in the mess tent. There was no one else to be seen, he must have been the only one still standing. We'd put him on mess duty to take care of us; he was a super guy, but he was awkward and noisy in the bush. And he had trouble killing, but he wanted to contribute. He could wheel and deal, so the mess hall was perfect for him. I looked again. "Kug, Tomo, here!" Tree was holding a big, well-used metal pan of—of—*steaks!* We were both on our feet and running in the door of the mess tent. Tree handed Tomo a pan and then me. Shiiit! We each had a two-by-three-foot metal pan of T-bones! Halle-fucking-lujah and we were racing back to sniper-ville on the double, right into the bunkers. Shells were still falling up in 175-land across the base. Most of the folks around there were still in the zigzags with Dickie. Fuck a little incoming when it came to T-bones! We called out for all the snipers in the area to come in for chow, but only five responded. Tough shit. We ate the meat right off the bones, like corn on the cob. And we mixed it with raw Bermuda onions that Tree had stolen for us the previous week. We ate them like apples. How good could it get? The bombing continued as the background music for our supper club. We ate 'til we damned near exploded, and then we ate some more.

Night was taking over when Dickie crawled to our bunker. "How the hell are ya?" Tomo asked, between bites of one of the few remaining T-bones. Dickie just sat in the corner, downtrodden and angry. Angry? "Come on," I said to Tomo, "this is his chance." But Dickie stormed out after telling us all the shit he had to take for being the sniper left behind. People were really furious that they'd lost all those steaks. Tough; the fucking REMFs didn't deserve steak anyway.

We went in to lie down. I was tired. Tomo, Huffer, and me, we were all flat on our asses. "Somebody turn the fuckin' light out!" I screamed to everyone in general and no one in particular. But no one moved. I got no answer at all except for the usual laughter from the masses. The light was just one bulb hanging in the middle of the tent, beckoning like a lighthouse. I was tired, short, and in no mood for bullshit that evening. I reached down, grabbed a jungle boot, and threw it half across the tent. A strike! Dead center. The bulb shattered and tiny bits of glass flew everywhere. It was dark, finally, and silent. I never could stand grab-ass.

A few hours later, we were rudely "thrown" awake by the largest barrage of incoming we had ever experienced. It seemed to go on forever, but it actually lasted just over an hour, covering the whole base of Carroll. My head hurt from all the noise. Dickie, Tomo, Huffer, and I were in a bunker, and arty was hitting all around us, dirt was falling, the world was shaking. Huffer, a good little Southern Baptist from the Carolinas, was at one end of our bunker. He had his hands folded, and was praying his heart out. At the other end, Dickie was half praying, half crying, and half whimpering. Tomo and I, the platoon's atheists, were in the middle. I was just hanging onto Mother Earth. The only reason I wasn't shitting myself was my ass was plugged tight with nerves trying to escape my body.

The shelling continued for what seemed like ever. So did Tomo's taunting of Huffer and Dickie. I was just trying to crawl inside myself, just to feel better . . . then it stopped. The stone cold silence was back, and it was eerie. The silence was broken by the familiar cry of "Corpsman up!" By that time, I was a lot more familiar with madness than I'd ever intended to be.

When we came out of the ground, it was a little after 0500, and the morning sky was just showing signs of life. I looked around. Our tent was Swiss cheese, just above the five-foot sandbag wall that surrounded it. The towers were standing tall at the perimeter's edge. But a truck was burning out front, a jeep had been severely modified behind us, and the number-two sniper tent was gone.

Luckily no snipers had left with it. I was not sure where they'd been, but all survived.

We set about cleaning up the mess that had been our camp. Usually the gooks didn't hit us back to back, and I hoped this was another of those times; I'd had it with work parties. Being a sniper wasn't work; digging and filling were work. And I didn't much like it. I had ten days left in country.

Tomo was hot on Dickie's ass; it was afternoon, and he'd just got word the Rogues were going out the next day. Finally! But . . . "Dickie, get your ass over here. I gotta toughen you up before we go out." Tomo laid it out for him. But shit, it wasn't happening. I liked the little asshole, but he wouldn't be there when you needed him. Hell, just because he wore that uniform didn't mean he "got it." And Dickie *didn't* get it when it came to war. I didn't think he should go, but I felt sorry for the little asshole.

A little while later, I heard a commotion. Someone yelled, "Tomo's stuffing Dickie in a fucking mailsack."

"Tomo, give the guy a break, man," I said, offering a little compassion. Tomo actually liked Dickie; he just wanted to make him tougher.

"Kug, I told him, 'Fight, or I'm putting your ass in this mailsack.' " And damned if Tomo didn't do it. Here was that skinny guy, about five foot eight and 150 pounds monsoon wet, in a canvas mailsack, maybe two feet around and four feet deep. How did he get him in there? Tomo hoisted him up on the sandbag wall around our hootch next to the ramp leading into our bunker.

"Don't move, Dickie; you'll roll off the wall," Tomo said. *Zzzzooooom! Kaboom! Bbboom!* "Incoming!" someone yelled. The earth was shaking one more time, and we ran for our lives down into the bunker. I looked around . . . "Tomo, where the hell's Dickie?"

"Oh, fuck!" and Tomo was scrambling out of the bunker.

Bboom, Kaboom! Dirt and debris was flying everywhere outside as he grabbed the strings on Dickie's mailsack and jerked him off the wall. Then he was moving forward, down into the bunker, before the sack hit the ground. Tomo dragged him down into the bunker with us. By the time we got Dickie out, he was hyperventilating. I couldn't blame him either. And he was pissed. Finally! He wouldn't speak to any of us, least of all me and Tomo. When the shit quit flying, Dickie was out of there and gone. Tomo looked at me and said, "Now what the fuck's wrong with him?"

Another day passed before we finally had work. They'd decided to open Highway 9 from Cam Lo to Khe Sanh to establish ground resupply. That was the plan anyway; it sounded like a pipe dream to me. That was some mean territory out there. But they were placing grunt companies all along the route to keep it open. Tomo was taking himself and five snipers down to work Highway 9. They'd stage out of the grunt locations the way we tried when we met the NVA band with the twin .50-calibers. Me? Well, I had eight days left, and Huffer had three weeks. They decided to put us up in the lighthouses—the perimeter towers—to look for bad guys. I bet they thought that was the next best thing to a tree. That's about how much some leaders knew about snipers; I thought they'd been watching too many World War II movies.

Tomo and I said our good-byes, farewells, and fuck-offs. I'd grown close to "his ugliness" and was going to miss him; he was one great Marine, and he was working on thirty months in Nam. Huffer and I finally copped out and climbed the lighthouse. I didn't like it up there, and they wanted us up there at night, for late night and early morning shots. And we could use the starlight scope they'd given us.

Our first night in the sky was a spooky one. Looking down thirty-five feet to the perimeter below gave us a great chance to conjure up all kinds of things that the NVA dickheads could do to us. The biggest one was imagining the gooks overrunning the perimeter while we were up top. And then there were the memories of recoilless rifles up on the Rockpile. Or the fan favorite, incoming artillery blows all the legs out from under our little cabin in the sky. Any of the above could ruin our young asses right before our own eyes. Our hearts could stop on the way down.

But that night nothing was happening except the lights on Dong Ha Mountain northwest of us across Highway 9. From our observation post, we could see forever. Our airborne outpost faced north, but had openings on four sides. And when we saw smoke out there, it usually meant a rocket was headed our way. We had a courtside seat over Mike's Hill, where Tomo and the rest of the Rogues were based. It was just below us to the northwest. Cam Lo village lay to our north, and the Rockpile and on to Khe Sanh were to the west.

Our second night up, we saw lights again on the mountain across from us. I called down to tanks. Nobody ever called them, and the tankers like to light things up. It was nearly straight across from them, so they should have been able to hit that sucker. They get all the coordinates, and we're ready for the big hunt. *Boom!* We heard them fire from across the base. *Boom!* Again, they called for an adjustment. Hell, I couldn't see out. "Look," I called to Huffer, who was asleep while I was on watch. "We're completely fogged in." He looked, and I had tanks calling me again. They wanted more direction. What a pain in the ass they were. I mean, we called them and gave them some business, and soon they were looking for lights every five minutes. By then, we couldn't see two feet outside of our cabin up there. After we received yet another call, I got on the radio. "That's an affirmative on the sightings; drop five zero and fire for effect." They were easy to please. They were happy to shoot all night long. I put the handset of the PRC-10 by my ear and went to sleep, high up in the fog. Whenever they called back, which was all night long, I'd wake up long enough to say "That's affirmative, lights still there. Fire for effect." At least that way, we kept everyone happy.

The third night was like the others, and I was bored as hell. Tanks were calling wanting to shoot every hour on the hour, so we gave it to them. The incoming that night was a little less, so we didn't worry as much about our tower getting knocked down. But the nights were long and gray up in the clouds. "Kug, Kug," Huffer was calling out. I sat up to the sounds of small-arms fire down along Highway 9. It was sporadic. Maybe it was a grunt ambush. Through the starlight, we could see muzzle flashes and, occasionally, lights. That didn't feel right to me. It was not stopping; instead, it picked up speed. Huffer changed the radio frequency to listen in on the grunts. Hell, their lines were being probed. Why would the NVA do that at that time? It was about 0430, and they always attacked in early evening and carried it into the night. Then all hell just broke loose at about 0515, still not daylight. Tracers were flying everywhere. The radio revealed that Mike's Hill was under full assault. Right before dawn.

Morning turned into a dark, overcast day, a sad looking

day. An ugly day ahead for all of us to see . . . and for those on Mike's Hill to try and live through. From our perch high above Carroll and with our telescope, we could watch the battle raging below. We were about a mile away. Mike's Hill sat right at the edge of Highway 9, halfway between Cam Lo and the Rockpile. Camp Carroll sat high above it on the east side, and Dong Ha Mountain was the shadow behind it on the west.

Mike's Hill had thick underbrush and had Mike company, reinforced, sitting on its back. Mike Company was under serious attack on all sides. Damn! Tomo, Det Cord, Dickie, and three real new snipers were right in there with the grunts. Explosions were going off everywhere as the battle got heavier. I felt like I was in the cheap seats at a big-time game of war, the nosebleed section, and my hands were tied. Where the hell was the air support? The weather, that's where the air support was. Hell, there were three more companies of Marines down on Highway 9. Why weren't they helping? Huffer and I didn't know the answers, but we did know the questions to ask when things were turning real ugly. And even from the nosebleed section, we could see the match was going downhill fast.

The NVA were attacking in broad daylight. It must have been their buddies we saw with the .50-calibers. The NVA were well organized. We could make out their assault lines from our tower. They looked like Marines from that distance. What the hell could we do? Nothing, that's what. The COC called up to find out what we could see. We told them. Here came the colonel. I hoped the NVA didn't have a brass-seeking missle out there someplace. He climbed up with the rest of us. He was nice, seemed a little aloof, and out of it, but he was okay. He told me the air support would come when the clouds lifted, which they expected to be soon.

By 1100 hours, the Marines were starting to hurt. Their perimeter was getting smaller and smaller. I hoped to hell Tomo and Det Cord were cool. The gooks were pushing in on three sides. What the hell was happening with Tomo? And the rest, especially Dickie? Damn. We were helping with some IDs and mortar directions, but that was about it. I wanted to do something. Arty was trying to get it to the NVA, but the gooks were so close they were not effective.

I overheard the colonel say that the NVA had apparently committed a whole regiment to the cause. From up there in the rafters, they seemed to be everywhere. Just after 1300, A-6 Intruders appeared. The skies were just breaking, and one came out of the clouds. I wanted to stand up and cheer. I didn't know if the guys down there had time to look up and see these beautiful silver birds. The pilot came right down the valley left to right, dropped down in front of the Rockpile, and with wings glistening beneath the little sun piercing the gray clouds, flew in lower than the crest of the mountain, then let loose with two canisters of napalm that just made my day. I mean, let's hear it for the makers of "crispy critters." It was like an interception with minutes to go in the game. Let's hope like hell the good guys took the ball back for a touchdown. Round two began with the second A-6 and another round of jelly fire rolling across the ground. We could see the mayhem that rolled in with it as the gooks scrambled away like ants from their trampled ant hill.

The lieutenant was now up here with us in the observation tower. The colonel called him over to check on us. They wanted to know if Huffer and I could work our way down behind the NVA. Hell yes! "The two of us are so short they'll never see us comin'," I said to Huffer, who was worried about leaving the security of Carroll at this point. We were a mile walk down some huge fingers that ran from our mountain down to the battle area. We were off on a hike to support Mike Company.

I took a 14 and a Remington 700 and so did Huffer. We walked as fast as we could. We could see the tide begin to turn after the visit by the Intruders, and the Marines began to regain some ground. The going for us was slower than I'd have liked. There wasn't any risk, even with just two of us; we were the least of the bad guys' worries. The terrain was downhill and flat, relatively open. Huffer packed our radio. It took us a good hour to reach an area from which we could see the battle, but we still weren't close enough. We crawled out on the finger, exposed as much as we dared, and were still fifteen hundred meters away. Oh man . . . I had to get me a little closer. I wanted one more kill before I left. With the 7×50s, we could see individual firefights. It was like watching a real-life movie. But from there, we couldn't help. So we crawled on forward to find a closer place to watch the war. What the hell was going on down there? The Marines on Mike's Hill were coming off with squad-size units, trying to mop up the sides of the highway. Then the F-4 Phantoms came in and really changed the balance of power. Then Hueys were in the area on the north side of the hill where a small landing area had been secured by a supporting grunt company. Ammunition was coming in while the most critically wounded were being shuttled out.

Finally, Huffer and I got a position about nine hundred yards out. We watched a Marine squad coming along the highway on the east side . . . our side . . . take a hit when an AK-47 opened up, killing their point man. We couldn't see where it had come from, though. Before I knew what had happened, another Marine was down, and another one was out of the game. One of them was still moving around, but an AK opened up, and he was history. So was the guy who was trying to reach him. There were four dead, at least that we could see. Finally, Huffer picked up a puff of smoke. It was under a bush right at the edge of the road. We called upstairs and told them to get word to those Marines. The reply was, "I'll try."

Huffer was on the 7×50s trying to spot in while I got ready for a shot. I would love to go out by taking that asshole under the bush. It was long, nine hundred yards at least. But I'd done it before. We saw the five remaining Marines cross to our side of Highway 9. They moved under cover from a blast of M-60 machine-gun fire. Their gunner was stepping up to the plate for that one as they started leapfrogging from bush to bush when *bbrrrp!* The AK did it again. One more Marine was gone. But now we knew which bush.

One by one, the little bastard in the spider trap was getting them all. I had to take a shot. I can do it. I lay it out . . . breathe, baby, breathe . . . squeeze the tit and . . . *boom!* What . . . Huffer picks it up, and it's a fucking hundred yards short. It fucking can't be my round. Down streetside, the grunt machine gunner must have had it. He was across the highway from the bad guy, then he jumped up. It was John Wayne with a belt of ammo around his shoulder. He was running, shooting . . . then he was right above the bush. He fired until he was empty, then he turned and ran back across the road. The NVA popped up and chucked a grenade at the gunner. *Boom!* We were close enough to hear it. The gunner hurled one back. *Boom!* For the next few minutes, the two warriors tossed grenades back and forth at each other to no good end. Meanwhile, everywhere but right there the Marines were taking control again.

I had to take another shot at the asshole. But I didn't want the Marines to think we were on the away team. I called back to COC and told them to pass the word. Again we got an "I'll try." Fuck! I took aim, went through the sniper's mantra, and *boom!* The report from Huffer was the same. The goddamn Remington 700 wouldn't shoot that far! To our right, a Huey gunship was hovering about three feet above the highway, two hundred yards north of the heavyweight fight. Inside, a Marine ran out to his window as the pilot set it down on Highway 9. Then the pilot fired that baby up and hovered his way west on the highway, about three feet above the ground. He hovered up to the bushes where the gook was holed up, and the door gunner let loose with a major blast from his M-60, shooting up the whole bush and all the ground around it. What balls those guys had! Then the chopper spun and headed back up station as a fresh squad came in to back up the lone machine gunner. Before they got there, he charged off to the spider hole, emptying another belt of ammo. We saw him kneel down, going berserk with a full belt, as he plowed headlong into his enemy. It was over. He collapsed as the squad moved in to help. Somebody was kneeling down, arm around the hero. It was probably the corpsman.

We were called back up to Carroll. I couldn't believe I'd had a last shot in the war and I couldn't shoot far enough. Son of a bitch. Going up was a lot harder than coming down. It was 1600 by the time we huffed and puffed to the top. We came in the perimeter, went straight to our tower, and climbed back up. The lieutenant was there, the colonel, and damn, Gen. Victor Krulak. Well, what a fucking party. Bet there were a lot of dead Marines nearby who would have enjoyed being up there that afternoon. Pissed me off! But it wasn't Krulak's fault. That was the problem: it wasn't anybody's fault; it just was. The general thanked *us* for the effort and shook our hands. Well, I'll be damned, the first general I'd had the pleasure to meet in two years, the first I'd seen who'd come remotely close to the front. Of course he was the only general I'd ever met, too. He was a nice man, smaller than I'd expected, but a gentleman.

It took another day to get word on our troops. The snipers all survived, but two were wounded. I'm not sure how they'd made it, but they had. Mike Company took heavy casualties. The word was the snipers performed admirably, defending the hill right alongside the grunts. I couldn't imagine what it had been like down there. I just knew it looked like hell from Camp Carroll.

I only had three days left, so nobody fucked with me. The lieutenant called me down to his digs to tell me I'd been awarded the Vietnamese Cross of Gallantry. "What the fuck is it?" I asked in disbelief. "And what the fuck are they givin' me something for?" It was for our last big deal in Co Bi Than Tan, the one where we quit counting at a-hundred-gooks-and-climbing and where we cheered on the guy who got vaporized on the five-yard line. He handed me a piece of paper, "The citation." I look at it, and, of course, the damned thing was written in gook. Makes sense, it was the Vietnamese Cross of Gallantry.

On my last day in country, the lieutenant called me in. He had a gook lieutenant, an ARVN, with him. The lieutenant said the ARVN would translate the citation for me. Well, hell, he started rattling this shit off, and I couldn't understand most of it. But, I remember the part about the "brave, fierce, fighting sergeant" and something about "the thirty-five killed." I didn't want to know about all that . . .

My last morning came, and I hopped the Carroll convoy. I'd ride down to Cam Lo on the first step of my journey back to the States. Kug, back in the World one more time. The idea of going back to Ohio scared me more than the battle for Mike's Hill had. The convoy went by Tomo and the sniper crew on Mike's Hill and stopped, so I hopped off to find my friends. This was it, the end of two years of something I couldn't explain. I had no time but to bid farewell. Tomo promised to write and stay alive to get together Stateside. I was dying to know the whole scoop about the battle from the inside. I had to admit, he looked good. Tired and worn, but good. He was staying to fight another day, and I was envious as I got on the six-by for my ride out. He'd made it. The asshole made it. I hadn't expected less. "What about Dickie?" I asked, as the truck was pulling away.

"Kug," Tomo said, "he done good, real good."

Well, I'll fucking be! I rode along, watching the mountains get smaller and smaller in the distance. It might be the last time I'd ever see the Rockpile. At Cam Lo, I changed trucks and headed on over to Dong Ha to catch a flight to Da Nang. *Fuck!* I couldn't believe it was over. What am I going to do? Be a mercenary? Race cars? Oh hell, I didn't even know what that meant anymore. But I did know that I had really done something. Unbelievable! I got off the convoy and took my seabag to the airstrip. Damn! They were even dressing up Dong Ha; it looked like Akron Airport on a bad day. I told the dude in the building, "I need to catch a C-130 to Da Nang. I'm goin' back to the World."

He said, "Marine, do you have your chit? Your chit for the ride?"

"A chit?" My achin' fuckin' ass. A damned chit to fly down to Da Nang? I'll be a son of a bitch if they ain't gonna fuck this up yet. What's this war comin' to?

Epilogue

I can see it all from here. The firing squad's off on a little rise in the distance. Oh man, there's the procession coming, and you're in it, Pearl. You're in the flag-draped coffin. Shiiit! You're lying there. I saw you on the table in 3d Med before you got here. I'm afraid of how they'll feel ... your parents are crying, and your younger brothers are sad, but I think they're supposed to look sad. You know that. Your friends are here, too. And the community's sad because that's the kind of community it is. It's just like you said it was, Pearl. It's a beautiful place, and you had a beautiful service, man. Beeeauutiful!

I stood up from the grave with my knees aching. Rivers of tears were running down my now heavy cheeks. I'd imagined the whole thing. I hope he heard my prayer. It'd been nineteen long years since this great kid of, ironically, nineteen years old, died in Vietnam. As he lay there in pieces on a stretcher, I promised him I'd come and visit the place he loved, his beloved hometown on Lake Superior. I'd finally made it. I prayed at his feet and watched his funeral ... the funeral that took place nineteen years before. I knew a lot about funerals. It was like all the funerals I'd done when I got back from my two years in Nam.

For the first time, the Marine Corps granted my request on a Dream Sheet. They sent me to Fort Wayne, Indiana, four hours from home in Ohio. I was assigned duty with the Reserve Center. The only catch was, since I didn't want to reenlist in the Corps, my only duty was helping to conduct military funerals. Our territory covered a hundred-mile radius of Fort Wayne. We did about four funerals a week for poor unfortunate Marines like the ones I once zipped into green body bags back in Nam. I don't know if the duty in Nam or the duty in Fort Wayne was tougher. I do know they both had a profound impact on my life.

The Marine Corps was the second best thing that ever happened to me. I still get choked up when I hear the Marine Corps Hymn, and the tears come on the National Anthem. I still think of World War II as the "Big One," and I believe the Korean War vets got the short end of a bad straw. I still think Vietnam was a good idea in the beginning and got screwed up by the politicians along the way. I think *Apocalypse Now* captured the mentality of Vietnam better than any other film. And *Full Metal Jacket* was a good portrayal of Marine boot camp and a damned close portrayal of the reality of combat. But *Platoon* was something I couldn't relate to; it was a Vietnam that I didn't see, know, understand, or experience. I'm not saying it didn't happen, but it didn't happen on my watch. I listen to "Imus in the Morning" and "Dr. Laura" because I think they're right. I don't listen to Rush Limbaugh because I think he's more self-serving than the local Chinese buffet. And yes, I came home with a lot of problems. But then, I went over with a lot of problems, too.

The kid from Mrs. Lyons's class and Lock Seventeen

did make it home. He lived to fight another day. But despite my "best intentions" at the time, I didn't go to Brussels, and although it took a few years to accept it, I didn't ever become a mercenary. Instead, I met the first best thing to ever happen to me, my wife of thirty years, Gloria Caroline Patterson Kugler. She stepped into the wild world of Marine snipers returning from war. And she stepped up to the plate and made a difference.

I came home to a world that didn't understand me but a wonderful young woman who did. Her unconditional love, kindness, acceptance, and support made all the difference in my life. She didn't judge me, for starters. Then she gave me three terrific kids. And somehow she handled the Rogue reunions with a smile on her face and a firm grip at the ready. She hosted the reunions and countless other visits for years. The Rogues came and went through her apartment, her trailer, and her houses. Most of all, though, she helped me see that whatever I was looking for could only be found by looking in the mirror. She helped me see that Vietnam was just a part of me. It was like grade school or going to the park on a picnic or, sometimes, a nightmare, but a nightmare that would go away. And she led me to the third best thing to ever happen to me, my acceptance of Jesus Christ into my life. My good lady had taken me from atheist to agnostic to acceptance. It was then that I began to reach back and pull all the good from a bad situation.

While I only made it to college for a couple of years by going at nights, I could use what I had become in the Marine Corps to help me succeed in spite of a lack of formal education. I've had a successful management career at three Fortune 500 companies, spanning the last twenty years, at the last of which I was a vice president of the world's fastest growing computer company, then senior vice president of a smaller computer company. That's not bad for a lowly grunt with about sixty college credits under his belt. And what happened to the other Rogues and snipers?

The list reads a little like the good, the bad, and the ugly. But it's mostly good, with an occasional bad streak and a little ugly thrown in now and then. Greek and I became fast friends, and our families stayed close until his untimely death from cancer a couple of years back. He struggled with drugs and alcohol, which he overcame after years of support from a wonderful wife. They reared two wonderful boys.

Stu came home wounded and didn't miss a stride. He and his wife are the parents of six kids and going strong after thirty years of marriage. He has the bar he always talked about back in Nam.

Crud came home and had lots of trouble with the "time machine" he so often put us to sleep with. He lived two hours from me our first few years back. We saw each other often. He never really left the war behind, and committed suicide two years after returning severely wounded. His mother told me at the funeral, "Kug, you boys were his life. He died in Vietnam, and we just buried him today." I never knew if it was Nam or the demons he brought with him. Greek was with me at the funeral, and the others called in. The bonds of combat grow stronger than one can describe.

Moe came home to his wife and kids and lived the American dream with all its triumph and its tragedy.

Tomo married, with me as his best man, and is only a year behind Gloria and me at twenty-nine years and counting. He has a wonderful son, which is a tribute to his wife; he's still mean and ugly.

Z kept his word and came home and had nothing to do with any of us.

Raid came home and took over the family business right where he left off.

Hoss was last heard of deep in the mountains of Montana.

Harley came home and divorced the wife that painted his bike. He's had four others since then and countless years he lost riding with the bikers. But a few years back, he got a great lady, and they started a business together, and things are going well.

And of course my main man, the Hood. We were in contact for many years, but he's MIA at this time. He bummed the States and did lots of things, including lots of drugs. But he straightened up and married a nice girl, and then rode off into the sunset. I'll always be indebted to him for the times he saved my life . . . wherever he is.

YaYa, last I heard, was married to his first wife for the fourth time—and she was his fifth wife. I know, I know, that's just the way it is sometimes.

Zulu was last heard of years ago, married and moving to the north woods. I'm sure he's doing just fine. It was him, his wife, and Nero Wolfe.

Wiener chose to leave well enough alone after what he'd been through. We talked to him during Crud's funeral and found out from his wife that he'd blacked out all memory of Vietnam. He was teaching school. Greek didn't think it'd be fair to tell him about the toad incident, or the burning boots. We decided that waking *that* sleeping dog might cause lots of folks a couple of bites.

Det Cord's alive and well, with a couple of college degrees, his continuing membership in Mensa, and, last I heard, he was driving trucks because that's what he wanted to do. He thought it would keep him in shape for the coming revolution. I know, I know . . .

I thought one time not long ago, I wonder if how we've done is about average? And you know what, I think it is. There were eighteen or twenty of us snipers who were real close over those two years. One suicide after a few years may be about average. I imagine four or five successful marriages is about average. One cancer death is about average. I think often of all the talk about what the government owes me for my service in such a dreadful place. What would the government owe me? They kept me well during those years and fed me. They paid me, not well, but enough. They protected me better than any soldier anywhere else in the world. They did for me exactly what they said they would when I signed up. Now I didn't say it was a lot, but it was what they said they'd do. So where is the issue?

I really think there is only one issue. The issue we struggled with the most was leadership. We live in a time of political correctness, when the thought police try to shape each of us as to what we can do and say. We can never prevent fifty-eight thousand names from adorning a wall again if we don't understand the nature of war and what takes place in the hearts and minds of those asked to fight it. It's a tough, ugly experience that impacts one for life. I don't think it's an excuse to go stand on a street corner and whine. But I also know that a lot of lives in Vietnam were wasted by the folks driving those big desks in Washington. It's easy to make a decision when you don't have to look the people in the eye who have to carry it out. And reminding people of that is my purpose with this book.

I wanted people to touch and feel what it's like inside the mind of a young man asked to play war. It changes you in ways you don't understand. I'm not proud of the language I used, or some of the things I did, and I am ashamed today of the attitude I had toward the Vietnamese. But at the time it was truly how we dealt with the business of killing. I shared the raw and true stories of events that actually took place. A few events, I dare say, some will find shocking and even take issue with. We did some absolutely crazy shit, if you'll pardon my language again here a minute. And we not only lived to tell about it, but for the most part, we came back and made a contribution to society. It's wild and weird and sick sometimes. But hey, that's my point, that happens in war, every war. And it's all made worse when our leaders pretend it's not so or have no idea what their decisions are doing to the people carrying out their "strategy." That's why it is so important to go to war only with a clear purpose.

If I came home with one passion in life, it was the passion to stop the bullshit wherever I find it. This passion extended to the bullshit in corporate America and severely slowed my career at times. But hey, it was the same bullshit that killed more people in Vietnam than all the bullets the enemy ever sent our way. I'm convinced that if Mr. McNamara and President Johnson had had kids out where we were who told them the truth about the bullshit, we would have had a quicker resolution to the war. I also know that you don't have to have all the brainpower nor the educational credentials of Mr. McNamara and his so-called Whiz Kids to figure out that his electronic barrier wasn't going to stop a single person from crossing the DMZ. Especially if that person was from the same army the French didn't think could get artillery over the mountains at Dien Bien Phu back in 1954, when I was in the second grade. Even a lowly Marine sniper and former Marine grunt like me can figure that out. Or to borrow a modern expression for Mr. Mc-Namara and his former band of merry men . . . *Duh!*

In the end, I hope only that this book has opened your eyes. I hope it has provided you with a new perspective on the Vietnam War specifically and just plain war in general. I hope you've felt the pain of loss and bloodshed that I felt; the love of comrades in arms who live and die for you and with you; the black humor born of survival under the most extreme and bizarre circumstances; and the overwhelming need to choose our future wars more carefully. Would I do it again? Hell yes, I surely would. I would expect my son also to stand front and center. And every other young, able-bodied man I know. And in return, I'd leave you with the hope that next time may the enemy kill more of us than the bullshit flowing out of Washington. Unfortunately, I haven't seen any indication that the river of stench is getting anything but worse up there.

It is said best by Danny Glover, playing Sam, in the movie *Dumbo Drop*, when he was consoling Lihn, a young Vietnamese orphan of the war. To Lihn's cries that the helicopters and weapons of war are causing the painful death he lives with every day, Sam says, "No, Lihn, the weapons didn't cause the deaths of your family. People cause these deaths, people far, far away who have never been here before."

May God help us all.